THE ARROGANCE OF AMERICAN POWER

THE ARROGANCE OF AMERICAN POWER

What U.S. Leaders Are Doing Wrong and Why It's Our Duty to Dissent

Nancy Snow

ROWMAN & LITTLEFIELD PUBLISHERS, INC.
Lanham • Boulder • New York • Toronto • Oxford

ROWMAN & LITTLEFIELD PUBLISHERS, INC.

Published in the United States of America
by Rowman & Littlefield Publishers, Inc.
A wholly owned subsidiary of The Rowman & Littlefield Publishing Group, Inc.
4501 Forbes Boulevard, Suite 200, Lanham, Maryland 20706
www.rowmanlittlefield.com

P.O. Box 317, Oxford OX2 9RU, UK

British Library Cataloguing in Publication Information Available

Library of Congress Cataloguing-in-Publication Data

Snow, Nancy.
  The arrogance of American power : what U.S. leaders are doing wrong and why
it's our duty to dissent / Nancy Snow.
      p.   cm.
  Includes bibliographical references and index.
  ISBN-13: 978-0-7425-5373-6 (cloth : alk. paper)
  ISBN-10: 0-7425-5373-6 (cloth : alk. paper)
  ISBN-13: 978-0-7425-5374-3 (pbk. : alk. paper)
  ISBN-10: 0-7425-5374-4 (pbk. : alk. paper)
  1. United States—Foreign relations—2001–   2. United States—Foreign
public opinion.   3. Anti-Americanism.   4. Propaganda, American.   5. Press
and politics—United States.   6. Mass media—Political aspects—United
States.   7. Diplomacy.   8. Public relations and politics—United States.
9. Freedom of speech—United States.   I. Title.
  E902.S59 2006
  303.48′2730090511—dc22   2006016644

Printed in the United States of America

♾™ The paper used in this publication meets the minimum requirements of
American National Standard for Information Sciences—Permanence of Paper for
Printed Library Materials, ANSI/NISO Z39.48-1992.

To Ensign Victor Donald Snow, Sr., USS *Missouri* 1946, who taught me the benefits of laughing every day, hard work, dedication to profession, moral character, selflessness, loyalty, and always putting family before oneself. What a gift it is to have a father whom I can also call such a dear friend. I miss and love you always, Dad.

And to all those Greatest Generation veterans who were dedicated to causes greater than their individual selves. I salute your service to country and to the spirit of America.

CONTENTS

ACKNOWLEDGMENTS

To all my students in global communications, opinion writing, and persuasion at California State University-Fullerton, Herbert Schiller, George Gerbner, Senator J. William Fulbright, and globally-mindful people everywhere, I gratefully acknowledge your insightful and thought-provoking contributions to my opinions and observations. Thanks for opening up my mind and keeping it open! To Cher on C-SPAN and "M.K.," the super-duper traveling cat who has walked on my dissertation to this writing project. And to the following students: Adam, Aliana, Allison, Amy, Andrea, Anna, Catherine, Christine, Courtney, Danielle, Jacqueline, Jason, Juliana, Jonathan, Katherine, Kelly, Kristy, Krystel, Marisol, Marissa, Michael C., Michael R., Nicole, Tim, and Trevor, in my fall 2005 "Anti-Americanism: Hating America at Home and Abroad" course at the Annenberg School for Communication, University of Southern California. You were amazing and made me more philosophical and introspective. I teach, therefore I am.

> Fear less, hope more; eat less, chew more; whine less, breathe more; talk less, say more; hate less, love more, and all good things will be yours.
>
> —Swedish Proverb

PROLOGUE

A TIN EAR AT HOME AND ABROAD

Is anyone really listening to anyone else in this country? Have public relations and image management replaced personal accountability? Whatever happened to honest and forthright communication, and dare I say it, acknowledgments of wrongdoing? As I watched James Frey, author of *A Million Little Pieces*, explain away his culpability in fabricating vast sections of his best-selling "memoir" on CNN's *Larry King Live* on January 11, 2006, I wondered if it were ever going to be possible for this country to present itself accurately and genuinely to the rest of the world. If we keep fooling ourselves at home, how can we expect anyone to be fooled by our slick packaging of America overseas?

Ex-presidential candidates John Kerry and Al Gore assail White House eavesdropping and incompetence but few seem to be listening to them outside of their Democratic supporters. Our nation is becoming a culture of non-listeners, just proclaimers and spinmeisters. For weeks, James Frey continued to proclaim his innocence, just some fudging of the facts, while his Doubleday editor Nan Talese proclaimed her elite publishing house free of any fact-checking accountability. In other words, if it's a good enough story and it will sell like hotcakes, then better to move on it before someone else can. While Frey and Talese made their meek mea culpa appearance on the *Oprah Winfrey* show, it seemed more as a means to save Oprah's billion-dollar credibility with her global audience than to address any structural problems in the business of American storytelling. If it sells, then all is well.

More often than not, we Americans don't seem to really care to hear what either critics or opponents have to say. We'd rather hire a good attorney, image consultant, or publicity agent to ward off the critics.

Imagine if we actually listened to each other, whether in the classroom, in the boardroom, or on the Senate floor. We might make some progress in coming up with some very much needed good ideas. Instead, we're reducing ourselves to reinforcement operatives that must choose a side in our win/lose debates. Consider the Bruin Alumni Association at the University of California, Los Angeles, where I once taught a class on media and social change. Formed in 2005 as a nonprofit lobbying organization with no active student members, its conservative GOP head James Jones offered UCLA students cash payments of $100 to record left-wing radical professors in the classroom. Dubbed the "Exposing UCLA's Radical Professors" initiative, it is designed to silence any faculty who actively proselytize their views and named a list of "Dirty 30" UCLA professors who support left-wing and liberal causes. This effort is just the latest in a national movement to expose critical faculty who are speaking too critically about U.S. foreign policy, the war in Iraq, President Bush, or the war on terror. It follows from post-9/11 efforts groups like the American Council of Trustees and Alumni and Americans for Victory over Terrorism to shame so-called unpatriotic Americans who don't join the bandwagon of support for Washington causes.

These efforts to "out" critical faculty is yet another chilling sign that professors who would dare to say anything disparaging of either President Bush or White House policies are being monitored. This is a new form of intellectual design that calls for professors to self-censor their remarks in the classroom out of fear some student might be taking copious notes to tattle on you. What would the Bruin Alumni Association prefer? That we just say nothing if we can't say anything nice? I've got the real news for them, and it's not good. As one of those nonpartisan but highly critical professors in the classroom, I'm not the one who is often doing the criticism. My own students are the ones quick on the draw to condemn the president. They argue with each other over the Bush administration's credibility and competence on a fairly regular basis. It is not I who eggs them on to do this. Now I'm left wondering if some are there as political bait.

What does any of this have to do with America's image in the world? Everything. So far things aren't looking very promising. The United States is actively engaged in learning more about what others think of us either at home or overseas. Secretary of State Condoleezza Rice and Under Secretary Karen Hughes are globetrotting to the Middle East and other countries engaged in the war on terror. While they talk democracy and freedom, the open society, and America's goodness, their wallpaper backdrop includes Muslim cartoon controversies, calls by the United Nations and European leaders to shut down the Guantanamo detention camp, and more pictures of Abu Ghraib torturing of prisoners. Embarrassing pictures on the Internet are being met with calls for more propaganda, not less. Secretary of Defense Donald Rumsfeld tells the Council on Foreign Relations that the U.S. government functions more like a five and dime store in a world run like eBay. What is needed, he argues, are more efforts by Americans inside and outside of government to challenge distorted pictures of America abroad. Trouble is, some of the pictures we abhor are accurate, and we cannot accuse our purported enemies for monopolizing lies and distortions while only Americans tell the truth. No one is buying it, and they aren't going to buy it if we don't take a long hard look in the mirror and first see ourselves as others see us, not just in our own good lighting.

Over sixty years ago, during the darkest days of World War II, Norman Rockwell was inspired by President Franklin Roosevelt to paint the Four Freedoms: freedom of speech, freedom of worship, freedom from want, and freedom from fear. The U.S. Treasury sent the completed paintings across the United States in a sixteen-city tour to promote the selling of war bonds. Over one million people who saw those paintings in person purchased $132 million in bonds to support a war effort in the cause of American democracy. The *Saturday Evening Post*, which originally published his paintings, reported that Rockwell would later carry his most revered work on his back to Moscow to tell the story of America through its love of freedom.

As I listen to Donald Rumsfeld call for multimedia efforts to engage the enemy in the war on terror, I worry that our basic stories, what the American people love the most about this country, will become lost in a global PR battle to win hearts and minds at all costs. This battle is being waged by multi-million dollar contracts with information warrior firms like Lincoln and Rendon that are given no-bid business to act as our citizen proxies in an information war. There is little, if any, public accountability, because the firms operate as military agents in mostly covert operations free of either Congressional or public scrutiny. Unlike some service delivery trucks with bumper stickers that ask other motorists, "How is my driving?" John Rendon isn't asking me or anyone else if his work is effective, much less ethical. He's just collecting his fat check while we're left with all the fact checking.

We need to get back to the fundamentals, whether we call them four freedoms or not. We need to start listening more to each other and acknowledging our differences within our borders as much as outside. If enough of us come together and build a critical dialogue, then we'll soon see the commonalities we have as a people who seek freedom from domination and control over our information sources and image. We need to realize that what is truly ailing us won't be cured by Blackberries, blogs, direct broadcast satellite, or Washington lobbyists. Mutual understanding doesn't require a publicity agent or even a website. It begins with one person sitting across the table from another. My hope is that we will continue to engage with each other and our counterparts abroad to circumvent and challenge, if not officially break up, the most harmful business, military, and state entanglements that are dominating our global landscape. More than Jennifer and Brad's, that's one break-up I'll gladly see covered in the press.

1

LIVING IN THE NUMBER ONE COUNTRY

WHY DO THEY (STILL) HATE US? OR DO THEY?

Within the matrix of American propaganda and the rise of anti-Americanism in the world lives a perplexed and, at times, ambivalent citizenry that wonders why other countries would ever hate the United States in the first place. The problem with such a self-reflection is that it rarely goes beyond a form of defense. We tell our fellow citizens that it is "they" who are mistaken. "We" are a good and righteous people. "They" are misinformed, while "we" are well intentioned. Our mainstream American media do a very poor job overall of attempting to overcome our own national myopia. For the most part, they manage to point out that hating America is on the rise, but offer little salvo in what we can do about it. Further, official U.S. government propaganda and public diplomacy campaigns in the new century have a direct relationship to the rise of anti-Americanism in the world—and yet doing nothing and hoping the problem will go away on its own is no answer either.

Anti-Americanism has become a particularly salient topic since September 2001, even though we rarely can settle on an acceptable definition or meaning, which makes it very well suited to being analyzed in the context of propaganda. The most effective propaganda is that which uses words that conceal, rather than reveal, meaning. What makes anti-Americanism a hot topic of discussion now is that, despite its ambivalent generality, *everyone* has something to say on the topic, whether informed or not in opinion. You don't bring up the topic and expect a shrug or a sigh. Nobody's neutral about America. It appears by the very existence of so powerful a label as "anti-Americanism" that there must be something about the idea of America that generates strong emotion. Having a discussion about anti-Americanism is not like discussing black-eyed peas in which one may have no opinion on likeability. Rather, there is something about America—its culture, people, ideals, politics, geographical divide between so-called Blue States and Red States—that is sure to get the blood boiling, both at home and abroad.

Everyone can identify some aspect of America that she doesn't like, no matter one's political persuasion. It may be the moral values, or lack thereof, perpetuated by American popular culture in general and as exemplified by the current "it" network TV show, *Desperate Housewives*, which depicts sexually frustrated or sexually aggressive women in back-biting domestic situations with their neighbors and spouses who live on Wisteria Lane. This show, despite its over-the-top suburban dysfunction mores, is currently the most in-demand U.S. television program in the global media market, offering yet another opportunity to misinform and stereotype America just as *Baywatch*, *Dallas*, and *Dynasty* did in the '80s and '90s.

America is a love-it-or-hate-it, like-it-or-leave-it maelstrom of public opinion. Maybe you view America as too absorbed in entertainment and selfish pursuits. You might see an America that overindulges in personal freedom where individual rights trump communal duties. To other critics, America is a triumph in political conformity in thought over vigorous free speech. Perhaps it is a particular American film director whose politics you disdain so you judge him anti-American. Think of Michael Moore, whose movie *Fahrenheit 9/11* started a riot of reaction in the news media and among the public in 2004. Michael Moore, like America, evokes no neutrality. If you are aware of Moore's existence, you have a positive or negative opinion about him based in part about how much you think he may or may not like America.

By its very syntax, anti-Americanism requires you to choose a side, to be pro- or anti- to this negatively defined concept. This rush to choose, or even to label another side as "pro-American" or "anti-American," makes it much harder to have a healthy debate or disagreement about American policies and perceptions from which we all could learn.

When I shared with friends and colleagues that I was working on a book about anti-Americanism and American propaganda and public diplomacy efforts to combat it, a number of my American friends said that they were anti-American in certain aspects and wanted me to make that point very strongly. Don't leave us out, they'd say. In other words, their sense was that the concept was viewed mostly from an outsider's perspective, in terms of non-Americans' negative attitudes toward the United States. It is true that most scholarly studies I've seen are discussions of anti-Americanism in the context of foreign attitudes toward the United States. Very few studies address the phenomenon of home-cooked anti-Americanism that is used to silence dissent and disagreement with the bandwagon point of view.

Consider a young American student I'll call Amy who says she's been a critic of American foreign policy and domestic practice her whole life, so contrary her thoughts and feelings are toward her government and the society in which she lives.[1] She thinks of herself as an idealist living in a cruelly realist world. In her view, the United States of America protects and promotes a Realpolitik view of the world based on what's going to protect "our" interests over others and uses the threat or use of military force to back up these national interests. Amy blames a number of institutions besides the government for her negative outlook, most notably the U.S. media system, which she feels does a very poor job in bringing the world to America, despite what ABC News's World News Tonight may say in its promotional voice-over. Not unsurprisingly, she is no fan of President Bush or the Bush Administration. She hated the way the press seemed to cow to governmental control and manipulation of information, particularly in the run-up to the 2003 invasion of Iraq when the American press took at face value the evidence the administration had of weapons of mass destruction. Amy also thinks that the world has no clue that many Americans share her feelings and are just as strong in their dissent against the foreign policies of the U.S. government as a European or Latin American citizen might be. I told her that I'd do what I could to get out the word that there is a community of dissenting and thinking people often labeled "anti-Americans" living in the number one country. Many are critics of what is and are working toward what can be. They believe, like Amy, that America can and should do better than it is now.

The most famous book on the topic of anti-Americanism is nearly fifty years old and is a dramatized fictional account of the actual experience of the authors. William J. Lederer and Eugene Burdick's 1958 book, *The Ugly American*, is credited with coining the term to describe the American aid worker and diplomat living abroad, in this particular case, U.S. military aid provided to South Vietnam to counter the Communist influence in the region. A copy of the book was sent to all members of Congress and it became a multi-million dollar bestseller in America. Then President Eisenhower later opened an investigation into how military aid was being received by the locals, in part prompted by the book's criticism. The Soviets were credited in the 1950s with doing a much finer job than Americans in adapting themselves to another culture and winning local hearts and minds. The Americans were not nimble in this process. "A mysterious change seems to come over Americans when they go to a foreign land. They isolate themselves socially. They live pretentiously. They're loud and ostentatious. Perhaps they're frightened and defensive; or maybe they're not properly trained and make mistakes out of ignorance."[2]

This tainted U.S. image, all these years later, dominates preconceptions of how Americans, whether tourist or diplomat, will be prone to behave toward foreign nationals. A very telling passage in the book informs the global perception gap between America and the rest of the world. When a Burmese journalist is asked to put herself in the position of the American president and what he might do to improve American prestige in Southeast Asia, she describes the work of a married American couple, the Martin family, who moved to Burma, and "brought no pamphlets, brochures, movies, or any of the other press-agent devices which are so offensive to most of us and on which most Americans rely . . . They came to Burma to help us, not to improve their own standard of living." Mindful today of the "stingy" remark by a U.N. diplomat about American aid following the Asian tsunami disaster, or of U.S. military efforts to convince Iraqis that they have come to liberate and not conquer their country, the journalist offers a prescription for credible public diplomacy efforts: "You don't need publicity if the results of what you are doing are visible and are valuable to the people. The steam from a pot of good soup is its best advertisement."[3] This prescription is the exact converse of what the American president and his administration are doing in their attempts to make a better case for America in the world.

Despite the Burmese journalist's good advice, the U.S. style of combating anti-Americanism is not to let stand the steam from a pot of good soup. It's to hire the best minds from Madison Avenue like Charlotte Beers, Under Secretary of State for Public Diplomacy and Public Affairs, a legend in brand stewardship, who the U.S. government thought could turn her pitching prowess from Uncle Ben's Rice to Uncle Sam's mission. Beers called government branding the most sophisticated branding assignment of her career. Secretary of State Powell told a House Budget Committee in March 2001: "I'm going to be bringing people into the public diplomacy function of the department who are going to change from just selling us in the old . . . way to really branding foreign policy, branding the department, marketing the department, marketing American values to the world."[4] After 9/11 and the chorus of "Why do they hate us?" abounded, President Bush expressed his bewilderment: "I am amazed that there is such misunderstanding of what our country is about, that people would hate us. Because I know how good we are. . . . "[5] This was later followed by Rep. Henry Hyde who expressed his own frustration: "How is it that the country that invented Hollywood and Madison Avenue has allowed such a destructive and parodied image of itself to become the intellectual coin of the realm overseas?"[6] Most recently, a group of business executives troubled with America's declining reputation in the world—Business for Diplomatic Action (BDA)—was founded in 2004 by another advertising legend Keith Reinhard to coordinate a Brand America campaign that it thinks is better led by the private sector and not by ex-Madison Avenue-turned government bureaucrats: "Anti-Americanism is, at least in part, a business problem that U.S. business, by virtue of its reach and resourcefulness, is uniquely qualified to address. Beyond pure profit concerns, American business leaders have a responsibility to use their influence to improve the overall reputation of the United States."[7]

Despite all this recognition that the ugly American isn't getting any more handsome, the cautionary message of *The Ugly American*—letting actions lead rhetoric, and showing respect for and understanding of the local culture customs—has been overlooked by government leadership in Washington that is zealously devoted to winning hearts and minds in the global war on terror. Because the United States has such a strong reputation for savvy and sophisticated marketing, advertising, and public relations, it has become our very own Achilles heel in how we project ourselves to the world. The world expects us to know better in how we apply our persuasion industries and let our models lead by softer example than heavy promotion. The war on terror has thus far clouded our good judgment and led us to measure our public diplomacy efforts by how much they protect our narrow security interests over common interests. Public diplomacy did not begin on September 11, 2001, nor did it end with the cold war. If the U.S. truly cares about what others think about America, then we need to care as much during peacetime as wartime, and care enough to invite full public participation in the effort, not just government-approved lackeys who pass ideological muster with the administration in power, or influentials and elites whom we always expect to be involved in the foreign affairs process. Understanding what the world thinks of America is too important to leave to the intellectuals and elites alone. It requires a full bottom-to-top effort, including the participation of nongovernmental organizations, the private sector, and individuals who heretofore may have been either taken for granted or not asked their opinion about what is to be done. And we must always be open to criticism from within if we are to gain strength to receive criticism from beyond our shores.

Our understanding of anti-Americanism and negative attitudes and opinions toward the United States is a necessity if we want to better inform, influence and engage each other. In other words, anti-Americanism may be good for democracy. I'm from the school of "no heads in the sand" when it comes to political hot potatoes. Like racism in the American South was to the public dialogue in the 1960s, anti-Americanism must be to the global dialogue in the 2000s. It's very convenient to point fingers at one's enemies or those you consider who don't love your country as much as you, but what do you really learn from such an exchange, except that you can point? In this book I analyze efforts underway to address the anti-Americanism of the 21st century, a period that has no parallel, so infused it is with recent developments like economic globalization and the global war on terror. The chapters to follow address the roles of the U.S. press and propaganda in shaping global attitudes and opinions as well as global media reactions to U.S. policies and practices. In the final chapter, I include recommendations and communication tips for thinking through our simple rhetorical labels and some alternatives to our current public diplomacy campaigns, several of which come from my own students who thoroughly analyzed this subject in our course examining anti-Americanism during the fall 2005 semester at the University of Southern California's Annenberg School for Communication.

TAKING INVENTORY OF WHERE LANGUAGE LEADS US

In the United States, we love to live by euphemism. Should a word like *propaganda* become too harsh to the taste, then we invent terms like *public diplomacy* to make the actual propaganda efforts that we engage in seem more like we're catering to the public's interest over political economy and national security Realpolitik state concerns. Social influence scholars Anthony Pratkanis and Eliot Aronson write in their book, *Age of Propaganda*, that the initial definition of propaganda was "the dissemination of biased ideas and opinions, often through the use of lies and deception" but has, since then, "evolved to mean mass 'suggestion' or influence through the manipulation of symbols and the psychology of the individual." They further explain propaganda as "the communication of a point of view with the ultimate goal of having the recipient of the appeal come to 'voluntarily' accept this position as if it were his or her own."[8] Generally speaking, most people would still accept the former negative association with propaganda (lies and deception) over the latter, more benign association with social influence and mass persuasion.

In *Persuasion, Social Influence and Compliance Gaining*, Robert Gass and John Seiter present five features of propaganda that separate it from education or straight information exchange. First, all propaganda has a strong ideological bent, which gives it its bad association with telling lies or making up stories. It does not serve a purely informational, "just the facts, ma'am" function, but is biased at the source. Second, because propaganda drives a certain agenda, its sponsors are purposively not trying to be neutral or objective, but rather hold up their own facts in the best light available. Third, propaganda is institutional in nature. It is manufactured and practiced by organized groups from across the political and economic spectrum like corporations (Disney, Microsoft, Wal-Mart), government agencies (State, Defense, White House), religious groups (churches, temples, mosques), terrorist cells (Al Qaeda), and social movements (Moveon.org). Fourth, in order to be most effective, propaganda must involve mass persuasion campaigns that target a mass audience and rely on mass media to persuade large-scale audiences. Finally, propaganda's "bad image" as a contested construct is based mostly on the ethics involved with mass persuasion methods used. With most propaganda, the ends justify the means, or at least the end results are primary while ethical considerations are often secondary.[9]

The term *public diplomacy* was coined by former Dean of the Fletcher School of Law and Diplomacy at Tufts University following the death of America's most legendary mid-century broadcast journalist Edward R. Murrow, who directed the United States Information Agency for two short years during the Kennedy Administration. The creation of the first independent U.S. government agency of public diplomacy in 1953, the United States Information Agency (USIA), itself followed on the heels of the first cold war with casualties, the Korean War. American public diplomacy became cast first in a national security and cold war framework. In many USIA publications public diplomacy was defined as seeking to promote the national interest and the national security of the United States through understanding, informing, and influencing foreign publics and broadening dialogue between American citizens and institutions and their counterparts abroad. This definition held up right through the end of USIA's independence in October 1999. Not until the attacks on the United States two years later did one hear about American public diplomacy and propaganda in so many media and public policy circles. What had been a mostly covert propaganda campaign or at least one directed exclusively at overseas audiences was now being discussed as a major part of the domestic and international information strategies of the war on terror.

The modern American manipulation of information began in full force at the outbreak of America's first major declaration of war in April 1917. On Friday, April 13, 1917, just one week after President Woodrow Wilson announced that the United States would no longer remain neutral regarding the hostilities in Europe, the Secretaries of State, War, and Navy sent a joint letter to the President calling for the creation of a Committee on Public Information (CPI) to both promote and censor all war information. Though the CPI would have a short two-year shelf life—it was disbanded following the war on June 30, 1919—its legacy and leadership have repercussions that continue to swirl around the direction of American public diplomacy efforts in this century, almost one hundred years later.

As told by the appointed director of the CPI, journalist George Creel, the newspapers of the day were reporting that with the involvement of America in the European war would come censorship in American news, and therefore CPI would serve to disclose and withhold information depending on whether or not it helped further the American cause of freedom and liberty. To Creel's credit, he did send a letter to Wilson with his preference for "expression over repression" and thought he was just the man to maintain the balance. The Washington, D.C. newspaper, *The Sunday Star*, announced his appointment with the front page headline, "President Names Censorship Chief," and described Creel as "a man of strongly progressive type who was formerly an active newspaperman in Denver and elsewhere, and was director of public safety in the Colorado city, at a time when he instituted reforms in penal institutions in that state."[10] Scholars Cedric Larson and James Mock, who completed an extensive study of the Creel Committee for *Public Opinion Quarterly*, describe it as "the first formal government committee to supervise the publication of news in American history."[11] Their study illustrates the uneasy nexus between press and propaganda as American newspapers, including the "newspaper of record," the *New York Times*, condemned the appointment of a formal censorship committee and chief information censor who would serve throughout the war period at the behest of the chief persuader, the American president. A little over eighty years later, the same newspaper of record would pillory the establishment of an Office of Strategic Influence (OSI) inside the now renamed War Department, Department of Defense, designed to engage in similar opinion control activities that supported the war on terror.[12]

AMERICA IN ATTITUDES AND OPINIONS

When we define anti-Americanism as negative attitudes toward the people, culture, and/or government of the United States, we need to understand how these attitudes develop. Attitudes are learned, and are generally viewed as a product of parenting, education, and the mass media. I've yet to come across anyone who has no opinion or attitude toward the United States, U.S. foreign policy, or its citizenry. In fact, the very nature of having an attitude is a predisposition to make an evaluative negative or positive judgment about some attitude object. What I've found in conducting interviews on the subject of America is that everyone has an attitude or opinion. You'd have to go to the ends of the earth to find someone who has had no experience with the United States, virtual or otherwise. The next question then is how are these attitudes formed?

Early research on communication in the 1930s was influenced by the political propagandists of the day like Hitler and Goebbels in Germany or Mussolini in Italy. The feeling was that mass populations were highly susceptible to mass persuasion tactics like public rallies, radio broadcasts, and feature films that were able to change the minds of the audience with little effort. A number of propaganda studies were conducted in the United

States to reveal the most prominent manipulative persuasion devices being used by demagogues, including those like Father Charles Coughlin,
the American priest who broadcast messages of social justice in the aftermath of the 1930s Depression. His radio diatribes included attacks on
prominent Jews and his national influence prompted an investigation by
the Institute for Propaganda Analysis (IPA) to identify the seven propaganda devices that Coughlin used to sway his audiences, including the
bandwagon ("everybody's doing it") approach, card-stacking (incomplete
information), name-calling, and glittering generalities (an ill-defined but
positive buzzword). It was naively assumed then "that propaganda could
be made almost irresistible with sufficiently clever use of propagandistic
gimmicks in the content of the communication." Edward Bernays, father
of modern public relations in America, offered this seemingly sanguine
interpretation of the power of the mass persuasion and propaganda industries in modern democracies: "The conscious and intelligent manipulation
of the organized habits and opinions of the masses is an important element
in democratic society. Those who manipulate this unseen mechanism of
society constitute an invisible government which is the true ruling power
of the country."

More sophisticated studies that followed showed that people by and
large are not easily persuaded and indeed have become rather skeptical
toward advertising and public relations strategies. Despite the avowed
skepticism, the United States remains the world's leader in advertising,
spending over $200 billion per year to commercially advertise through
mass media campaigns, or about $700 per person. In contrast, the U.S.
State Department's public diplomacy budget is about $1 billion per year,
about 4 percent of the overall international affairs budget, and half is spent
on international broadcasting efforts. Would commercial advertisers risk
the expense if they didn't think they were getting something for their
money? They are certainly getting something—recognition, repetition,
and reputation, but it's much more difficult to do the same for Uncle Sam
as one does for a Pepsi. You can air a car or soda commercial hundreds
of times to an audience in the United States and not get the negative
response you would airing a government-sponsored ad a few times in a
foreign country. Why? Because we expect commercial advertisers to be
aggressive and to try to outsell their competitors through constant media
carpet bombing. When a government tries the same, the public's guard
goes up and the propaganda filters go on.

Fifty years ago it was thought that the public was easily malleable and basically putty in the hands of the hidden persuaders. Today it is widely believed that mass media have limited effects on attitude and opinion changes. People consume media for a host of reasons—distraction, entertainment, social contact, probably least so to change attitudes and opinions. In fact, some studies of mass media consumption suggest that even with new media like the Internet, people choose sites that reinforce their attitudes, not challenge them, a concept called selective exposure. Even though the Internet may offer a myriad of choices, both pro and con, the user has the power to point and click where he wishes to go, just as one does with a television remote. This power of self-maneuvering leads us to select information favorable to our point of view, even though we may know subconsciously that there is opposing information available. Oskamp and Schultz argue that "it is clear that most people most of the time are surrounded by a higher proportion of supportive information than of opposing information."[13]

Face-to-face communication remains the best opportunity for persuasion attempts, but it is the poorer cousin in public diplomacy to much-hyped international broadcasting and advertising campaigns. Because U.S. public diplomacy has become fused with the U.S.-led war on terror, face-to-face efforts are seen as too long-term, labor-intensive (they require selection of candidates, interaction, follow-up), and less crisis-driven than broadcast media that can challenge hate media and target populations influenced by the enemy. The two flagship face-to-face programs of the State Department are the Fulbright educational exchange program, now in its seventh decade, and the International Visitors Leadership Program (IVLP), known as the IVP during my USIA and State days. These programs, though widely touted, have not received adequate funding since 9/11, while funding for international broadcasting to the Middle East region has expanded. Mass media campaigns used in conjunction with other persuasive attempts have some effect, but alone they are insufficient to garner much of any attitude shift. The global population is still mostly exposed to mass-mediated images of the United States, which is why the U.S. government's marketing and public relations strategies are more mass-media driven than interpersonal, despite what research tells us about their effects on attitude change. The rationale is that it's better to try to reach as many people as possible and hope that something positive sticks. Most studies show, however, that attitudes toward one's own nation and other nations are acquired often very early in life and then get reinforced throughout one's life, with little altering shaped by new information.

So why does the U.S. government continue to push mass-media approaches over face-to-face international exchanges? The influence of Al Jazeera and Al Arabiya TV, among other new media in the Middle East, is so pervasive and prominent in shaping regional attitudes that the United States wants to be a player among these global media, not a spectator. The problem is that the U.S. government lacks credibility in the Middle East and is seen by many Arabs and Muslims in about as favorable a light as they see their own governments. Nevertheless, because the Middle East media are characterized as anti-American and pro-Arab in their graphic coverage of the civilian casualties of the war in Iraq, credibility or not, the United States would like to have a voice to attempt to lend some balance to a region of public opinion that tilts away from U.S. interests, Israel excepted. So far, Middle East media consumption is favoring the regional over the U.S. media, and it's doubtful that the U.S. broadcasting efforts will be able to tip the balance in the region as long as the United States remains so heavily militarily involved in the region.

ON DISSENT AND FREE SPEECH

Any confrontation of anti-Americanism at its most harmful and destructive must be predicated by a rise in introspection within the United States. We don't have a global reputation as a self-searching and self-critical people in this country and these have been characteristics recognized by many international visitors throughout the ages. There are two common criticisms leveled at the United States. One is the ignorance about and lack of conscious awareness of how U.S.-directed actions in the world affect others. The second criticism, related to the first, is that the average American citizen believes that anyone, if given the opportunity, would want to become an American citizen, a position unique to the American character and not shared by our industrial democratic counterparts. These perceptions of the American people and American power lead to commonly-held outside perceptions that the United States is both arrogant in its ignorance and thinks of itself as exceptional in its political economy and cultural traits.

A most famous observation about American discourse and dissent was made by French writer, Alexis de Tocqueville, in his four volume series,

Democracy in America (1835–1840), whose lengthy treatise is culled for support by both conservative and liberal philosophers and practitioners:

> I know no country in which there is so little true independence of mind and freedom of discussion as in America . . . In America, the majority raises very formidable barriers to the liberty of opinion: within these barriers an author may write whatever he pleases, but he will repent it if he ever step beyond them. Not that he is exposed to the terrors of an auto-da-fé, but he is tormented by the slights and persecutions of daily obloquy. His political career is closed forever, since he has offended the only authority which is able to promote his success. Every sort of compensation, even that of celebrity, is refused to him. Before he published his opinions he imagined that he held them in common with many others; but no sooner has he declared them openly than he is loudly censured by his overbearing opponents, while those who think like him, without having the courage to speak, abandon him in silence. He yields at length, oppressed by the daily efforts he has been making, and he subsides into silence, as if he was tormented by remorse for having spoken the truth.[14]

Over one hundred years later, American Senator and Fulbright program creator J. William Fulbright would observe, "The discharge of the duty of dissent is handicapped in America by an unworthy tendency to fear serious criticism of our government."[15] At the time Fulbright published *The Arrogance of Power* in 1966, the war in Vietnam was well underway while the anti-war movement on American streets and on American campuses had not yet come to its full fruition. Both men offer insights into how the American image and reputation in the world in the twenty-first century is a consequence of a lack of critical investigation of the American character and American cultural values. Fulbright writes in his chapter "The Citizen and the University" that "in the abstract we celebrate freedom of opinion as part of our patriotic liturgy; it is only when some Americans exercise it that other Americans are shocked."[16] Similarly, de Tocqueville said Americans were quick to fall in line with the acceptable opinion of the day, thereby creating the condition of the bandwagon (everybody's doing it) effect: "When an opinion has taken root in a democracy and established itself in the minds of the majority, it afterward persists by itself, needing no effort to maintain it since no one attacks it. Those who at first rejected it as false come in the end to adopt it as accepted, and even those who still at the bottom of their hearts oppose it keep their views to themselves, taking great care to avoid a dangerous and futile contest."[17]

To most Americans, First Amendment protections of free speech are sacrosanct and at the top of any list of our most cherished values, but in much of our civic discussion of the protections it provides, we tend to focus on the institutional rights of private, commercial media to be "free from" government intervention and not on the individual rights to free speech. John Merrill states that the "Americanized core definition is basically that freedom is freedom from government interference . . . Americans seldom talk about interference by corporate powers, advertisers, civil pressure groups, publishers, editors, and so on. The concern is with government, and with the press being autonomous or independent of government."[18]

Because Americans have a deeply ingrained mistrust of institutions with too much power, be they government, business, or labor, this may help explain why such a large percentage of young people in America in the new century and particularly after the events of 9/11 still don't even recognize the basic human rights and individual protections that the First Amendment provides. A January 2005 poll released by the John S. and James L. Knight Foundation surveyed 100,000 American high school students, about 8,000 teachers and 500 principals and administrators at U.S. secondary education schools over two years. The results show that over a third (35%) of the students surveyed thought that the U.S. First Amendment went "too far" in guaranteeing freedom of speech, press, worship and assembly. This was after having the text of the First Amendment read to them: *Congress shall make no law respecting an establishment of religion, or prohibiting the free exercise thereof; or abridging the freedom of speech, or of the press; or the right of the people peaceably to assemble, and to petition the government for a redress of grievances.*

Another half of the students thought that the U.S. government had the right to censor indecent material over the Internet. It does not. Two-thirds thought that it was illegal in the United States to burn the flag. It is not. Students were less likely than school administrators and teachers to think that people have the right to express unpopular opinions. Just 51 percent of students agreed with the following (compared to 80 percent of teachers and principals): "Newspapers should be allowed to publish freely without government approval of stories."[19]

These students might want to take a long, hard look at modern times in America—for the times, they are a changin' for the narrower—in terms of the parameters of what we can say. Although flag burning is legal as symbolic expression of free speech, the U.S. House of Representatives overwhelmingly passed a measure in June 2005 that, if signed into law, will give Congress power to "prohibit the physical desecration of the flag of the United States." Burning of the American flag may be a popular way to exhibit political protest overseas, but it's not exactly an epidemic inside the United States. In 2004, there were two cases of flag burning reported. Nevertheless, supporters of this flag burning prohibition seem to believe that if one sanctifies the physical flag itself, then one can stomp out the concomitant thoughts and words associated with the flag burners. One goal of House Joint Resolution 10 is to limit free expression to designated "free speech zones" defined by the government. Obviously, antiwar activist Cindy Sheehan was not in a free speech zone at the president's 2006 State of the Union Address when she was hustled away by Capitol Hill Police for displaying her own symbolic speech—in her case, a tee shirt with the words: "2,245 Dead. How Many More?" Despite Sheehan's having a legitimate ticket for the event supplied by her district Rep. Lynn Woolsey, Sheehan was handcuffed and held for questioning for hours. Beverly Young, no FOC (friend of Cindy), is the wife of Republican Rep. C.W. Bill Young of Florida. She too wore a tee shirt that mightily displeased the fashion, er, Capitol Police. Young was removed from the House visitors' gallery during Bush's SOTU address. Her sin: A tee shirt that said, "Support the Troops." Capitol Hill police later apologized to both women and acknowledged that "mistakes were made" that denied the women access, but the damage was already done, and this time the criticism was an equal opportunity bipartisan sing-a-long. What these incidents show is that America in 2006 is a country as in conflict with its own self-image as it is with the rest of the world. You can't blame this one on the French.

Alexis De Tocqueville also observed that the Anglo-American Christian religion and American patriotism fit together like a hand in glove, creating conditions that modify individual dissent from the moral norm. "The Americans, having admitted the principal doctrines of the Christian religion without inquiry, are obliged to accept in like manner a great number of moral truths originating in it and connected with it. Hence the activity of individual analysis is restrained within narrow limits, and many of the most important of human opinions are removed from the range of its influence."[20]

Despite the First Amendment separation of an officially sanctioned church from the state, American religious values permeate government and commercial transactions, with even the phrase, "In God We Trust," found on the back of the U.S. dollar. It is not at all unusual to see the American President carrying a Bible to church, praying in public, attending a prayer breakfast, or ending a public address with "God Bless America." In individual lives, religion matters a lot to most Americans and religious values often direct public policy outcomes, most famously in the election of 2004 when "moral values" were considered the most important factor impacting the vote. Polls by Gallup and by the National Opinion Research Center indicate that the United States is the most religious country in the modern industrialized world. Eight out of ten Americans (84%) identify as Christian (Catholic, Protestant, Mormon) while just 9 percent have no religion.[21] Over 40 percent of voters surveyed in 2003 and 2004 indicated that they were "born again" or "evangelical" Christians.[22] This religiosity is much higher than our European counterparts where paradoxically there are more state and national religions. According to the World Values Survey, 80 percent of Americans consider religion important or very important to their everyday lives, while less than half (45%) of Europeans do (Germany, France, Austria, Netherlands, Italy, and Great Britain).[23]

Despite the high importance of religion as a cultural characteristic in America, the United States' image to the world that is most often criticized is American secularism and materialism. The United States, unlike other modern industrialized democracies, has no official Socialist party and deeply distrusts a centralized government or resolving problems through collective means (which smacks of socialism and communism, two very different political economies). The private sector, represented by Wall Street, American banks and financial firms, is exalted as almost a secular religion. This explains why the anti-globalization movement activists are quick to blame the United States for a lot of the world's economic ills. They believe that the U.S. true religion is represented by the dollar and by privatization of trade and services that favor the rich nations and individual elites of the world. This dichotomy between the charge card and a higher charge in America makes it very difficult to decide what common values we share with the rest of the world. If we emphasize our religious beliefs, we risk coming across as the Christian crusaders who are heaven-bent on shaping the world to our point of view and belief system. If we underemphasize our faith, then we play into the stereotypical picture that we are the most materialistic, greedy, and pleasure-seeking nation on the planet, bereft of a moral compass. Which way do we proceed?

PROMOTING AMERICAN CULTURAL VALUES TO THE WORLD

In the American self-image, American business and the corporate sector are considered more efficient and more risk-taking sectors than the public sector. They are seen as the most responsible sectors for American economic success in the twenty-first century, but it wasn't always so. There was a worrisome time when American government was beginning to have some inroad in curbing American profit excess. The War Advertising Council's original aims before Pearl Harbor and the outbreak of World War II was to promote the mantra, "the business of America is business," which had been lost during the social and labor movements period of the 1930s Depression era and the early administrations of FDR. We now know it better as the Advertising Council.

According to American University intercultural communication scholar Gary Weaver, when it comes to the political economy of the United States today, "the dominant economic belief is laissez faire capitalism, in which government should not interfere in the economy and it is up to the individual to succeed or fail."[24] If there were a secular Bible, it would probably be Adam Smith's *The Wealth of Nations*, which was published the same year as the establishment of the United States of America. This exaltation of American capitalism is seen as a threat to many cultures and national economies that do not ascribe to the same political economy plans. In the cultural realm, American popular culture and the worldwide dominance of Hollywood film and television distribution have led to a backlash against U.S. products and cries of cultural imperialism, a term that is almost alien to the thinking of an American citizen but not at all uncommon in discourse outside the United States.

What other cultural traits besides those observed by de Tocqueville and homegrown Senator Fulbright are both treasured and criticized by non-Americans? Intercultural communications "guru" Dr. Robert Kohls, a former Foreign Service officer and author of *The Survival Kit for Overseas Living*, developed a general list of common cultural traits in the United States over twenty years ago (1984) while serving as the Executive

Director of the Washington International Center that hosted thousands of international visitors. His list of thirteen American cultural traits, "The Values Americans Live By," is still widely referenced by both American students and businesspeople preparing for living and studying overseas and for incoming visitors to the United States. It is not a foolproof list and carries with it a tendency to generalize, but it is nevertheless useful as a starting off point for dialogue about what makes Americans tick in comparison to other nationalities. Kohl's cultural traits are an extension of yet another Alexis de Tocqueville observation about American discourse 150 years ago: "An American cannot converse, but he can discuss, and his talk falls into a dissertation. He speaks to you as if he was addressing a meeting; and if he should chance to become warm in the discussion, he will say 'Gentlemen' to the person with whom he is conversing."

Kohls and other intercultural communication observers like Weaver say that Americans prefer a direct approach in information and communication strategies, an approach that creates a number of problems with cultures that use indirect means to make their point. In the United States, anything less than a direct style of communication is associated often with manipulation and/or dishonesty. Ting-Toomey and Chung, authors of *Understanding Intercultural Communication*, say that "the overall U.S. American verbal style often calls for clear and direct communication. Phrases such as 'be very clear,' 'don't beat around the bush,' and 'what is the point' are some examples."[25] This may be why de Tocqueville thought that Americans were not masters of the art of conversation, which is more of a back-and-forth style of discourse rather than a lecture format.[26] In American public diplomacy strategies since 9/11, we see how the direct style of communication plays out. The U.S. government favors the mass-mediated style of communicating with target audiences through international radio and television broadcasting and advertising campaigns rather than interpersonal communication, although in the post-9/11 era some opportunities (like expanding high school exchanges and the Fulbright Program) are arising to promote more interpersonal, exchange-oriented strategies that build mutual understanding. The vast majority of taxpayer resources are designated for television and radio broadcasting, which are more direct and targeted, but which, according to attitude and opinion researchers Oskamp and Shultz, "are not generally very effective in changing public attitudes."[27]

Dr. Kohls's list of thirteen common American values is designed neither to convert visitors to the United States nor to stand as superior over the values of other countries. These powerful generalizations listed here do not substitute for personal experience but serve as exemplars that help explain what gives the United States its particular uniquely American qualities. They are seen as positive traits by the majority of Americans and mostly negative traits in many non-Western, developing countries with less democratic traditions. They include an individual's having personal control or mastery over his/her environment; orientation toward change; controlling time; support for equality/egalitarianism; support for individualism and privacy; push for self-help over community support; emphasis on competition and free enterprise; orientation toward the future over the past; emphasis on action/work; informality in social interaction; communication style that emphasizes directness, openness, and honesty; practicality and efficiency; and finally, materialism and acquisition. That last trait might be called a Keeping Up with the Jones's mentality or a symbol that all that hard work has payed off in consumer stuff. In the United States, there is now such an emphasis on acquisition that it has led to a modern illness, hoarding, in which some people cannot throw anything out, so emotionally attached they are to inanimate objects.

Kohls identifies personal control over the environment and change seen as natural and positive in the same manner that de Tocqueville observed on his mid-19th century visit to the United States, a time in which Americans arguably had even much less personal control over their destiny. Many Americans today consider their individual actions to be a result of their direct control and consider anyone who wants to hold others' responsible for their actions as slothful or lazy. Think of any American fictionalized or reality-based court show on television or the 24-hour cable network version, Court TV, and you will see countless courtroom scenarios in which the jury or attending judge holds the defendant completely responsible for the deed. If the defendant doesn't accept responsibility for his behavior, he is often given a verbal dressing down by the judge or a look of disdain and eye-rolling from the audience. When an attorney seeks to defend her client, she may point out so-called mitigating factors (childhood abuse, neglect) that may account for why the person behaved so badly, but which are not used to justify the action. Globally, it is not uncommon to come across much more fatalistic outlooks—that the conditions into which you are born are not easily changeable. In countries with vast amounts of poverty and no middle class, people may be less inclined to grow up with a sense of personal destiny or strong beliefs that just by taking control of their environmental conditions, they can improve their futures. In contrast, Americans who don't act on their environment to produce positive changes are seen often as backward or too primitive to adapt to the demands of a dynamic culture that exists in the United States. De Tocqueville observed that Americans are neither fatalistic nor passive about their lot in life:

> The whole life of an American is passed like a game of chance, a revolutionary crisis, or a battle. As the same causes are continually in operation throughout the country, they ultimately impart an irresistible impulse to the national character. The American, taken as a chance specimen of his countrymen, must then be a man of singular warmth in his desires, enterprising, fond of adventure, and, above all, of innovation. The same bent is manifest in all that he does; he introduces it into his political laws, his religious doctrines, his theories of social economy, and his domestic occupations; he bears it with him in the depths of the backwoods, as well as in the business of the city. It is this same passion, applied to maritime commerce, which makes him the cheapest and the quickest trader in the world.[28]

De Tocqueville sees the American spirit as essentially dynamic, restless, and embracing of change: "Born often under another sky, placed in the middle of an always moving scene, himself driven by the irresistible torrent which draws all about him, the American has no time to tie himself to anything, he grows accustomed only to change, and ends by regarding it as the natural state of man. He feels the need of it, more he loves it; for the instability; instead of meaning disaster to him, seems to give birth only to miracles all about him."

A strongly held belief in competition and American free enterprise often translates overseas into a love for wealth over happiness. De Tocqueville notes, "As one digs deeper into the national character of the Americans, one sees that they have sought the value of everything in this world only in the answer to this single question: how much money will it bring in?" Kohls agrees that Americans are material and acquisitive more than inquisitive, but he notes that material wealth is viewed in the United States as something integrated with the "American Dream," that anyone who works hard enough can enjoy the "natural benefit" of wealth, including holding property. De Tocqueville seems to agree: "In no other country in the world is the love of property keener or more alert than in the United States, and nowhere else does the majority display less inclination toward doctrines which in any way threaten the way property is owned."[29]

Kohls views the support for equality and egalitarianism as operating almost at the point of religious fervor in the United States, even if it doesn't always play out in reality. In the U.S. context, all men are created equal as set out in the Declaration of Independence, knowing of course that at the time of that document's first publication, women and minorities, including enslaved and indentured servants, were not seen as equal in the eyes of the law as white male property owners. It would take centuries of war, changing attitudes and mores, Congressional legislation, and presidential order to make that ideal closer to reality. De Tocqueville says, "Americans are so enamored of equality that they would rather be equal in slavery than unequal in freedom." This is not the case the world over where personal status and state authority may be stronger values. At a personal level, in many non-Western societies, being equal is an insult because there are people born into their fate and their lives are predetermined by their social heritage, place of birth, and acceptance or rejection by the collective community. Kohls explains that many international visitors to the United States are struck by its informality and equality values, which may be seen by some very important international visitors as a social insult to their high status in their home communities. Being treated "just like everybody else" is not valued everywhere.

The value of intercultural communication research and observation is that it reminds us that some of the enmity for the United States is really a reflection of misunderstandings and misperceptions about what the American people value. So much of the U.S. image in the world is a projected image of the U.S. government, which doesn't always do the most effective job of explaining the motivations of U.S. policy in terms of American cultural values. As an American citizen who is deeply affected by my own growing up in this highly individualistic, competitive culture, I know that the onus is on me to keep explaining and informing others about American values in the context of seeking understanding of how differences inform and offer common ground from which to better communicate with each other.

WASHINGTON AND THE WAR, STRUGGLE, BATTLE OVER ISMS

The April 2002 issue of the *Foreign Service Journal* asked the question, "How is the war selling?" in reference to the post-9/11 war on terrorism and its relationship to the U.S. public diplomacy campaign to win over hearts and minds to the war's mission. It included frank commentaries from five Washington, D.C.-based international journalists, all of whom agreed "that much of the world harbors serious doubts about both the objectives and conduct of the anti-terrorist campaign."[30]

At the time it was quite common among Washington policymakers to link a rise in anti-Americanism to a root cause of terrorism against the United States and its interests. This view was not widely shared outside the shores of the United States. Khaled Abdulkareem, Washington correspondent of Egypt's Middle East News Agency (MENA), said that anti-American sentiment isn't tied to the events of 9/11 or to the respondent Bush administration war on terror policy. "Over the past decade, many in the Muslim world have developed a strong belief that since the demise of communism as a viable blueprint for the right ideological foundation for any given group of nations, Islam has been painted as the West's Enemy No. 1."[31] On the streets of Egypt, he explains, it is not uncommon for someone to ask, "Is it genuine or American?" so untrusting and unbelievable the U.S. mission in the region comes across to many Arabs and Muslims. Israel's crackdown policy against Arab Palestinian resistance, and its close association with the U.S. war on terror, only helped to fuel the suspicions toward the United States that it doesn't play a fair hand in that region. Once you added President Bush's bellicose terror rhetoric, "either with us or with the terrorists," and "dead or alive," you had the ingredients for a meteoric rise in anti-Americanism that was already in full force before 9/11. Tying the two together just exacerbates the problem and sends a message to the Middle East that any open criticism of U.S. policies in the region will be judged as fuel for terrorism.

Ronald Spiers, a career Foreign Service officer, said that when he worked at the State Department under Secretary of State George Schultz, everyone knew to avoid the use of the tired cliché, "one man's terrorist is another man's freedom fighter," when engaging the Secretary on definitions of terrorism. Spiers did ask the Secretary why the United States considered the efforts of the French underground in World War II as freedom fighting, even though they utilized bombs and political assassinations to resist the Nazis and the pro-Nazi Vichy regime in France. To the Nazis, the underground activities were terroristic. To the United States, they were, in Schultz's words, "not terrorists."[32]

What makes terrorism a twin linguistic concept to anti-Americanism is that both conjure up similar visual images in people's heads: A terrorist becomes anyone whose objectives are in direct contrast to your own non-terrorist objectives. Anti-Americanism becomes a belief or behavior that is in contrast to pro-American values. But what do all these pro/con positions really mean? As Speirs notes, Gavrillo Princip, the person responsible for assassinating Austria-Hungarian Crown Prince Ferdinand, was considered a hero, perhaps even a freedom fighter to his fellow Serbs, a terrorist to the Austrian people, and the igniter of World War I to the world.

The need to shift labels away from terrorism wasn't lost on the White House in the summer of 2005 when all of sudden it seemed we started hearing "Global Struggle Against Violent Extremism" (GSAVE) over "Global War on Terrorism" (GWOT). The Bush administration decided that we needed more words of explanation for what we were up against. I took note, as any rhetorical critic would, and told radio host Warren Olney on "To the Point" that the reason for the name change was based in part on a failure to get more countries on board with the U.S.-led war on terror and the failing war in Iraq. Not only that, but the American people were registering their own negative impressions in recent Gallup polls that the war on terror was itself a failure. The phrase, according to the *New Yorker* columnist George Packer, had "outlived its political usefulness."[33] Just after the July 2005 London bombings, the Bush folks were expanding their vocabulary in order to de-emphasize focus on Iraq (and Abu Ghraib, Guantanamo Bay, and Koran desecration stories) and to invite more public participation in the struggle of ideas. A "war on terror" label invited critical questions like, "When will it end?" while a global struggle is ongoing and doesn't really have a perceived ending. Plus, war on terror was always a misnomer. Terrorism is a tactical method in violence. Declaring a war on terrorism is like declaring war on kamikazes. Good luck! A global struggle conjures up pictures of good guys versus bad guys whereas a war on terror might invite others (and has) to indict the United States for engaging in its own state-sponsored terrorism in Iraq and Afghanistan. As General Richard B. Myers, chairman of the Joint Chiefs of Staff, said of the old phrase, "if you call it a war, then you think of people in uniform as being the solution. . . . The long-term problem is as much diplomatic, as much economic—in fact, more diplomatic, more economic, more political than it is military."[34]

A global struggle against violent extremists is more inclusive and broader than just military engagement, but doesn't GSAVE replace one generic name with another, GWOT? How many of us can even picture either phrase in our heads? Author Victor David Hanson thinks that the new phrase isn't precise enough. The target of the global struggle should be identified as radical Islam or radical Islamism, a term many policymakers in Washington, D.C. use to describe ideological opponents of the United States who advocate violence against U.S. targets in the name of their religion. To Hanson, this is not singling out Islam as a religion, only those who use their Islamic identification to incite terror and violence. Whatever the new phrase means to the individual, it is a signal that Washington is motivated more by a struggle over ideas and ideology. But will it work? Packer has ambivalent feelings:

> The Administration is right to reconsider its strategy, starting with the language. Will anything else follow? The global struggle against violent extremism would inspire more confidence if, for example, the Administration hadn't failed to include funding for democracy programs in Iraq beyond the second next round of elections there; or if Karen Hughes hadn't left the job empty for five months while waiting for her son to graduate from high school; or if the White House weren't resisting attempts by Congress to regulate the treatment of prisoners; or if Karl Rove would stop using 9/11 to raise money and smear Democrats. No one really knows how American influence can be used to disinfect Islamist politics of violent ideas. This is the first problem. The second is that the Bush team has shown such bad faith, arrogance and incompetence since September 11th that it seems unlikely to figure it out.[35]

All of this is to suggest that we'll be fighting over the semantics of loaded labels like terrorism and anti-Americanism for years to come, which means that we must continue to define and dissect these name-calling labels to enlighten and not hinder understanding.

AMERICA AND FOREIGN ISMS

Frank Luntz is a Republican pollster and master language meister for what works and doesn't work with the American public. One of the words he cautions members of Congress to stop using is the word "foreigner."

In a memo entitled, "International Trade: Promoting America's Competitiveness," he begins with a communication recommendation away from the use of "foreign" or "global" trade and to "international trade." In his view, "foreign" is a very negative concept in America. "Since Americans are more 'pro international' than they are 'pro-foreign' or 'pro-global,' (globalization is a particularly frightening term to Americans), we suggest you accept this terminology. International trade is favored over foreign trade by 68% of Americans."[36]

The same antipathy toward what those foreigners are saying about us might be applied in the realm of the anti-American debate. In the post-WWII 1940s, U.S. Senator J. William Fulbright found himself at odds with members of Congress who wouldn't support his namesake international exchange program, arguing that they didn't want "American youth corrupted by foreign isms."[37] In the Congressional record, there exists no lofty speech from Fulbright about the importance of seeing the world as others see it or strengthening intercultural relations on the heels of a major world war. In fact, Fulbright doubts that the bill would ever have passed had it come to a full debate on the Senate floor. He explains, "When Senator McKellar of Tennessee found out about it, he said that if he had been aware of the issue, he would have objected because it was a very dangerous thing to send our fine young men and women abroad to be exposed to those foreign 'isms.' He meant it. He thought it was dangerous to expose young Americans to countries whose governments advocated socialism, communism, or any alternative to our American way."[38] As a result, Fulbright's international ism in the United States Senate was decidedly low-key. The former Rhodes Scholar kept his remarks brief and slipped the Fulbright exchange bill into a surplus assets recovery program for war debtor countries.

This suspicion of what others have to say about the United States continues today and is certainly more intense in the post-9/11, post-Iraq war environment. In a special report on anti-Americanism, *The Economist* writes, "Ever since the days of the Founding Fathers, America has regarded what George Washington called 'the foreign world' with a degree of suspicion, and the foreign world has often reciprocated. Never more than now, it seems."[39] The anti-American sentiment is hard to pinpoint, however. Is it directed at a person like Bush? Is it directed toward a place or state of mind like Hollywood? Is America a place to study for an international student? Is it a political image like Globo Cop? When it comes to anti-America anything, it is easy to fall into the paradox trap: one can hate the American president on the one hand and love American popular culture on the other. Perhaps it is best illustrated by the picture of "the incandescent third-world demonstrator, shrieking 'Down with America!' in one breath and 'Can you get me a green card?' in the next."[40]

The evergreen "Yankee Go Home" sentiment was for a moment in 2006 shifted against, of all places, those tolerant non-imperial Danes, who first published twelve caricatures of the Prophet Mohammed that were later reprinted in dozens of European newspapers. One image showed the Prophet wearing a bomb-shaped turban while another depicted him turning away suicide bombers from paradise with the words, "There are no more virgins." Islamic faith prohibits any visual images of the Prophet for fear of spreading idolatry, and, in this case, Muslims throughout the world condemned not only the violation of Islamic doctrine but also the linkage between Islam and terrorism. To them, it was no different than showing Jesus with an AK-47 automatic rifle. (Coincidentally, just days earlier, some American Christians were offended by a *Rolling Stone* magazine cover showing controversial rap artist Kanye West wearing a crown of thorns.)

The European press took a public stance of support for the Danish press by reprinting the "offensive" material in the name of free expression. The U.S. State Department, for once, off the hook in responding to standard anti-American fare, agreed with the Muslim protesters that such cartoons were offensive, but said that such offensive images are protected speech and can be printed by the media. The enormity of the global protests against these cartoons signaled that for all our American and European secular faith in the First Amendment and leap of faith that the world wants to be more like us, a new world order that embraces the Western concept of free speech is not a sure thing.

In the days leading up to war in Iraq, no country came under so much finger pointing in the United States than France, where anti-American sentiment is less contradictory and more national pastime. This is not to say that the French people don't respond to American culture. They do. France has its Euro Disney and the French frequent McDonalds and Starbucks, but they have a national cultural rivalry with the United States that surpasses Great Britain. American culture is also characterized as Anglo-American, not French-American in inspiration and political heritage. America regularly salutes the Statue of Liberty in the New York harbor, one of the world's most recognized freedom icons and a gift of international friendship by the French government to the United States in 1886, but the French want more than passing credit for promoting liberty and equality in the first place. What emerges from the French antipathy toward America is an ongoing cultural rivalry. As the *Economist* writes, "the two countries both think they invented the rights of man, have a unique calling to spread liberty round the world and hold a variety of other attributes that make them utterly and admirably exceptional. Jealousy also plays a part."[41]

The Pew Research Center for the People and the Press, a Washington, D.C.-based think tank, notes in a recent compilation of its post-9/11 Global Attitudes Surveys that "anti-Americanism is deeper and broader now than at any time in modern history... Simply put, the rest of the world both fears and resents the unrivaled power that the United States has amassed since the Cold War ended. In the eyes of others, the U.S. is a worrisome colossus: It is too quick to act unilaterally, it doesn't do a good job of addressing the world's problems, and it widens the global gulf between rich and poor."[42] When President Bush says that the real reason the United States invaded Iraq to remove Saddam Hussein has more to do with advancing democracy in the world, global public opinion just doesn't buy that argument. More likely, global publics would question U.S. motives and likely frame international events in terms of retaining power through a hunt for additional resources, in the case of the Middle East, oil.

The Pew global surveys continue to show a picture of America's image in the world that is not easily comprehended, but rather full of contradictions and complements. Even within a framework of global military and economic domination, "a majority of people around the world admire America's democratic values and much about its way of life. While they express deep misgivings about the U.S.-led war on terror, they feel more secure living in a world in which no other nation can challenge the United States militarily. In short, while they chafe at the U.S. roles as the world's super cop, they're also relieved that no one else is walking the beat."[43] This has been a rather steady global opinion and attitude assessment since the end of the Cold War. The difference now is that the shining city on the hill is losing its shimmer as the best model for the free-spirited, democratic and pluralist society in the twenty-first century. There are more democracy models to follow, including the 25-member state European Union that has a collective economic wealth and population size that surpasses the United States.

Particularly worrisome to many Europeans is the U.S. strong support for the death penalty, much stronger religious values expression in public life, and strong opposition to multilateral institutions such as the United Nations. Even though a December 2004 BBC poll indicated that much of European anti-Americanism is driven more by the reelection of President Bush (42% said the presidential results "made them feel worse toward Americans"), Americans shouldn't necessarily hold their breaths and wait until a more globally palatable president is elected. What is becoming more widespread and not necessarily tied to opposition to Bush is a feeling that "American is losing its allure as a model society. Whereas much of the rest of the world once looked to the United States as a beacon, it is argued, non-Americans are now turning away."[44]

AMERICA AND THE UNITED NATIONS

Ron Paul is a medical doctor and Republican member of Congress from the 14th Congressional District in Texas that stretches from the Gulf Coast near Galveston almost to Corpus Christi. The district prides itself as "where Texas began," since Texas founding father Stephen F. Austin grew up in the district town of Jones Creek. Dr. Paul is a libertarian and proponent of "The Ron Paul Freedom Principles" that are displayed prominently on his website:

- Rights belong to individuals, not groups.
- Property should be owned by people, not government.
- All voluntary associations should be permissible—economic and social.
- The government's monetary role is to maintain the integrity of the monetary unit, not participate in fraud.
- Government exists to protect liberty, not to redistribute wealth or to grant special privileges.
- The lives and actions of people are their own responsibility, not the government's.

As a member of the Committee on International Relations, Dr. Paul is an outspoken foe of the United Nations. His April 18, 2005 "Texas Straight Talk" weekly column entitled "Why do we fund UNESCO?" criticizes the

Bush Administration for rejoining UNESCO, the United Nations Educational, Scientific, and Cultural Organization, in 2002 after nearly a 20-year absence. The United States had left UNESCO in 1984 after the Reagan Administration accused the agency of being anti-American, particularly against American sacrosanct philosophics of liberty, freedom, and the free market, and fiscally unsound with its seemingly ever-growing budget, 25% of which the United States was funding. Reagan certainly had no use for having U.S. taxpayers support an international organization that wasn't completely beholden to U.S. interests. Now Congressman Paul wondered why the United States had decided in the post-9/11 environment to make good on its lapsed membership.

He writes, "Rejoining UNESCO, of course, means paying for it. Our new commitment to UNESCO costs $60 million annually for starters, fully one-quarter of the agency's budget. Sadly, I believe the administration made this decision as a concession to our globalist critics, who decry supposed American unilateralism."[45] Though the name of the organization "sounds lofty . . . the agency is nothing but a mouthpiece for the usual UN causes, including international abortion and population control; politically correct UN curriculum for American schools; and UN control of federal land in America through so-called World Heritage sites." Paul accuses UNESCO of being anti-American from birth. "From its inception UNESCO has been openly hostile to American values, our Constitution, and western culture. Why in the world should we send tax dollars to an organization that actively promotes values so contrary to those of most Americans? Is it worth spending $60 million every year on an organization with such a terrible history of waste, corruption, and anti-Americanism?"

Dr. Paul promised to attach an amendment to get the U.S. out of the UNESCO in a foreign aid spending bill in the summer of 2005. Though such an amendment failed passage, it is worth examining the validity of the anti-American label Paul uses against UNESCO. In his original column, Paul criticizes UNESCO's founding director, Sir Julian Huxley, brother to Aldous Huxley. Aldous is the more famous of the two brothers, a popular British essayist and author of *Brave New World* and *Brave New World Revisited*, which deal with the propaganda in dictatorships and democracies that undermine human freedom. Julian Huxley had said that an organization like UNESCO would certainly challenge national sovereignty and that UNESCO's focus on political unification may require some sort of world government. It is that phrase, "world government," that is often the euphemistic hook for "anti-Americanism," and most any anti-UN person is quick to denounce the United Nations as nothing but a world body that pokes its nose into individual member countries' business. But just how justified are the charges that Paul makes of the UN in general or UNESCO in particular? Why is it that international organizations that we know do a lot of good in the world are so quickly labeled as anti-American for having globalist tendencies? Only a world body can tackle some of the most pressing global problems of the day, be they AIDS, SARS, polio, foreign debt, nuclear proliferation. There is no question that the United Nations is an organization fraught with waste, fraud, and abuse, not unlike any large government bureaucracy. Is the United Nations any more inefficient because of its global membership? It could possibly be, given the reality that while 190 countries are members, there is no one CEO or COO responsible for holding it accountable. Not even the Secretary General of the UN can possibly manage such a large bureaucracy. Nevertheless, I think it's too simplistic to characterize this global organization as inherently anti-American or too fraught with abuse to justify its continuation.

As a former U.S. government official, I was initially surprised at the levels of inefficiency and wasted taxpayer resources in the two organizations with which I was working, the U.S. Information Agency and the U.S. State Department. Much of my work consisted of monitoring what our subcontracting organizations were doing on the government's behalf, which almost made me feel like my job was superfluous. In the case of USIA, there were two primary private nonprofit organizations that worked to carry out the Fulbright international exchange mission of the agency as part of its overall mission, "telling America's story to the world." These were the Institute for International Education (IIE) ironically located directly across the street from the United Nations in mid-Manhattan, and the Council for International Exchange of Scholars (CIES), located in Washington, D.C. I always thought it was these organizations that were truly responsible for the day-to-day activities of the Fulbright program. They were its face. We were the hidden bureaucrats pushing paper behind the scenes, with rare opportunities to meet face-to-face with our Fulbright recipients.

One impetus for my leaving government service was because I'm much too hands-on to ever enjoy a job that didn't include a lot of interpersonal contact. This is why teaching has worked out wonderfully and my federal government service is fast becoming a fading memory. I tell this story because it dispels the myth that only global organizations are inefficient. Waste, fraud, and abuse are alive and well in the most pro-American organizations, and they exist in organizations accused by freedom-loving Texas Congressmen as fronts for world government.

NOTES

1. This passage is based on a conversation with a USC Annenberg School for Communication student on January 17, 2005, whose real name is not used to protect the student's privacy.

2. William J. Lederer and Eugene Burdick, *The Ugly American* (New York: W.W. Norton and Company, 1958), 145.

3. Lederer, *The Ugly American*, 145.

4. Colin Powell, "Testimony Before the House Budget Committee," March 15, 2001.

5. George W. Bush, Televised National Press Conference, October 11, 2001.

6. Henry Hyde, "Speaking to our Silent Allies: The Role of Public Diplomacy in U.S. Foreign Policy," speech delivered to the Council on Foreign Relations, June 17, 2002. Quote is taken from press statement released by Rep. Hyde's office on June 18, 2002.

7. See www.businessfordiplomaticaction.org mission statement.

8. Anthony Pratkanis and Elliot Aronson, *Age of Propaganda* (New York: W.H. Freeman & Company, 2001), 11.

9. Robert H. Gass and John S. Seiter, *Persuasion, Social Influence and Compliance Gaining*, 2nd ed. (Boston: Allyn & Bacon, 2003), 12.

10. Cedric Larson and James R. Mock, "The Lost Files of the Creel Committee of 1917–1919," *Public Opinion Quarterly* 3, no. 1 (January 1939): 8.

11. Larson and Mock, 8.

12. See James Dao and Eric Schmitt, "Pentagon Readies Efforts to Sway Sentiment Abroad," *New York Times*, February 19, 2002 www.commondreams .org/headlines02/0219-01.htm; Nancy Snow, "Déjà Vu All Over Again," Common Dreams, February 20, 2002 www.commondreams.org/views02/0220-03.htm; The BBC News story, "Pentagon Plans Propaganda War," news.bbc.co.uk/2/hi/ americas/1830500.stm; "New Pentagon Office to Spear Information War" in CNN archives archives.cnn.com/2002/US/02/19/gen.strategic.influence; "Strategic Influence Office 'Closed Down,' Says Rumsfeld" by Gerry J. Gilmore, American Forces Press Service www.defenselink.mil/news/Feb2002/n02262002 _200202263.html.

13. Stuart Oskamp and P. Wesley Schultz, *Attitudes and Opinions*, third ed. (Mahwah, NJ: Lawrence Erlbaum Associates, 2005), 188.

14. Alexis de Tocqueville, *Democracy in America*, Volume 1. Contributors: John Bigelow, Henry Reeve, translator. (New York: D. Appleton and Company, 1899), 280–281.

15. J. William Fulbright, *The Arrogance of Power* (New York: Vintage Books, 1966), 27.

16. Fulbright, *The Arrogance of Power*, 27.

17. De Tocqueville, *Democracy in America*, 753.

18. Arnold S. de Beer and John C. Merrill, *Global Journalism* (New York: Pearson, 2004), 8.

19. Knight Foundation, "First Amendment Survey," January 2005; results available at www.firstamendmentfuture.org/main.html.

20. Alexis de Tocqeville, *Democracy in America*, Volume 2 (New York: D. Appleton and Co., 1899), 488.

21. Frank Newport, "Update: Americans and Religion," December 23, 2004. Available in Gallup archive at www.gallup.com.

22. Albert L. Winseman, "Who Has Been Born Again?" January 18, 2005. Available for Gallup subscribers at www.gallup.com/poll/content/default.aspx?ci= 14632.

23. Ronald Inglehart, "1990 World Values Survey" (Ann Arbor, MI: Institute for Social Research, 1990), question 3 F.

24. Gary R. Weaver, "American Cultural Values." This piece was originally published in *Kokusai Bunka Kenshu* (*Intercultural Training*) 14 (Winter 1997): 14–20.

25. Stella Ting-Toomey and Leeva C. Chung, *Intercultural Communication* (Los Angeles, CA: Roxbury, 2005), 176.

26. L. Robert Kohls, *Survival Kit for Overseas Living* (Yarmouth, ME: Intercultural Press, 2001). See also Gary Althen, Ed., *Learning Across Cultures* (Washington, D.C.: NAFSA, Association of International Educators, 1994).

27. Oskamp and Schultz, *Attitudes and Opinions*, 206.

28. De Tocqueville, 472.

29. De Tocqueville, 747.

30. American Foreign Service Association, *Foreign Service Journal*, Focus on "How is the War Selling?" April 2002.

31. Khaled Abdulkareem, "U.S. War on Terror—A Middle Eastern Perspective," *Foreign Service Journal*, 2002, 17.

32. Ronald Spiers, "The Anatomy of Terrorism," *Foreign Service Journal*, September 2004, 43.

33. George Packer, "Name Calling," *The New Yorker*, August 1, 2005. Online version.

34. Robin Abcarian, " 'War'? Oh, that's over," *Los Angeles Times*, August 1, 2005.

35. Packer, *The New Yorker*.

36. Bidisha Banerjee, "GOP Master Plan Revealed," *Slate*, February 23, 2005. Available at slate.msn.com/id/2113945/.

37. J. William Fulbright, *The Price of Empire* (New York: Pantheon, 1989), 212.

38. Fulbright, *Price of Empire*, 213.

39. "Anti-Americanism: The View From Abroad," *The Economist*, February 19th, 2005, 24–26.

40. *The Economist*, 24.

41. *The Economist*, 25.

42. Pew Research Center for People and the Press, "Trends 2005," January 2005, 106. Available at pewresearch.org/trends/trends2005.pdf.

43. Pew, "Trends 2005," 107.

44. *The Economist*, "Anti-Americanism," 26.

45. Ron Paul, "Why Do We Fund UNESCO?" www.house.gov/paul/tst/tst2005/tst041805.htm.

2

PERCEPTION IS REALITY IN MARKETING THE NUMBER ONE

SELLING AMERICAN DEMOCRACY, THEN AND NOW

It really is a wonder that a few short months after 9/11, America became viewed as the aggressor and not the victim to the world. To some, America was never a victim, even on September 11, 2001. The American image in the world is now at rock bottom, despite record-breaking public diplomacy efforts to improve its image through information, engagement, and social influence strategies with international audiences. The Government Accountability Office (GAO) sharply criticized this failed effort to persuade in its April 2005 report. Coordinated efforts to forge an international communications strategy have withered away with the demise of the Pentagon's Office of Strategic Influence (OSI) in 2002 and the end of the White House's Office of Global Communications (OGC) in 2005. Similarly, the public face of public diplomacy keeps changing. Charlotte Beers was on board just eighteen months followed by the six-month reign of Margaret Tutwiler. Even President Bush's chief domestic confidante, Karen Hughes, who took over in the third quarter of 2005 as under secretary of state for public diplomacy, wasn't expected to change the nation's image overnight. Hughes is viewed as more adept at domestic spin necessary in the battleground of American political campaigns, but not geared toward the cultural and contextualized complexities of international relations.

According to *U.S. News and World Report* writer David E. Kaplan, the U.S. government is embarking on a reinvigorated effort to win hearts and minds. In a four-month investigative report titled "Hearts, Minds and Dollars," Kaplan reports that top government officials have grown tired of the global media bashing about America's failed information war strategies.[1] The government is now re-launching covert and overt multimedia efforts to engage the world in a battle for a moderate Islam that partners, rather than spars, with America. The U.S. Department of Defense announced in February 2006 that psychological operations (Psy/Ops) would be significantly increased in the war on terror. Psychological operations are defined by the U.S. military as "conveying messages to selected foreign groups to promote particular themes that result in desired foreign attitudes and behaviors."[2] They include activities such as dropping information leaflets or training personnel to integrate into the local population to counter disinformation from the enemy. Whether we call it Psy/Ops or public diplomacy, it may have been unofficially launched by the hand-holding seen 'round the world, with President George W. Bush and Jordan's King Abdallah showing great affection and mutual admiration during the king's visit to Bush's Crawford ranch in spring 2005. This love, American-style, approach to global engagement came at a most precarious time when American credibility and respectability in the world was in decline. According to a survey of 23,519 people in twenty-three countries conducted by the Program on International Policy Attitudes (PIPA) in December 2004 and released in April 2005, the United States was viewed in 20 of the 23 countries as less influential than Europe in world affairs. Almost 60 percent of those surveyed thought that Europe should become more influential than the United States in world affairs, with just the Philippines and the United States showing majorities opposed to the rise in European influence. France was viewed most positively in 20 countries, even though its favorability in the United States is a minority opinion. Steven Kull, director of PIPA, found it noteworthy that the areas registering as mostly positive influences were Europe and China, "which have engaged the world primarily through economic relations—or soft power," while the United States and Russia, which "have very large militaries and have recently used them in a prominent way" were "more often seen as having a negative influence." Said Kull, "Some have argued U.S. military power deserves appreciation for making the global economic order possible, but with the Cold War a fading memory, this perspective seems to be fading as well. While trade might buy you love, guns clearly do not."[3]

Doug Miller, president of GlobeScan, concluded from the research that "Europe's star has risen as America's reputation has declined under the Bush Administration. Americans really must worry when it is the wealthy of the world and the youth of the world that are the most upset with them."

It may seem to be a singular obsession with us Americans, but we do get quite worked up about how others view us. Even President Bush first cast the attacks of 9/11 in terms of American antipathy. Other countries think that Americans are a bit taken with our own national image, which is very true, but this vanity is very much a symbolic representation of who we are, a very confident people in general, as much as it is about how others see us. I know of no other country on the planet that so worries over its own national reputation in the world. For instance, there seems to be no equivalent to the contested term "anti-Americanism" in our modern lexicon outside of the often linked concept, "anti-Semitism." Indeed, to those highly critical of U.S. foreign policy, they are often equally critical of Israeli foreign and domestic policy, but this joint criticism may not speak of any hatred toward a particular religious or national group; rather, such criticism is to many a reflection of what it means to live in a democratic society where dissent and open debate are expected and welcomed.

America's preoccupation with saving face in the eyes of the world may seem at times to be a bit overdone, like some glamour diva who cannot resist stopping to check out her image in every mirror. Much of this national image concern has deep-seated historical ties. We are a nation that has been involved in two world wars from which we emerged victorious. The victory was won in blood and publicity. *New York Times* writer Victoria de Grazia noted in an article published just a year after 9/11, this merging of Madison Avenue with war is neither new nor even exclusively an American phenomenon. "The Romans demonstrated their power from Gaul to Galilee by stamping the emperor's face on their coins," she wrote, "and Her Majesty's government publicized the Pax Britannica by celebrating Queen Victoria's Diamond Jubilee with global distribution of figurines and cups with her image." But, she said, there is no country that has "developed as close a link between statesmanship and salesmanship as the United States."[4]

So the United States went from President Bush's "Why do they hate us?" to "How do we reposition the brand?"[5] It was Charlotte Beers, the first post-9/11 public diplomacy czar, who argued that it was America's poor perception in the world that led to unrest, which in turn leads to threats to our nation's security. Beers regarded the emotional connection between the advertiser and the audience as paramount. A rational message alone wouldn't cut it. The problem for the United States in the new century is that try as we might to "sell" the War on Terror as an extension of the Cold War or to recast the information war strategies of post-September 11, 2001, with that of Pearl Harbor or the immediate post-WWII period, the two centuries and events are too distinct and too far apart in cultural make-up.

At times the United States is very good with the hard sell, even when our nation engages in war. Throughout most of the twentieth century, it was our century alone, as media icon Henry Luce declared. America was living in a world of its own making. We were the white hats standing firm against the black hat totalitarians ruling Eastern Europe, the Soviet Union, North Korea, Cuba, and the Viet Cong. Harry Truman, who presided over America's nuclear solution to end World War II, would less than a month later see his nation's top brass gather aboard the USS *Missouri* September 2, 1945 to accept the surrender of Japan. World War II officially ended on the deck of the USS *Missouri*, anchored in Tokyo Bay on that date, when representatives of ten nations—the United States, Australia, Canada, China, France, the Netherlands, New Zealand, Russia, United Kingdom, and Japan—assembled on her deck to sign the surrender.

Within a few short months, the Cold War had begun and the *Missouri* was involved in a most important diplomatic mission the following spring to seize the theater of persuasion away from the Soviet Union that craved a stronghold in Greece and Turkey. My father Victor D. Snow, Sr., was aboard the *Missouri* for this soft power campaign. After receiving the remains of the Turkish Ambassador to the United States, Melmet Munir Ertegun, the ship departed New York for Gibraltar. By April 5, 1946, it was anchored off Istanbul and rendered full military honors. This included a nineteen-gun salute during the ceremony to transfer the Ambassador's remains from ship to funeral ashore. On April 9, the *Missouri* departed Istanbul for Phaleron Bay, Piraeus, Greece, where on the following day the Greek government and Greek people welcomed the great battleship with open arms. As the USS *Missouri* Memorial Association reports:

> She had arrived in a year when there were ominous Russian overtures and activities in the entire Balkan area. Greece had become the scene of a Communist-inspired civil war, as Russia sought every possible extension of Soviet influence throughout the Mediterranean region. Demands were made that Turkey grant the Soviets a base of sea power in the Dodecanese Islands and joint control of the Turkish Strait leading from the Black Sea into the Mediterranean. The voyage of *Missouri* to the eastern Mediterranean gave comfort to both Greece and Turkey. News media proclaimed her a symbol of U.S. interest in preserving Greek and Turkish liberty. With an August decision to deploy a strong fleet to the Mediterranean, it became obvious that the United States intended to use her naval sea and air power to stand firm against the tide of Soviet subversion.[6]

The *Missouri* made its case for America without firing a shot. It didn't have to. And America came out the good guys.

On June 5, 1947, U.S. Secretary of State George C. Marshall delivered one of the most significant commencement addresses in American history to the country's elite, Harvard Class of '47. Less than two years had passed since cessation of hostilities in the Pacific theater with the dropping of the atomic bombs on the Japanese cities of Nagasaki and Hiroshima. As the *Washington Post* headlined the occasion, "Marshall Sees Europe in Need of Vast New U.S. Aid; Urges Self-Help in Reconstruction,"[7] he called on the American people, specifically its most enterprising and entrepreneurial business people and farmers, to help reconstruct the devastated countries of Europe. The vision was innovative in that it was not designed to be charity or top-down in style. Rather, the idea was to allow the European countries to help themselves through partnering with assisting organizations from the United States. The Marshall Plan was not strictly about America's Cold War needs in a narrow national security context, though indeed it was that in part, but was marketed mostly under a regional security framework that included how domestic populations would be fed, clothed, housed, and made well enough to build up their own economies:

> Our policy is directed not against any country or doctrine but against hunger, poverty, desperation and chaos. Its purpose should be the revival of a working economy in the world so as to permit the emergence of political and social

conditions in which free institutions can exist ... Any government that is willing to assist in the task of recovery will find full cooperation, I am sure, on the part of the United States Government. Any government which maneuvers to block the recovery of other countries cannot expect help from us. Furthermore, governments, political parties or groups which seek to perpetuate human misery in order to profit therefrom politically or otherwise will encounter opposition of the United States.[8]

According to a Library of Congress fiftieth anniversary exhibit of the Marshall Plan, it had two major aims: "to prevent the spread of communism in Western Europe and to stabilize the international order in a way favorable to the development of political democracy and free-market economies."[9] Some scholars have referred to the Marshall Plan, otherwise known as the European Recovery Program (ERP), as a program of American enlightened self-interest. It wasn't just about us and our needs, a telling narrative that may help to inform American public diplomacy aims and objectives of the twenty-first century. Amy Garrett, now a scholar-in-residence at the U.S. State Department, argues in her doctoral dissertation, "Marketing America: Public Culture and Public Diplomacy in the Marshall Plan Era, 1947–1954," the Marshall Plan was marketed as helping the Europeans help themselves, but in reality included efforts "that could reform European work habits until the economies of Western Europe operated according to the received American economic wisdom and conformed to U.S. foreign policy goals."[10] These U.S. foreign policy goals were anti-communist and pro-American free market economy. However initially embedded U.S. foreign policy and ideological goals were with the Marshall Plan, sixteen countries of Western Europe were enthusiastically on board to accept U.S. aid.

We were the one victorious country that was able to pull up defeated countries by their proverbial bootstraps through economic security programs like the Marshall Plan. Amy Garrett notes that the Marshall Plan was viewed quite differently through European and American eyes. What many Americans saw as generosity, some Europeans saw as "a Trojan horse, opening the gates to laissez-faire capitalism."[11] American-style capitalism was infused with anti-Communism ideology. Paul Hoffman, who once headed Studebaker Motor Co. before taking over the reins of the Marshall Plan, ordered some of the Marshall funds for a remarkably inventive range of events, films and publications, many propagandizing the "high standard of living" of "Joe Smith, America's average worker"—his tidy home, clean denim overalls, shiny tools, his car. All would be accessible to Europeans, provided they worked hard and voted anti-Communist.

The Marshall Plan was a high point in American's image in Europe, despite the reticence among some Europeans toward America's true motives. The important point was that Europe was getting back on its feet and the ERP was even supporting trade unionism against the traditionally Communist-controlled labor unions in Italy, France, and Greece. The tougher sell was surely the North Atlantic Treaty Organization (NATO), which unlike the Marshall Plan's beneficient "Grapes of Wrath" approach to feeding Europe's starving, had more hard power overtones. De Grazia notes in the *New York Times* that J. Walter Thompson, then the world's advertising giant, took over the NATO account at a time when many Americans in the mid-1950s were growing weary of their overseas commitments:

> The ad men's advice was that for its 10th anniversary, in 1959, NATO should be reshaped "to forge a history of community and tradition," and "make clear to the world the striking superiority, as much moral as material, of the Western conception of Man and his dignity." The campaign called for a NATO birthday celebration, a NATO song featuring Rosemary Clooney, Bing Crosby, Frank Sinatra and Harry Belafonte, among others, and slogans like "Good night, sleep tight, NATO stands on guard" and "N-A-T-O—four letters that spell peace."

China was not a worry then because it had not become the economic behemoth of today. Japan was still in a post-WWII adolescence as a nation surviving a nuclear holocaust and later demilitarized. It was far from the Japan, Inc. of the mid-1990s. The Soviet Union was a formidable opponent but secretly we believed that it would come to its own ruination in time. Give the people MTV and they'll beg for more.

Another incident, the famous "kitchen debate" between then Vice President Richard Nixon and Soviet premier Nikita Khrushchev illustrated the persuasion power that America enjoyed in the decades after World War II and before Vietnam. In this case, it was 1959 and the United States and Soviet Union had agreed to share exhibitions to introduce each country's culture, society, and way of life to the people. On the two leaders' visit to a Moscow exhibit of a model American kitchen, Khrushchev denounced the scene and Nixon responded by pointing a finger at Khrushchev's chest and telling him not to expect any favors at the next round of diplomatic meetings. Khrushchev complained he had been threatened by the American, but still photographs showed America standing up to the Big Bear. Nixon's legendary status as a crusading anti-Communist would work to his favor in the 1968 presidential elections and the "kitchen debate" legend would go down in history as an opportunity for America to show up its consumer advancements and challenge Soviet propaganda that sought to debase so-called American crass commercialism.[12]

America's history of greatness in the 20th century makes me all the more ambivalent about current U.S. policies in the world. We can love that America has the capacity and mission to do much good in the world. America has been a force for good, emphasis on force and good. We are simultaneously a Rock Star Nation that can generate millions of donations for some humanitarian need in a nanosecond and part Bombs Bursting Bright, the only nation that can so arrogantly call our military operations "Operation Shock and Awe" and expect others to support it. When we are good, we are very good at what we do. I'm thinking of World War II in particular, which is foremost in my thoughts as I write this book the same year that I lost my father, Victor Donald Snow, Sr., whose entire life was defined by his being part of the Greatest Generation and Great Depression. I did not know him to be particularly political, although I'm comforted by his lack of support for the war in Iraq, which he saw as an elective and unnecessary war that did far more harm than good. I did know that Dad served his country at a time when many men and women saw it as a calling to give back to a nation that had helped that generation through an economic depression. One didn't so much question the government's actions then; one served. Part of Dad's college education was paid for by the U.S. Navy and Dad enjoyed the best in education at some of the nation's best universities, including Rice, Notre Dame, and MIT. He earned his engineering degree from Rice within days of turning 20 and was in less than a year on board the Mighty Mo as a Navy ensign steering toward the Mediterranean. He retired honorably from the Naval Reserve as lieutenant in 1956. My father was a most selfless man and exemplified a time in our history when we were perceived as a most selfless do-gooder nation. While my Dad's service on the USS *Missouri* followed the end of conflict in 1945, he did participate in that global mission to exert American influence in the Mediterranean region. Would America be met with so much enthusiasm were it to send its top battleship into Turkish or Greek waters today? It's highly doubtful.

At that period after World War II, America was truly great because she was seen as good. We were a good society because we seemed to take others' interests into account and not just our own. This period of goodwill would be followed shortly thereafter by the Marshall Plan and the Berlin Airlift when so many Europeans accepted American help with open arms. The American government dubbed its 324-day airlift "Operation Vittles," a far cry from "Operation Shock and Awe" that named the war on Iraq. It was a time for "The Yanks Are Here" over "Yankee Go Home." International ambivalence would come much later.

It is with fading nostalgia that I look back on that post-WWII period. I can see why President Bush tried to build on that good ole time feeling when he referred to September 11th as this generation's Pearl Harbor. It did not stick. We had Pearl Harbor, but no World War II, no Marshall Plan, and no kitchen debate drama. I do not think that the United States will ever again enjoy the goodwill it had in that immediate post–World War II period. Our times are so much more deeply cynical and driven by rumor, innuendo, irrelevant media, harsh imagery available for immediate download, and loss of credibility from the corporate suite to the government corridor. Even our public institutions of higher learning, so strapped for cash, are driven to distraction by a search for external support and revenue from students than they are for higher meaning. We don't generally have time to live the life of the mind because we are too worried about keeping our jobs! Despite these limitations, I do think that these times are so precarious that they are heightening our awareness of what's really going on in media, language, and mind space. The reflections to follow are my attempt to push the envelope of our thinking about what it means to be an American in a world increasingly in doubt of its superiority or moral leadership.

PROPAGANDA AND THE PERCEPTION GAP

There exists a global gap in perception perpetuated by propaganda—namely, how Americans view themselves as basically good and well-intentioned in their behavior toward the outside world and how non-Americans see us, both negatively and positively. While we see ourselves as basically a good people, if not a far superior people who make only unintentional mistakes, other nations view the United States as they would any other, full of people and policies that can either help or hurt the world, but certainly not save it due to any superior moral turpitude ingrained in our national psyche.

As a United States citizen and one who spends her professional focus on all things American persuasion, influence, and propaganda, I view my national identity as a fortunate accident-of-birth condition that has shaped my lifelong devotion to what it means to be an American in a world where my nation of birth impacts so many. I often wonder, do Canadians, British, Japanese, or Brazilians wake up every day and think about their respective nations' impact on the world? I would doubt that any other nation of people so obsesses over its international reputation as we do in the United States, but the problem, you'll see, is that our national obsession is very much focused on how we can improve our image in the world, not understand any grievances or our own shortcomings. So often I read international op-eds or essays about America's role in the world that conclude with "you just don't get it" or "it's not all about you" sentiments. I hope that this book will help to enlighten both Americans and non-Americans about how we can better understand each other and what we can do to overcome our misperceptions.

Because most Americans get a heavy dosage of how great it is to live in America from the time we are born and receive a lot of indoctrination in defending the actions and intentions of Americans in the world, we are quick to protect our young cubs like mother lions when others want to criticize. We even do that with each other. Have problems with the whys or why nots of the American war in Iraq? Then you must be against the troops! Left out is any critical discussion and debate about those whys or why nots. I correct myself. We did eventually learn about the why nots— weapons of mass destruction—but have yet to learn why we went to war in the first place.

My USA citizenship is fortunate in that I have many more constitutional and legal protections as a woman and professional writer, author, and academic than I would have in the world's majority countries. It is also accidental in that I did not decide one day to immigrate to the United States for greater opportunity. I was born here, grew up here, and have lived mostly in the United States with one year's exception, my Fulbright exchange year during the mid-1980s to the former Federal Republic of Germany, known better as West Germany. I have traveled throughout the world quite extensively however, having visited or given public lectures in more than thirty countries, but the majority of my life has been spent residing in the United States. At the time I lived abroad in West Germany, the United States was in a very pro-American phase. It's "morning in America," said one ad for Republican candidate Ronald W. Reagan. President Reagan was reelected for a second term in part for his ability to make Americans feel good about themselves again and was wildly popular among conservatives and Republicans at home. Reagan was also criticized often in the American press and inspired many a protest in Washington for his Cold War and Central American policies.

I got my citizen protest "sea legs" during the Reagan years that coincided with my college years. I recall being downright afraid that a nuclear war would break out because the United States seemed to be at an impasse with its negotiations with the Soviet Union and Reagan's rhetoric reinforced the picture in the world of American "arrogance of power," to use Fulbright's term. Equally worrisome was American intervention in Central America, including Nicaragua, El Salvador, and Grenada. Reagan told America that Communist insurgents were just days away from marching into Texas, another variation on the dominoes theory of Vietnam. I couldn't see how little defenseless Grenada could take us, but I knew that Reagan would win points for standing up to these countries, many of which were challenging the pro-market capitalist economy we favored. It was with a curiosity to learn more outside my college textbooks and comparative politics courses that I joined a local peace group in my college town of Clemson, South Carolina. I'm thankful to that group, comprised of local townspeople and retired college professors, that helped to educate its one college student member about U.S. foreign policy in the world.

Reagan was not a favorite president of mine, to be sure, but he must be acknowledged for having a conversion to global humanity in his second term. By the time of Reagan's nuclear arms talks with Gorbachev, he seemed to be thinking long and hard about his posthumous legacy, and not about Iranian arms for Central American hostages as he later admitted in a subpoenaed deposition. Reagan wished to be viewed as the American president who was so rabid an anti-Communist that he best could help shape the transformation of the Soviet Union from tyranny to democracy. For that, I think he deserves his due credit in changing his hardened stance toward the USSR, but like any other American president, he should be viewed in his complete chronology and not just credited with helping to bring down the Soviet Union.

When I began my Fulbright program exchange study in the Federal Republic of Germany (West Germany) in the mid-1980s, it was the reelection campaign season for Reagan. Reagan's decisive presidential victory in November 1984 was not very well received in the European press or public, even though many governments like Margaret Thatcher's Great Britain or Helmut Kohl's Germany were solid U.S. allies and shared Reagan's strongly anti-Communist views. Reagan was friendly with Chancellor Helmut Kohl despite the opposition from many German citizens, particularly the youth, who were worried about Reagan's aggressive anti-Communist and warrior rhetoric directed at the Soviet Union. They viewed Kohl as Reagan's lapdog, not unlike the criticism in 2003 of Tony Blair as loyal canine to big dog George W. Bush over Iraq.

Generally, Reagan was viewed by most European citizens I encountered as having a Cowboy-style approach to foreign policy, an inclination to go on the offensive militarily rather than negotiate international problems, and an overly confident view of American ideals. A week after I arrived in Germany, the left-leaning *Stern* magazine had a cover of Reagan dressed like Bozo the Clown with the caption, *Der Spinnt* (He's Crazy), in response to Reagan's joking comment caught over an open mike during a sound check of his weekly radio address: "My fellow Americans, I'm pleased to tell you today that I've signed legislation that will outlaw Russia forever. We begin bombing in five minutes." His seeming insensitivity to real fears evoked during the Cold War created a global media stir and provided the USSR with appropriate propaganda fodder for the bipolar information and ideology war. Now the world could see that the presidential cowboy, like a reckless sheriff in a town gone scared, was ready to make a unilateral decision to fire on innocents. Reagan's supporters said he was a man with great humor and meant nothing by it, but for America's public diplomacy corps, it didn't help their efforts to win global hearts and minds to have the chief CEO of the USA project an image of America as a country gone mad. It would be several years before the softer image of the so-called Great Communicator would emerge, reflected in his summit meetings with Mikhail Gorbachev where both men displayed a mutual respect for each other and a shared interest in reducing the world's dependency on nuclear weapons.

The topic of American propaganda in a world of anti-Americanism began to influence my professional direction as long as twenty years ago when I was deciding between a career in law and one in academia as an international relations Ph.D. with an emphasis in intercultural communication, peace and conflict resolution, and U.S. foreign policy. [I guess you know what I decided!] While still in college and before my Fulbright year, I had spent part of a summer traveling with a small group of students and our German language professors to Eastern and Western Europe, including a rare look behind the Iron Curtain in East Germany and Czechoslovakia. In the Soviet Bloc, anti-American sentiment was expected and experienced. In Leipzig, Germany, we spent an afternoon with a group of college students debating the liberating attributes of Western-style capitalism against the forced conformity of Soviet-led communism. While we didn't come to any common ground over ideology and political economy or win over any converts, we did share a love for American Rock and Roll and had the most fun dancing to the beats.

In the early to mid-1990s, I worked at the U.S. Information Agency (USIA), an independent agency of the U.S. government, whose Cold War heyday was over. It still had the responsibility to tell America's story to the world in a post-Cold War era where it seemed by now the U.S. culture and political economy served as the preferred model for the world. In the summer of 1993, there were two widely circulated articles throughout USIA and its "big sister" Department of State that laid out two alternative foreign policy visions for the future. First, there was the established "end of history" optimism of Francis Fukuyama, whose 1989 article in *The National Interest* foreshadowed the triumph of a market-driven liberal democracy over communism and socialism: "We may be witnessing...the end of history as such: that is, the end point of mankind's ideological evolution and the universalization of Western liberal democracy as the final form of human government." His thesis was being challenged that summer by Samuel Huntington's premise that the war of ideas was heating up, this time under a different guise: "It is my hypothesis that the fundamental source of conflict in this new world will not be primarily ideological or primarily economic. The great divisions among humankind and the dominating source of conflict will be cultural." Some of us at the agency at the time used the Huntington warning to keep pressing the global promise of American values of entrepreneurship, individualism, free press, and free enterprise, that although not exclusive to the United States, set a cultural standard for the rest of the world to follow. With no recognizable enemy state to challenge, however, it was a tall order for a billion dollar agency to convince Congress that promoting America was justifiable on its own merits. In 1999, just five years after I left USIA, its life had been cut short at 46 and there was no longer an independent government agency involved in the pro-America business.

Fast forward from the 1990s to the 2000s. The topic of anti-Americanism began in earnest when I saw high level Washington officials express amazement, bewilderment, and confusion about anti-American sentiment and a poor image of the U.S. overseas after 9/11. Most famously, Representative Henry Hyde's questioning how Hollywood and Madison Avenue had dropped the ball on American antipathy overseas and President Bush's amazed incredulity one month after 9/11 that some people, somewhere, might actually hate the United States. To both expressions, I remember thinking, they just don't get it. The United States is considered a world leader in the persuasion industries—advertising, film, marketing, and public relations—and yet it is these practices that are seen wanting in stemming the tide of 21st century anti-Americanism. Advocacy of a message can backfire if the receiver feels overwhelmed by the message. As an American who had by now lived and traveled abroad for two decades, I knew that the world was deeply ambivalent about American power projection and efforts to promote that power. This is why to this day the United States is more at a disadvantage than other less powerful (and therefore less threatening) countries in getting its story across. Just because we can speak louder along with carrying that big stick doesn't mean that we can make ourselves liked any better or understood any more. At times, an expression of humility, even in jest, seems appreciated. I recall an opening conversation with a Greek woman scholar, Circe "Kirki" Kefalea, at an Athens conference on media and globalization in 1998. We introduced ourselves and she immediately asked where I was from. I answered, "the United States," to which she scrunched up her nose. In an effort to break the tension, I added, "I'm sorry, we rule the world." We both broke out laughing and used that interchange as an opening for some lively discussion about U.S.-Greek relations and intercultural perceptions.

ANTI-AMERICAN AS ISM: DECONSTRUCTING A LABEL

Since September 11, 2001, to the war in Afghanistan through the Iraq elections of January 2005, there has been much heated debate both inside and outside the United States about its image, power, reputation, and credibility in the world and the attitudes and opinions that develop in response to these source variables. Most of the discourse has been about the negative attitudes reflected in a concept we call "anti-Americanism," defined most generally as hostility directed at the government, culture, history and/or people of the United States of America. Authors Barry and Judith Colp Rubin, unlike many others who write on the topic, define anti-Americanism quite precisely within several parameters: "An antagonism to the United States that is systemic, seeing it as completely and inevitably evil; A view that greatly exaggerates America's shortcomings; The deliberate misrepresentation of the nature and policies of the United States for political purposes; A misperception of American society, policies, or goals which falsely portrays them as ridiculous or malevolent."[13]

The Rubins restrict their book, *Hating America: A History*, to discussing anti-Americanism in the context of illegitimate and strictly negative attitudes or opinions from non-Americans, which limits a broader exploration of the topic from either within the United States or from overseas opposition to U.S. policies. Many of my students found their framework for discussion of the topic to be too narrow and defensive, especially when we considered the very real, headline-grabbing global opposition to very specific U.S. policies in Iraq, Guantanamo Bay, and Abu Ghraib. Does global criticism of U.S. practices equate with the Rubins' definition of anti-Americanism? The Rubins elect to make a distinction between opposition, which may be but is not always justified, and anti-Americanism, which they define as illegitimate and extremist:

> Of course, opposition to specific American actions or policies is easily understandable and may well be justifiable, but anti-Americanism as a whole is not. The reason for this conclusion is simply that the United States is not a terrible or evil society, whatever its shortcomings. It does not seek world domination and its citizens do not take pleasure in deliberately injuring others. There are many occasions when decisions inevitably have drawbacks or bad effects. There are equally many times when mistakes are made. But here is where the line can be drawn between legitimate criticism and anti-Americanism.[14]

Of course, anti-American sentiment is nothing new. The Rubins lay out a two-hundred-year festivity of America bashing from our overseas brothers and sisters. The present phase of anti-Americanism, the Rubins would argue, is the most virile and vitriolic because "those who hold anti-Americanism views see the U.S. domination, both as a great power and as a terrible model for civilization (as the centerpiece of globalization, modernization, and Westernization), to be an established fact."[15] The Rubins' last phase defined in that quote, the post–September 2001 era, is the major focus of this book. I'm especially intrigued that the Rubins would limit their discussion to just so-called anti-Americanism views held outside the United States, for many Americans, including a solid number who backed Senator Kerry (or any Democrat for that matter) against President Bush would probably consider many policies of the United States to be a "terrible model" for civilization. I'm not talking here about views held solely by Michael Moore or the Left Coast (California, Oregon, Washington), Barbra Streisand or Sean Penn. Rather, the direction of American policy in the new century is too serious to worry too much about whether or not one's criticisms of American policy will be cast as either "un-American" or "anti-American" in purpose. I certainly don't. Progress on American policy, whether it is civil rights and civil liberties, protesting the war in Iraq, or expanding rights for women and minorities, is often met with fierce resistance, including opponents who use the label "anti-American" to attempt to chill dissent or shut down all debate. I would add several dimensions to the parameters of anti-Americanism set by the Rubins. These include: (1) a rhetorical label designed to mark an opponent as working against the best interests of the United States; (2) one of the seven classic propaganda devices known as name-calling when a person or idea is linked to a negative symbol, in this case, anti-Americanism. Calling a person anti-American can at times be as bad in flavor as labeling someone by another "ism," namely Communist, Socialist, Fascist, Leftist, Terrorist, or even Feminist. When used in a propagandistic or rhetorical manner, anti-Americanism is most revealing because it forces one to peel away at the superficial layer of name-calling to find the intended meaning.[16]

It isn't then enough for the purposes of our discussion here to say that anti-Americanism is housed in the exclusive domain of the four-part parameters presented by the Rubins. While theirs is a very necessary definition, it is certainly insufficient. It doesn't consider the unique position of the United States as the sole superpower in the world and as a country that, rightly or wrongly, is seen as the very front face of economic globalization. The United States is in its most powerful position since the height of the Cold War, and British author Stephen Howe explains well in his book, *Empire*, how delicate the balance is between Benevolent Superpower and Global Superbully:

> On a global scale, only one country could now even dream of maintaining an informal empire. And it is of course immensely contentious whether the power and policies of the United States represent either the fact of such an empire or an aspiration towards it. . . . The new idea of empire is like the ancient Roman and medieval Christian ones, unlike the imperial systems that rose and fell in between, in that it is, or aspires to be, a universal order. The United States, with its closest allies, is the only force that can maintain global peace and justice—if necessary, by force—not in pursuit of a nationalist or a power-hungry agenda, but to uphold those universal values. [17]

This association of American values with universal values is not new. It seems to come with the position of superpower, whether acquired through territorial conquest or simply assumed through military and economic prowess. In the case of the United States, promoting the universality of democratic values like equality, egalitarianism, rule of law, human rights, civil liberties, and freedom are problematic, particularly in the Middle East, which has witnessed three Arab and Muslim country invasions by the United States in the last 14 years. The first Gulf War, though it did divide opinion in the United States, was viewed by the Arab Street (a term that is commonly used for that region's public opinion) as mostly acceptable given that Iraq had invaded Kuwait, which in turn asked the United States to intervene and kick out the perpetrator. Plus, there were many more nations of the world involved and the invasion of Iraq had the backing of the United Nations, something which only George Bush, Sr. was able to secure, not the son. Even the war in Afghanistan was viewed as somewhat of a "just war" in that it followed from an unprovoked attack on the United States and the organizers of the attack were thought to be staging their operation inside Afghanistan.

The war in Iraq, however, has become the most deeply divisive policy for not only the United States but the world. It is not just the Middle East population that is heavily against the U.S. presence in Iraq, but also many populations in allied countries of Europe and Japan that think the United States has overstepped its superpower privileges. Even the Bush Doctrine of preventive war isn't convincing global public opinion that the war in Iraq was a just war. Current public diplomacy and propaganda strategies to overcome negative attitudes and opinions toward the United States are bereft of vision and a central role for the American public. The

U.S. government is not going to win any battle of international reputation struggles without allowing its own citizenry an opportunity to speak on its own terms with people overseas.

AMERICA AND THE PATRIOTIC DUTY OF DISSENT

Much of what I learned initially about American propaganda was formed by reading the works of a man who still informs my thinking about America's role in the new century. This role is defined by limits on free expression and increases in sponsored information at home, and a fear-driven security-conscious and never-ending global declaration of war on terrorism. It is couched in a context of moral superiority and a renewed intolerant Puritanism. The first "person of influence" is an American, Senator J. William Fulbright, author of a number of books about the workings of America at home and abroad including his most famous, *The Arrogance of Power*, *The Price of Empire*, and a more obscure book, *The Pentagon Propaganda Machine*. The latter is an interpretation of the U.S. military's involvement in "selling" the military establishment to a believing American audience. The book's jacket sounds eerily forewarning though it was directed at the Cold War times: "Fulbright's well-documented expose shows how the heated climate of fear of world communism was fanned by the publicly-financed propaganda of an increasingly political and unregulated military establishment." You might substitute fear of communism then for fear of terrorism today. He writes in 1970:

> It is interesting to compare American government's only official propaganda organization, the U.S. Information Agency, with the Defense Department's apparatus. USIA is so circumscribed by Congress that it cannot, with the rarest of exceptions, distribute its materials within this country. Since much USIA output is composed of a filtered view of the United States and its policies, such a prohibition is eminently sensible. But the Defense Department, with more than twice as many people engaged in public relations as USIA has in all of its posts abroad, operates to distribute its propaganda within this country without control other than the executive, and floods the domestic scene with its special, narrow view of the military establishment and its role in the world.[18]

I read *The Arrogance of Power* periodically to remind myself of how history informs and enlightens, especially how our government continues to offer up false analogies during wartime. President Bush announced shortly after 9/11 that the attacks were "our generation's Pearl Harbor," which made many an American take notice of the gravity of the situation. While it is true that September 11, 2001 is, to use Franklin D. Roosevelt's words about Pearl Harbor, "a date which will live in infamy," this is where the comparison runs dry. One attack prompted only one acceptable option, a global military response. The other prompted a unilateral military response that was better suited to a police and intelligence investigation that would garner punishment within international jurisprudence. President Bush's calling September 11th a new Pearl Harbor was a naming device that prevented any debate about how America could or should respond to it. Pearl Harbor is a sacred place of mourning in Honolulu harbor and a sacred term in the American lexicon that symbolizes the start of America's entry into World War II. It should stand alone and on its own terms, in its own historical context. Fulbright explains why governments use false historical analogies, saying that Americans are "uniquely inflicted" with this tendency: "North Vietnam's involvement in South Vietnam, for example, is equated with Hitler's invasion of Poland and a parley with the Viet Cong would represent 'another Munich.'" Such analogies, he said, are based on "slight and superficial resemblances" and misguided views "of history 'repeating itself,'" and their use is merely "a substitute for thinking and a misuse of history."[19]

In many other areas Fulbright offers light over heat in explaining why the United States continues to generate opposition so widely. In matters of public diplomacy and our mission to win hearts and minds in the Middle East, he writes: "We all like telling people what to do, which is perfectly all right except that most people do not like being told what to do." And in U.S. foreign policy, America has wavered in mission.

> Throughout our history two strands have coexisted uneasily—a dominant strand of democratic humanism and a lesser but durable strand of intolerant Puritanism. There has been a tendency through the years for reasons and moderation to prevail as long as things are going tolerably well or as long as our problems seem clear and finite and manageable. But when things have gone badly for any length of time, or when the reasons for adversity have seemed obscure, or simply when some event or leader of opinion has aroused the people to a state of high emotion, our puritan spirit has tended to break through, leading us to look at the world through a distorting prism of harsh and angry moralism.[20]

This moral superiority is part of the arrogance of power that persists in American thinking. Because we are the world's sole superpower, we tend to associate that power with an idea that this power is due to our being given Divine Will to act on other nations and make them in our own image. Fulbright writes, "Power confuses itself with virtue and tends also to take itself for omnipotence. Once imbued with the idea of a mission, a great nation easily assumes that it has the means as well as the duty to do God's work."

I was always quite enamored of Senator Fulbright, knowing as well that he was no progressive on civil rights in America. I was honored to have known the Senator and met him on a number of occasions in Washington, D.C. where I lived for nine years. In fact, I interviewed Senator Fulbright shortly after Bill Clinton's election in order to get his take on his young protégé. Clinton had first interned in Fulbright's office while attending Georgetown University. It was Senator Fulbright who helped Clinton secure a Rhodes scholarship to Oxford. Fulbright's own experience as a Rhodes scholar inspired his vision of the Fulbright program, often referred to as the "little Rhodes" but very prestigious nonetheless and still going strong today.[21] I've met many a foreign Fulbrighter in my day who responded to Fulbright like a Dead Head might respond to meeting Jerry Garcia. Perhaps this is a poor analogy but Fulbright was the Rock Star head of international exchange, and when he died in 1995, America lost a great man who understood how important it was for Americans to seek truth and honor dissent.

Fulbright is such a well-recognized brand for international exchange that it garnered a dialogue among college characters in American writer Tom Wolfe's book, *I Am Charlotte Simmons*. Note that Fulbright, though second tier to a Rhodes, is "okay," but is linked to imperialistic ambition. I suppose my own positive bias toward my Fulbright experience prevents me from associating such a negative connotation between empire and government exchange as Charlotte's friend Adam.

> Charlotte said. "There are only thirty-two Rhodes scholarships?" Adam nodded yes. "Well, golly, that's not very many. What if...that's what you're counting on and you don't get one?" "In that case," said Adam, "you go after a Fulbright. That's a pretty long way down from a Rhodes, but it's okay. There's also the Marshall Fellowships, they're the last resort. I mean that's bottom-fishing. During the cold war a bad-ass couldn't have accepted a Fulbright or a Marshall, because they're government programs, and that

would've made you look like a tool of imperialism. A Rhodes was okay because there was no British Empire left, and you couldn't be accused of being
a tool of something that wasn't there anymore. Today the only empire is the
American empire, and it's omnipresent, and so if you don't get the Rhodes
you have to make use of it, the new empire. It's okay as long as you're using
it for the sake of your own goals and not theirs."[22]

Senator Fulbright was a great international visionary who saw beyond the
borders of his accident-of-birth condition. This condition is something
that is both a privilege and an infliction. It is a privilege in that it comes
with enormous advantages that the world's majority does not have. It is
an infliction in that the privileges I have sitting comfortably before my
computer with its cable modem Internet, 24-hour access to international
databases, cable TV, cell phone, digital camera, and many other amenities
can, at times, give one a feeling of natural superiority. It seems as if being
an American of at least middle-class privilege comes with a special card
access to comfort and pleasure not afforded to many. It's easy to fall into
a mind trap, "Thank God I'm an American" but not follow that with, "To
much is given, much is expected." Many Americans may wonder, "why do
they (continue to) hate us," and it is partly this attitude: We tend to exude
a feeling of natural born superiority that inflames enmity and a sense of
humiliation.

I am equally inspired by the memory of my friend and fellow scholar
Herbert Schiller, who wrote the introduction to my first book, *Propaganda, Inc.* Herb was a scholarly mentor, and his last book, *Living in the
Number One Country*, may say something about the scholar's devotion to
dependency theory. It does say something about how I title book chapters!
Herb authored many books, notably *Culture, Inc.*, *Mass Communications
and American Empire*, and *Information Inequality*. Described by scholar
Lai-Si Tsui as a "clarion voice against cultural hegemony," his work both
influenced scholarship on cultural imperialism and information disparities
between the developed West and the developing world, and the United
Nations' and UNESCO drive for a new world information and international order in the early 1970s.[23] In his last book published right after his
death on January 29, 2000, Herb wrote something that would foreshadow
our post-September 11 realities: "[H]ow the world sees us may not be
as revealing as how we see ourselves. How do those who reside in this
globally preeminent territory understand their own and their country's
situation? Is it, in fact, so obvious to everyone, as they go about their

daily routines, that they are part of a dominating global order? When, if at all, do people in this ruling core society express indignation at, or resistance to, the burdens their order imposes on others—and frequently on themselves as well?"[24]

Schiller was a world-renowned scholar in critical media studies, whose writings constantly prodded leaders in government and industry to challenge the tendency for public information efforts to be commercialized and devoted to culturally imperialistic endeavors. His prescription for change was a non-dominating communications model that provided an alternative model to the Western class-conscious, profit-driven system:

> Informational resources . . . available to help people recognize false labeling and enable them to deconstruct propaganda of the dominating sectors which, for example, calls bombs "peace-keepers," multinational corporations "global citizens," or cultural policy "prior censorship" and so on. This suggests a public information environment with vigilant checks and corrections of what George Orwell termed "double-speak" and "news-speak." News can be a liberating consciousness-shaping process when at least two conditions are present: 1) that journalists and media workers make the understanding of liberation movements worldwide a top priority, relating the stories and strategies of resistance to all forms of oppression, cultural, informational, political, etc.; 2) news can only do this if it is not presented in "fragmented, minute, anti-historical accounts" that typify the professional commercial broadcasting systems.[25]

There are far too few academics like Herbert Schiller who, like Fulbright, dared to keep asking the more unpopular questions about empire, affluence, domination, and misperception that shape our mind battles. We need to encourage such dissenting perspectives in order to air a far more balanced representation of diverse opinion than is presently supported.

FEAR APPEALS AT HOME AND ABROAD

On Wednesday, February 2, 2005, President Bush delivered the first State of the Union speech of his second administration, the fifth since he took office in January 2001. Not since his "Axis of Evil" address in 2002 had a speech so stirred up the global press. The *Christian Science Reporter* said the reaction was mixed between those media that saw a president more open than ever in U.S. foreign policy and those that saw business as usual in a proactive, aggressively militaristic foreign policy that now had Iran and Syria in its sights.[26] In response to Bush's charge that Iran was now the "the world's primary state sponsor of terror," Iran's supreme leader Ayatollah Ali Khamenei was quoted on Iranian state-run television as saying, "The Islamic Republic of Iran, because of supporting the oppressed and confronting oppressors, is being attacked by the global tyrants. . . . America is like one of the big heads of a seven-headed dragon. The brains directing it are Zionist and non-Zionist capitalists who brought Bush to power to meet their own interests."[27] Radio Netherlands, making note that Bush had mentioned September 11 just once in his speech, said that "the president's foreign policy remains rooted in the trauma of that day."[28] Indeed, reflecting the sentiment of his second term Inaugural Address of January 20, 2005, the fight this time seemed less confined to the 9/11 terrorists and their supporters but more about advancing the cause of democracy against its own enemies:

> The United States has no right, no desire and no intention to impose our form of government on anyone else. That is one of the main differences between us and our enemies. They seek to impose and expand an empire of oppression, in which a tiny group of brutal, self-appointed rulers control every aspect of every life. Our aim is to build and preserve a community of free and independent nations, with governments that answer to their citizens and reflect their own cultures. And because democracies respect their own people and their neighbors, the advance of freedom will lead to peace.[29]

Aljazeera.com, an independent media website that has no formal tie to the well-known Arab satellite television network, Al Jazeera, reported that President Bush had "prepared the world for more death and destruction on Wednesday when he warned Iran and Syria that they were next in his sight and that he would confront them" and that, in the State of the Union address "the U.S. president revealed the agenda of his second presidential term in which he branded the Middle East countries as supporters of 'terror and tyranny.' "[30]

In a column titled "A man of his word like it or lump it," Australian writer Greg Sheridan said that the American President had a global strategic communication advantage—stubborn continuity—that the world has to live with, like it or not: "Bush's stubbornness—resolve to his admirers, inflexibility and simpleton certitudes to his detractors—is in fact one of his greatest strategic assets. So much of strategic policy is about influencing the psychology of the battlefield. Bush's enemies have to contend with the fact that he doesn't change his position, he doesn't give up and he doesn't give in."[31]

In 2002 President Bush had singled out an "axis of evil" that included North Korea, Syria, Iran, and Iraq. That bellicose rhetoric, in light of the Iraq invasion just over a year later, helped to refuel anti-American sentiment throughout the world, and not just in the targeted axis countries. In 2005, President Bush seemed to be willing to show his softer power side, especially with the part of his speech that promised $350 million in aid and assistance to the Palestinian region. There seemed to be a greater effort this time for a sustainable two-state solution in the fifty-year struggle between Jewish and Palestinian inhabitants of Israel. This conflict, and especially America's close ties to Jewish Israel, many scholars claim is the major contributing factor to anti-American feelings in the Middle East, notwithstanding the anti-Semitic charges from Iran's top leader that the U.S. is beholden strictly to Zionist interests.

During the 2004 presidential election, it became clear that fear appeals work better at home than they work abroad. Michael Moore's *Fahrenheit 9/11* was playing strong to anti-Bush audiences who were standing on their feet and cheering his satirical and critical take on the administration that couldn't shoot straight. To many of the Moore supporter voters, the only rational choice for president was ABB (Anybody But Bush). The Democratic nominee would have to do, even if he didn't conjure up the most enthusiasm and made Al Gore seem almost loose in his delivery. Kerry's greatest appeal was that he wasn't Bush and history tells us that being the un-candidate is like being the un-cola, second best. For another subset of Americans, the un-Fahrenheit crowd, the global war on terrorism was in the forefront of their continued support for the commander-in-chief, whom they credited for managing to keep America safe from 9/12. Decision 2004 therefore turned on fear and stay-the-course decision making and no amount of dissent or questioning of America's policy in Iraq would trump the war on terror. After all, a majority of Americans still connected the war in Iraq with the war on terrorism that was declared on 9/11.

In foreign policy, both Senator John Kerry and President George W. Bush appealed to voters' fears that Bin Laden was still at large and must be caught, that global terrorism was still the greatest threat to America's national security, and that Iraq was not yet a mission accomplished. Senator

Kerry was emphasizing his more "sensitive" approach to the war on terror, which is not what many voters wanted to hear. The nation needed a commander-in-chief, not a therapist. On top of everything going against Kerry, he was slow to respond to a well-orchestrated domestic propaganda campaign by the Swift Boat Veterans for Truth who challenged his heroism in the Vietnam War. To many of these fellow Vietnam veterans, Kerry, like Jane Fonda, had forever sullied his image and reputation by not just questioning the morality of the war, which many Americans were doing at the time, but in a very public campaign that seemed to paint all Vietnam veterans in a negative broad stroke as war criminals. Even Kerry's appeal to voters that he would be the better choice to negotiate with our allies overseas because Bush was in so much global disfavor seemed to cement even more support for the American president. Americans are concerned with presidential reputation and national image in the world but not as much as they are concerned with their own immediate national security concerns. In the end, the fear rhetoric and get tough strategy of the Bush Administration earned re-election from voters who chose to stick with what they knew rather than replace an untested commander midstream.

Rule number one: what works at home does not translate abroad. What may have worked to win hearts and minds of most Americans was not very effective on hearts and minds overseas. In fact, if anything, these hearts were hardening and minds were well made up. As Carlos Fuentes reported in the *Los Angeles Times*, in Latin America many who were following the U.S. election were stunned by the war rhetoric that was working to great effect in the United States but scaring the international community. The message from abroad was "you scare us," while at home it seemed to be "strength with us." At home, America may view itself as strong and united, but the message heard abroad was a strong and united America means that weaker countries will have to just go along with U.S. policy, however unpopular it may be. Fuentes wrote, "There is a measure of suspicion balanced by an enormous admiration for the culture of Herman Melville to Walt Whitman to William Faulkner, of Hollywood and jazz, of Eugene O'Neill to Arthur Miller ... The problem lies in foreign policy. Too often, the United States is seen as a benevolent Dr. Jekyll at home and a malevolent Mr. Hyde abroad."[32]

America's involvement in the summer Olympics in Athens, Greece, just three months earlier had itself been a lesson in global humility. Whereas

American athletes may have been seen in gatherings past as our country's goodwill ambassadors in (mostly) amateur athletics, this time U.S. Olympic athletes were trained in the art of celebratory humility. The training center offered voluntary workshops to outgoing Olympic athletes in the art of celebrating American victories without overdoing it. The athletes were being instructed that America's image in the world was mostly negative and that an American athlete who plays up American success and achievement may just add fuel to the negative flames. The war in Iraq seemed to be the tipping point in the negative turn away from goodwill. As Frederic Morton wrote in an op-ed, "From Role Model to International Bully in Three Short Years," in the *Los Angeles Times*,

> Before Iraq, America's formidable appeal continued largely unabated.... America has meant promise to just about every age group and political species.... If this rainbow array of hopes is indeed dying now, it is not the terrorists but the recent cumulative acts of the United States itself that are the slayers. What previously could have been excused as wild oats sown by a young superpower have now, unmistakably, hardened into systematic global bullying. To Europeans of every stripe, the statue in New York harbor brandishes not a torch but a Tommy gun.[33]

Most Americans would probably not agree with Morton's critical redressing of what Lady Liberty is holding in her hand or what she symbolizes here as well as abroad. After all, they might say, while it may be harder to gain entry into the United States through new restrictive immigration and visa laws in the homeland security era, new immigrants, both legal and illegal, are coming in record numbers to the United States. America is still the number one immigrant nation and no amount of loss in global popularity is going to override the drive of those who wish to study, work, or raise their families here. What Morton does capture is a popular sentiment abroad—that America has the force and will to shape the world to our liking—and while it is popular to hate the most rich and powerful who live among us, we may still want that rich uncle's money and the opportunities he affords us.

America's credibility problem with the world is the "soft underbelly" of U.S. leadership in the global war on terrorism. Our credibility problem is shaped by a number of inconsistencies and missteps in how we present ourselves. The American ideals of freedom, democracy, liberty, and equality do not match our policies toward other countries. A free and moral society (how we see ourselves) continues to buttress up regimes of some of the worst human rights abusers in the world (how others see our actions in the world). Think of Saudi Arabia, Saddam Hussein in the Iran/Iraq war of the 1980s, Noriega in Panama, Marcos in the Philippines, among many others. Where is the global moral authority of a self-perceived free and moral society that is not afraid to address grievances head-on when we have not fully investigated prisoner abuse allegations in internment camps of Guantanamo Bay and Abu Ghraib prison? The world was so angry at us for the Abu Ghraib prisoner scandal that President Bush appeared on Al Hurra, the U.S. government's Arab-language television network, and Dubai-based Al-Arabiya TV, a Saudi-funded broadcast TV network that is considered much more credible in the Middle East. He spoke directly to Arab and Muslims about the Iraqi prisoner abuse in Abu Ghraib prison, not by Saddam Hussein's henchmen, but by U.S. soldiers. In his remarks, President Bush gave a clear picture of what American democracy and American jurisprudence ideally represent and why so many the world over continue to hold us to this higher standard. "In a democracy," he said, "there will be a full investigation. In other words, we want to know the truth. In our country, when there's an allegation of abuse—more than an allegation in this case, actual abuse, we saw the pictures—there will be a full investigation and justice will be delivered. We have a presumption of innocent until you're guilty in our system, but the system will be transparent, it will be open and people will see the results."

At the time of this writing not one high-ranked military official has been punished for the Abu Ghraib abuses. At home, we continue to scratch our heads and wonder how it is that the number one propaganda nation in the world, the country that invented advertising, sales, marketing, and hype, could manage to fan the flames of hatred overseas. It is in part due to a perceived arrogance of power expressed in our public diplomacy campaigns designed to win the hearts and minds of the Arab and Muslim audiences who seem the most disengaged from America.

TELLING OUR STORY TO THE WORLD FROM A GRITS PERSPECTIVE

Too often in the United States, U.S. foreign policy becomes a movie with good guys and bad guys, where America prevails, and where the world eventually comes over to the good guys' side, etc. In December

2001, the American war film *Black Hawk Down* was released. Based on the Mark Bowden book about the failed American mission in Somalia in 1993, the film project included Pentagon advisers and told the story of American soldiers in the region from their own perspective. While it was both Hollywood entertaining and compelling, the story was incomplete. As is often the case with how Americans view our policies in the world, *Black Hawk Down* offered little if any perspective on why the United States was in Somalia in the first place, why the Somalian people had grown to resent the American presence, or what were the numbers of civilian dead. Another film and yet another opportunity lost to educate an American audience to the need to listen more and dictate less at the international level. *Black Hawk Down* serves as a metaphor for America's image problem in the world: Don't ask, don't tell. It wasn't until December 2005 that President Bush first notified the American public that there were about 30,000 civilian casualties in the war in Iraq, an extremely low estimate when a well-regarded British medical journal *Lancet* reported nearly one hundred thousand Iraqi civilian casualties as of fall 2004.

When I worked at the U.S. Information Agency from 1992–1994, my boss for most of that time was Joseph Duffey. As the last director of the government's propaganda agency before its demise in 1999, Duffey might now label the perhaps unintended consequences of American public diplomacy after 9/11 as a disaster. It's not really a stretch to say that young Army Pfc. Lynndie England of West Virginia became the new face of U.S. public diplomacy in the Middle East in 2004, with her cigarette-dangling smiling face and thumbs up posing next to a leashed Iraqi prisoner of war. It looks as much fun to her as an *Animal House* reunion party. Whether or not she was instructed by higher ups above to "soften up" the prisoners seems beside the point. What really matters is that the images of American workers in Iraq so humiliating Iraq men were images played around the clock by Al-Jazeera and Al-Arabiya TV in cafes, living rooms, and meeting places. That's the real story of America to the world unless and until we come up with a plan to re-engage and re-build trust with the Iraqi people.

And what is America's story to the world, according to at least dozens of surveys published since 9/11? Edward Djerejian, director of the James A. Baker III Institute for Public Policy at Rice University and chair of a U.S. government–sponsored commission that investigated U.S. public diplomacy to the Middle East in 2003, is equally as apoplectic in his pleas about American public diplomacy as Joseph Duffey. He told Copley News

Service, "Where I come out is with the old Woody Allen adage: '90 percent of life is showing up.' And we're not showing up in a significant manner in the Arab and Muslim world in promoting and explaining... (to) these populations our values, our policies, and much more needs to be done." Djerejian is the same person who endorsed the following in "Changing Minds, Winning Peace" that was submitted to the U.S. House Subcommittee on Appropriations on October 1, 2003. The report revealed a lot about why so often we hide policy differences behind positive labels:

> Arabs and Muslims admire the universal values for which the United States stands. They admire, as well, our technology, entrepreneurial zeal, and the achievements of Americans as individuals. We were told many times in our travels in Arab countries that "we like Americans but not what the American government is doing." This distinction is unrealistic, since Americans elect their government and broadly support its foreign policy, but the assertion that "we like you but don't like your policies" offers hope for transformed public diplomacy.

In no place in Djerejian's report was there any discussion of U.S. foreign policy to the Middle East. American foreign policy is always off the table when America is trying to influence, engage, and win hearts and minds. The pro-Israel government tilt in the Arab-Israeli conflict and a steady media diet of dying and humiliated Iraqis is what many Arab and Muslim leaders want to discuss with U.S. political leadership but so far the U.S. government's response has been to amplify its own position or try to make a stronger case to the rest of the world that we're likable because we are so good.

At the time in 2003 when Margaret Tutwiler, former Ambassador of Morocco, was being nominated by the Bush Administration as the new undersecretary of state for public diplomacy and public affairs, I published an open letter in Tutwiler's hometown newspaper, *The Birmingham News*. Though Tutwiler was ultimately just six months on the job, I thought it necessary to conjure up some American values propagated in the South that might be of help in her new public diplomacy style. What the United States needed was a southern-style charm offensive modeled on the "Welcome Wagon" of old, when new neighbors were greeted by their neighbors with food, assistance, and a friendly smile. We weren't making any headway, it seemed, because U.S. public diplomacy was being conducted like a corporate boardroom focus group from an uptown, top-down, and inside-the-beltway of Washington, D.C., perspective. Instead of reaching out to Arabs and Muslims through meaningful contact, active listening, and continuing dialogue, we had chosen the easier path: packaging public diplomacy in commercials and slick packaging. So far, this fancy packaging wasn't improving America's image in the world and seemed to reinforce the negative perception that when it comes to public diplomacy, "it's all about us."

I told Tutwiler, woman-to-woman, and Southerner-to-Southerner, that we needed to get back to the basic glue that holds people together— friendliness, openness, and making a guest feel at home, a Southern charm offensive based on discussion and dialogue with those people who are at times skeptical toward the United States and with others who are downright hostile. We needed to listen and learn more than dictate and declare. In her own confirmation hearing before the Senate Foreign Relations Committee October 29, 2003, Margaret Tutwiler herself pointed out the lessons she learned from serving in an Arab Muslim country:

> Much of what I learned about our country, from listening, engaging and interacting with Moroccans from all walks of life, was troubling and disturbing. I would never have known how our country is really viewed, both the positives and the negatives, had I not been serving overseas for the last two turbulent years. . . . There is not one magic bullet, magic program or magic solution. As much as we would like to think Washington knows best, we have to be honest and admit we do not necessarily always have all the answers.

In that same vein, American public diplomacy would serve itself well if the United States accepted that we hold no patent on democracy and freedom. While we hold no patent, we are part of a larger and majority global neighborhood of civic- and human rights–oriented nations that cherish the democratic process and democratic ideals over tyranny and dictatorial control. In that spirit, the United States should roll out a welcome sign of inclusiveness that what the world most admires about us (productivity, entrepreneurial spirit, education, freedom to practice religion, free speech) is what we want to share and help them build on in their own homelands. This means specifically that a public diplomacy in Iraq must be led with an attitude of respect for individual dignity that we are guests in the homes of the Iraqi people, not the other way around.

YOU CAN CALL ME AL JAZEERA

"We know that Al Jazeera has a pattern of playing propaganda over and over and over again."

—Secretary of Defense Donald Rumsfeld

Before September 11, 2001, I doubt any non-Arab American would have ever heard of Al Jazeera. After 9/11, I doubt any American hadn't heard of it. Within days of the attacks on the World Trade Center and Pentagon, the Bush Administration was openly criticizing this Middle East television network based in Qatar, a small Persian Gulf country, for its biased, pro-Arab and anti-American programming of the war on terror and U.S. presence in the Middle East. Jehane Noujaim, the Egyptian-American director of the Academy award–nominated documentary, *Control Room,* became aware during her overseas travels of how differently the global press and U.S. press were covering the same news stories, particularly the most important war story of the day in 2003, Iraq. She decided to tell the story of how the Iraqi war was being covered by Al Jazeera and CentCom's Coalition Provisional Authority, located just miles from each other in Doha, Qatar. The result is a deeply personal movie that illustrates how simplistic any accusation is that Al Jazeera is just an anti-American press organization with no credibility. In the words of one Al Jazeera executive, "we wanted to show every war has a human cost."[34] This victim perspective is exactly why the United States government seems to be so frustrated with Al Jazeera's programming; it doesn't sanitize the Iraq war but shows the gruesome pictures of the Arab and Muslim victims, many women and children, who are helpless to defend life and home from overwhelming force, what the Bush Administration calls "Shock and Awe." In contrast, the U.S. media choose to exclude these Iraqi victims from nightly news coverage, while showing instead almost a bloodless liberation with few American casualties. The film makes you think that the U.S. public is being propagandized by American media in terms of their sanitized coverage of when nations go to war.

The Pentagon lens on the war is revealed through several characters like Lt. Josh Rushing, the CENTCOM press spokesman, who had the thankless task of briefing the Arab press about the U.S. position on the war. He shows sensitivity to the civilian casualties of the war in Iraq, but believes that the war and Saddam Hussein's capture and removal from power will make life for the Iraqis better in the long run. Rushing's Arab press audience is skeptical of the U.S. military and tends to doubt anything Rushing has to say since he represents the military perspective. Through the course of the film, one sees Rushing draw parallels between Arab and U.S. media institutions. He suggests that Al Jazeera's Arab nationalist coverage may not be all that different from Fox News Channel's American nationalism. After the film was released, Rushing left the military and returned to civilian life, in part because he was not allowed to comment on the film. I met Rushing at a Goethe Institute seminar in Los Angeles spring 2005 where panelists discussed the impact of the Marshall Plan films on the German people. Though not a historian, he talked about his experience trying to be as truthful and balanced as possible to the press in wartime. His balanced and culturally-sensitive approach to the Arab media must have gotten noticed, since he was later hired as an anchor/reporter by none other than the English-language version of Al Jazeera.

The film introduces a human side to Al Jazeera through two of its re-porters, Hassan Ibrahim and Samir Khader, who manage to destigmatize the stereotype that many Americans have that Al Jazeera is just an anti-American propaganda organ of the Arab Street. Samir Khader is a senior producer for Al Jazeera who is critical of the war and who also loves Amer-ican values of free press and free expression. He expresses a desire in the film to leave the Middle East, move to America, and allow his children to attend American universities so that they "can exchange the Arab night-mare for the American dream " He's not even opposed to taking a job with conservative Fox News Channel, if they offered it to him. Regarding the propaganda image of Al Jazeera, Khader defends his station: "We don't want to alienate the Americans . . . we are what they want for the region, an Arab channel with Western mentality."[35]

Hassan Ibrahim reflects the mosaic nature of many of the global press. Married to a British woman, he grew up in Saudi Arabia where he attended grade school with one Osama Bin Laden. He attended college in the United States and worked for the BBC Arab News Service before being hired by Al Jazeera. He thinks of himself as a strong Arab nationalist who is vehemently opposed to the war in Iraq as well as U.S. presence in the Middle East region. "Eventually you will have to find a solution that doesn't involve bombing people into submission," he says in the film, and predicts that once the American people see the full spectrum of what personal devastation the war is reaping, they will stop the U.S military from acting.[36] At the same time, just like Samir Khader, Ibrahim shows a strong appreciation for the U.S. Constitution and U.S. ideals.

Most all of the Western media journalists working at CentCom were contractually prohibited by their American broadcasters from expressing their personal opinion about the war, and the timing of the film during the first six weeks of the war in 2003 was particularly sensitive. Pulitzer prize-winning journalist Peter Arnett had just been fired by CNN for doing a one-on-one interview with Iraqi state television. Two U.S. journalists, Tom Mintier from CNN and David Shuster from NBC News, do agree to speak with Noujaim about their perspectives of covering the war through the prism of the daily Pentagon press briefings and Al Jazeera. Mintier feels that American journalists are being favored in CentCom press briefings and asks that his turn to ask a question be given to a foreign journalist, while Shuster views Al Jazeera as a member of the Western press and "one of the most important cultural and sociological developments in the Arab world." Filmmaker Noujaim concludes that nationality may impact how the press covers war, but it is not necessarily a case of a chess match between the propaganda Arab press on one side versus a free American press on the other. In many respects, how different nationalities cover the same war depends on how personally impacted the journalist involved. For instance, the war in Iraq to most Arabs and Muslims is seen through the context of U.S. support for Israel and the ongoing Israeli/Palestinian conflict, while an American reporter or American citizen would rarely view the war in that context:

> When you have an Iraqi translator at Al Jazeera translating Bush announcing the freeing of the Iraqi people, and then calling home to see if his family was okay, the war was really part of their lives though they weren't in the center of things. There were such strong emotions about what was happening which really contrasted with many Western journalists who had never been to the Middle East and [whose] jobs were mainly to try and get the most out of the [CentCom] press officers. . . . It's the same difference that you'd find if you followed Al Jazeera journalists in New York after 9/11 versus American journalists at the same time. American journalists were very emotional about what happened and went into a kind of emotional depth that foreign journalists would not have been able to connect with quite as clearly. This is why the Al Jazeera reporters focused so much on the victims of war, which they were harshly criticized for.[37]

When *Control Room* was first screened across the United States in 2004, Noujaim was accused of being anti-American and unpatriotic. She said that her identity is neither solely American nor Egyptian but a product of her Egyptian background and American heritage. When watching the film screened back in the States, she, like many of the Arab journalists she covered, questioned whether or not the war in Iraq was really worth it. "But this is exactly what the Arab world is seeing. In this way, the film could be labeled 'unpatriotic,' but I feel like the most patriotic thing I can do is try to express what I perceive the Arab world to be seeing, feeling, etc., and Al Jazeera's broadcasts play such a huge role in this right now."[38]

WE AREN'T THE WORLD

More than two decades ago on January 28, 1985, a stellar group of top Hollywood performers of the day including Bruce Springsteen, Michael Jackson, Lionel Ritchie, and Stevie Wonder came together to record the song, "We Are the World (USA for Africa)." It was the night of the American Music Awards in Los Angeles, and singers were told by producer Quincy Jones to check their egos at the door in order to do something that would benefit the starving victims of famine in Africa. By March when the song was released, over 800,000 copies were sold in the first weekend, and it would go on to win two Grammy awards for song of the year and record of the year. The song became the highest debuting recording in American music history since John Lennon's "Imagine," and the lyrics by Michael Jackson and Lionel Ritchie expressed a similar sentiment of peace and hope.

Fast forward twenty years and three presidents later, the United States is not in the same definitional position. Reputation and image wise, we are, most decisively, not the world, in Africa or the Middle East and from Canada to Latin America. A 2004 poll conducted by the Pew Global Attitudes Project of four Muslim and four European countries showed that resentment toward the United States has strengthened since the start of the Iraq war in 2003. President Bush was less popular than Osama Bin Laden in Jordan, Pakistan, and Morocco. The survey showed high approval ratings in all three countries for suicide bombings against the Israelis and Americans in Iraq.

The survey of 8,000 people was conducted in February 2004 in four European countries (France, Germany, Great Britain, and Russia) and four Muslim-majority countries (Jordan, Morocco, Pakistan, and Turkey). It indicated an amazing amount of anti-religious bias over religious tolerance. Christians and Jews faired poorly in Pakistan, Morocco, and Turkey, while nearly a third of Americans signaled an anti-Muslim bias. In Europe, the anti-Muslim sentiment was higher in places like Germany and Russia. The European and Muslim-majority states had something in common—a growing dislike for the United States and its leadership in the world.

Madeleine Albright, the former Clinton administration secretary of state who chairs the Pew Global Attitudes Project, said that the survey showed that U.S. credibility in the world was sinking. Even in Europe, public opinion toward the United States after Iraq is skeptical and a majority thinks Bush and Blair lied about the motivations for war with Iraq. In Germany and France, overwhelming majorities want the European Union to serve as a counterweight, perhaps even a wedge, between the United States and the world.

Albright gave a nod to Bin Ladenism for having the communications capacity "to do something that 40 years of communism was unable to do, which is to divide Europe from the United States." She offered a quick Diplomacy 101 lesson: "It's nice to be feared by your enemies, but it's not nice to be feared by your friends." She added, however, "it's nice to be popular, but it's not a popularity contest. It's a matter of making sure that many other countries come along with your policies." Or is it? Therein lies the rub. The world doesn't want U.S. policies, if what they only see are policies of unilateralism over multilateralism, military intervention over international cooperation, the arrogance of American power over humble self-examination of our power projections.

In his book, *The Price of Empire*, Senator J. William Fulbright wrote that "countries that achieve great power have long had a tendency to identify themselves with the deity or with high standards of virtue, and, on the basis of this identification, to develop a form of messianism, a conviction that it is their duty to take their message to other people."[39] His namesake Fulbright exchange program was designed to downplay the American tendency toward messianic mission. Better to understand one's own ideological limitations and learn how to mutually understand others through their own perceptions and belief systems.

It was what he called the Fulbright difference in international relations—the opportunity to come together not always as affectionate
friends but at least to build a sense of common humanity and shared
purpose. He represented the message that the United States is indeed
part of the world, not its emperor.

The Pew Global Attitudes Survey, coupled with the *State of the News
Media 2004* report, show that the United States' position in the world vis-
à-vis our global politics and communications is truly despairing, but worse,
offers no signs that we will see any significant change from the current
direction. A State Department spokesman Gregg Sullivan responded to
the Pew survey with a "slow and steady wins the race. That's the approach
we are going to take." And White House spokesman Jim Morrell said that
"the president doesn't base his decisions on polls. He bases his decisions
on the best interests of the safety and security of the American people."

It isn't good enough to know we are in such a sorry state. Why aren't
we trying to right this ship by rethinking our country's directions and projections? There are times when government doesn't have all the answers.
Can we, to use the words of President Lincoln, "think anew and act anew"
in our public diplomacy programs so that we emphasize the best human
relations programs we have to offer the world through the arts, culture,
and education over mass media broadcasts by "the free one"? Must we
make sure that other countries come along with our policies or can we
approach the world with a set of new eyes and ears? Are we still trying
to make the world in our own image? Can the hard sell become the soft
tell? Lincoln warned this nation at one time that "we must disenthrall
ourselves, and then we shall save our own country." We aren't the world
and the world is no longer as enthralled with us as we are of ourselves.
Anybody have a tune to go along with that?

HOLLYWOOD PROPAGANDA

Most every week, I travel along the 110 freeway to the campus of the
University of Southern California in downtown Los Angeles. The 110
freeway intersects with Highway 101, known in that part as the Hollywood Freeway, and on a clear day, the Hollywood sign dominates the
hills overlooking Los Angeles. The origins of that world-famous icon are
anything but glamorous. True to America's inclination for hucksterism, it

derives from a 1924 real estate builder's flashing metal sign consisting of thirteen letters fifty feet tall and four thousand twenty-watt light bulbs to announce a new tract of homes in a 500-acre subdivision of Los Angeles known then as Hollywoodland. Today, refurbished and four letters short, Hollywood stands out as a euphemism for all that is American culture in its global, commercial, reach.

Along with the American Left, there is no other sector of American culture so derided or accused of hating America than the dream factory known as Hollywood. Hollywood is part place and part idea. It is first a euphemism for the film and television industry that dominates Hollywood, California, more in history than in modern practice. So much of the commercial media industry has followed the path of globalization and cheaper labor markets from New York and Los Angeles to Vancouver, Louisiana and North Carolina. The Hollywood of Old is about as accessible as the condemned Ambassador Hotel on Wilshire Boulevard that contains the ghosts of Robert F. Kennedy and the Academy Awards in the Cocoanut Grove nightclub. But just like its counterpart America that is used interchangeably in brand-speak as the United States, popular culture in America is used interchangeably with the stamp, Hollywood. And the perception of American popular culture in Hollywood is that what gets produced and distributed there is more secular, more obscene, and more over-the-top than what the real Main Street American culture offers.

Michael Medved has written at length about Hollywood's deleterious affect on the American image in the world and how Hollywood, in turn, chooses not to take responsibility for its own actions. In his essay "That's Entertainment? Hollywood's Contribution to Anti-Americanism Abroad," he writes, "Of course, apologists for the entertainment industry decry all attempts to blame Hollywood for anti-Americanism, insisting that American pop culture merely reports reality, accurately reflecting the promise and problems of the United States, and allowing the worldwide audience to respond as they may to the best and worst aspects of our society."

Medved tells of a forum he attended on movie violence that featured movie director Paul Verhoeven of *Robocop* and *Basic Instinct* fame, or, to Medved, more like infamy. Verhoeven said that Hollywood films, like all art, just reflected reality. If what is reflected back to the world is bad, you cannot blame the messenger. To Medved and many other conservatives, and some liberals like Senator Joseph Lieberman, this is a Robocop-out.

Hollywood has enormous projection power value over American society. Most of what people overseas know about America comes across a film screen and not from a handshake. Hollywood must take even more responsibility for its images then the average Joe on the street. Further, Medved points to work by George Gerbner and many other media violence scholars who argue that a celluloid mean world is much darker, more excessive, and more dramatic than any American reality and accounts for far more victims of violence in the name of entertainment than real crime statistics present.[40]

Along with the distorted picture Hollywood brings to the global table, the widely held viewpoint of many cultural critics is that being too patriotic or too religious in the Hollywood market spells a death knell for getting your project green lighted and accepted by the powers-that-be. Australian-born film actor and director Mel Gibson made this point famous when he individually financed his film, *The Passion of the Christ*, and bypassed Hollywood big-budgeted marketing altogether. Using primarily word-of-mouth, Internet-based and pre-release screenings in Christian churches across America, Gibson promoted a film about the last twelve hours of Jesus Christ that broke all records in ticket sales for 2004 and grossed the ninth highest domestic gross ahead of *Jurassic Park* and two of the *The Lord of the Rings* trilogy. According to Boxofficemojo.com, with a production budget of $30 million and an even smaller marketing budget of $25 million, *The Passion of the Christ* has grossed over $600 million ($370 million domestic, $241 million international).

Given the obvious appeal that a traditional religious-based film has both home and abroad, why isn't Hollywood answering the call? Doesn't it want to make money? Part of the problem may be the dominant values of the Hollywood insider culture. Born-again Christians do not necessarily flock to the industry, and the dirty little secret about the American film industry is that pornography is the highest-grossing sector, not the type of film the family or teenagers flock to at the multiplex theater every weekend. According to the National Coalition for the Protection of Children & Families, American porn industry revenues in 2003 alone were over 12 billion, more than double the combined profits of the Big Three networks, ABC, CBS, and NBC (6.2 billion). American porn is more profitable than the combined revenues from the Big Three sports entertainment franchises of professional baseball, basketball, and football. It is more profitable than annual revenues generated from American popular music genres like Rock-n-Roll, Country, Jazz, and Classical music combined. It dwarfs the annual revenue from Broadway productions. This accounts for a legally protected adult entertainment industry that generates annual worldwide revenue of over $60 billion. Closer to the American home is a mainstream Hollywood market that is still out of touch and over the top. Michael Medved writes in his book, *Hollywood vs. America*, that the film and television industry is equivalent to a "poison factory" that promotes filth, favors the outlandish over the mundane, all but ignores the religiosity of the American people, and maligns the American nuclear family while spreading offensive language, sexual promiscuity and addictive violence across the globe. Hollywood is a land of popular sleaze and indulgence, a picture of America that infects a most negative stereotype about the American people in the minds of our overseas counterparts who are impacted the most in their attitudes and opinions about America through its popular media. "As a nation, we no longer believe that popular culture enriches our lives," he writes. "Few of us view the show business capital as a magical source of uplifting entertainment, romantic inspiration, or even harmless fun. Instead, tens of millions of Americans now see the entertainment industry as an all-powerful enemy, an alien force that assaults our most cherished values and corrupts our children. The dream factory has become the poison factory."[41]

This picture of Hollywood as sleaze central does not apply to military campaigns and American soldiers stationed in Iraq. Shortly after 9/11, the Bush Administration extended an olive branch to Hollywood in order to engage this industry in the newly declared war on terror. The president's chief advisors, including Karl Rove, met in Los Angeles with top Hollywood producers and directors to discuss a plan to use film to engage in the information and image battle to win global hearts and minds susceptible to ideologies of terrorist leaders like Osama Bin Laden. Nothing fully coordinated between the political power center and the cultural power center ever came from these 2001 meetings, though Hollywood did delay the release of feature films like Arnold Schwarzennegger's *Collateral Damage* and Jerry Bruckheimer's *Black Hawk Down* due to the sensitivity of the content in the aftermath of the World Trade Center and Pentagon attacks. The advance of time seemed to make a difference in accepting that branch. In 2005, just two years after the start of the war in Iraq, Hollywood had finally come to answer Washington's call. No less than four feature films about the U.S. military and the Iraq war were scheduled to film or had completed, including *No True Glory: The Battle of Fallujah*, starring A-list actor Harrison Ford of "Indiana Jones" fame, and *Jarhead*, which opened on Veterans Day 2005. A documentary film, *Gunner Palace*, was told from the point of view of U.S. soldiers serving in Iraq, reality-based youth at war, Baghdad style. Michael Moore's critical op-ed style documentary about Iraq, *Fahrenheit 9/11*, released during the election campaign of 2004, was left in the dust of the Hollywood-Washington nexus in 2005. *USA Today* reported that

> not since World War II has Hollywood so embraced an ongoing global conflict. It took years for pop culture to tackle the Korean and Vietnam wars, and it took time before the country was ready to be entertained by those politically charged conflicts. . . . But not any and every angle of war is being depicted. One aspect is glaringly absent from most projects: negativity. The U.S. soldier is the hero; his cause is just. Storylines featuring the Abu Ghraib prisoner abuse scandal or war protests are no-nos.[42]

Phil Strub, head of the Pentagon's film liaison office, says that presently "there is an unwillingness to criticize individual servicemen and women, which was quite common in the Vietnam era. Americans are very disinclined to do that now, and we're very glad this attitude tends to pervade all entertainment."[43]

It's not clear that the present pro-military bandwagon in Hollywood will either last or is reflective of patriotic values. The follow-up to show is business, and Hollywood producers, directors, and marketers know the power of films with traditional heroic themes to draw crowds both domestically and internationally. The average movie costs over $100 million in production and marketing, and most American films don't even turn a profit until they distribute the film overseas where at least half of all grosses come from these days. What sells well on the global media marketplace will undoubtedly contribute more to the bottom-line decision making in Hollywood than how patriotic the theme. Just ask Namrata Singh Gujral, an ethnic Indian actress who began working in Hollywood shortly before 9/11 and was moved to respond to the Bush Administration's call for Hollywood to help in the war on terror. She and her Naval Reserve pilot screenwriting partner, Joe Cooper, penned *Americanizing Shelley*, a pro-U.S. romantic comedy, which they shopped around Hollywood to no avail. The film's dedication to "our troops who laid their lives on the line

for our freedom," was especially criticized. What to do? They "pulled a
Mel Gibson" and formed their own film production company, American
Pride Films Group. Its mission statement boldly goes where other film
production and distribution companies haven't dared to go—at the heart
of Hollywood's alleged Achilles' heel: "Hollywood is doing a shoddy job of
portraying the many blessings and freedoms our nation offers—not just to
Americans, but to people worldwide."[44] On the menu of their films is an
effort to overcome the most negative images of Americans in the world.
America may be a wealthy nation, which Hollywood shows to a strong degree, but it is also a nation of values beyond material wealth, according to
Gujral, and these include to "portray Americans as decent, generous people," which "will be handy tools in combating anti-Americanism abroad."
Military pilot Cooper says, "When's the last time you saw a war movie
where the top brass aren't villains?"[45] He may need look no further than
the year 2005.

So, in answer to the present question, "Is Hollywood anti-American?"
the answer seems to be a gray bag, not as stark a black and white picture
that Michael Medved paints, particularly in propagating a pro-military
stance for the world's top military culture. *Los Angeles Times* reporter
Ronald Brownstein writes in his book, *The Power and the Glitter*, that Hollywood and Washington have a common feature, propaganda. One may
sell an ideology of political substance, military prowess, and hard power,
while the other sells an ideology of glitz, fame, enormous wealth, and
soft power, but both delve into respective fantasy worlds. Richard Stengel
writes that "the two cities are the source of much American mythology.
Washington promulgated the fable that any boy—or girl—could grow up
to be President; Hollywood invented the fantasy that the same boy or girl
could become a movie star. Both cities must appeal to hearts and minds;
both require a mass audience; both thrive on applause."[46] Similarly, David
Culbert writes, "Feature film is a wonderful medium for the propagandist.
Every feature film—good or bad; lavish or spartan in its production values;
frivolous or earnest—is loaded with cultural propaganda for the country
or society that produced it."[47] This power of film to change attitudes and
opinions has never been lost on modern American presidential administrations from Woodrow Wilson's screening of D. W. Griffith's Civil War
revisionist epic film, *The Birth of a Nation*, to Franklin Delano Roosevelt's
Office of War Information series, *Why We Fight*, directed by legendary
Hollywood film maker, Frank Capra.

While the epic films of Griffith and Capra are lost to Hollywood's heyday history, what is not lost is the paradox of Americanism that is Hollywood. Part advertiser for America, part propaganda machine, it can avoid marketing a Christian blockbuster like *The Passion of the Christ* but join the pro-military call for movies that celebrate the American hero in combat. Like the paradox that is anti-American sentiment, Hollywood is a puzzle and contradictory in tone and content. It is not anti-values because Hollywood is anything but neutral on social issues from militarism to gender, race, and sex. It is at times messianic in its pro-military stance and, at other times, seemingly conflicted by America's war history, as films like *Saving Private Ryan*, *The Deer Hunter*, and *Apocalypse Now* have shown. What will stand the test of time is that Hollywood will remain a symbol of America's image in the world—glamour, glitz, power, and domination, full of inspiration one moment, and at other times, dread.

NOTES

1. David E. Kaplan, "Hearts, Minds and Dollars," *U.S. News and World Report*, April 25, 2005. www.usnews.com/usnews/news/articles/050425/25roots.htm.

2. Jason Vest, "US: The Booming Business for Psy/Ops," *Government Executive*, November 30, 2005.

3. Program on International Policy Attitudes (PIPA), "In 20 of 23 Countries Polled Citizens Want Europe to Be More Influential Than US," April 6, 2005. Available online at www.pipa.org/OnlineReports/europe/040605/html/new_4_06_05.html#1

4. Victoria de Grazia, "Bush team enlists Madison Avenue in war on terror," *New York Times*, August 26, 2002.

5. Victoria de Grazia, *New York Times*.

6. www.ussmissouri.org/13.pdf

7. *Washington Post*, June 6, 1947, 1,3.

8. George C. Marshall speaking at Harvard University, June 5, 1947.

9. Library of Congress, "For European Recovery: The Fiftieth Anniversary of the Marshall Plan"; www.loc.gov/exhibits/marshall/mars0.html.

10. Amy C. Garrett, "Marketing America: Public Culture and Public Diplomacy in the Marshall Plan Era, 1947–1954," University of Pennsylvania, unpublished doctoral dissertation, 2004, 1–2.

11. Garrett, "Marketing America."

12. Martin Manning, *Historical Dictionary of American Propaganda* (Westport, CT: Greenwood Press, 2004), 10–11.

13. Barry and Judith Colp Rubin, *Hating America: A History* (New York: Oxford University Press, 2004), ix.

14. Barry and Judith Colp Rubin, *Hating America*.

15. Rubin and Rubin, *Hating America*, preface, x.

16. For further discussion, see www.propagandacritic.com/articles/ct.wg.name.html

17. Stephen Howe, *Empire* (London: Oxford University Press), 116–117.

18. Senator J. William Fulbright, *The Pentagon Propaganda Machine* (New York: Liveright, 1970), 149–150.

19. Senator J. William Fulbright, *The Arrogance of Power*, (New York: Vintage Books, 1966.)

20. Fulbright, *The Arrogance of Power*, 250.

21. I'm a proud lifetime member of the Fulbright Association.

22. Tom Wolfe, *I Am Charlotte Simmons*, on campus life in America, 258.

23. Quoted description is in John A. Lent, ed., *A Different Road Taken: Profiles in Critical Communication* (Boulder, CO: Westview, 1995), 155.

24. Herbert I. Schiller, *Living in the Number One Country* (New York: Seven Stories Press, 2000), 150.

25. As quoted in Richard Maxwell, *Herbert Schiller* (Lanham, MD: Rowman and Littlefield, 2003), 127–128. See also, Herbert I. Schiller, *Communication and Cultural Domination* (New York: International Arts and Sciences Press, 1976), 85–94.

26. Tom Regan, "Bush Speech Divides Foreign Media," *Christian Science Monitor*, February 3, 2005.

27. Nasser Karimi, "Iran Condemns Bush Speech on Terrorism," Associated Press, February 3, 2005.

28. Reinout van Wagtendonk, "State of the Union Warning for Syria and Iran," Radio Netherlands, February 3, 2005, www2.rnw.nl/rnw/en/currentaffairs/region/northamerica/usa050203.

29. George W. Bush, State of the Union Address, February 2, 2005.

30. Aljazeera.com editorial, "Bush issues staunch warning against Iran and Syria," International English Language Edition, February 3, 2005.

31. Greg Sheridan, "A man of his word like it or lump it," *The Australian*, February 3, 2005.

32. Carlos Fuentes, "Bush is giving Latin America the willies," *Los Angeles Times*, September 26, 2004.

33. Frederic Morton, "From Role Model to International Bully in Three Short Years," *Los Angeles Times*, September 28, 2004.

34. Mark Caro, "Movie Review: Control Room," *Chicago Tribune*, June 11, 2004.

35. www.controlroommovie.com character bios.

36. Caro, *Chicago Tribune*.

37. Caro, *Chicago Tribune*, from text of interview with the director.

38. Noujaim interview posted on documentary film website www.controlroommovie.com.

39. J. William Fulbright, *The Price of Empire* (New York: Pantheon, 1989).

40. Michael Medved, "That's Entertainment? Hollywood's Contribution to Anti-Americanism Abroad," *The National Interest*, Summer 2002.

41. Michael Medved, *Hollywood vs. America* (New York: Perennial, 1993), 1.

42. Cesar G. Soriano and Ann Oldenburg, "With America at war, Hollywood follows," *USA Today*, February 7, 2005.

43. Soriano and Oldenburg, *USA Today*.

44. Scott Galupo, "Positively clueless," *Washington Times*, March 4, 2005.

45. Galupo, *Washington Times*.

46. Richard Stengel, "Books: Rival Capitals of Fantasy: The Power and the Glitter by Ronald Brownstein," *Time*, February 4, 1991.

47. David Culbert, "Film (Feature)," in *Propaganda and Mass Persuasion: A Historical Encyclopedia, 1500 to the Present*, ed. Nicholas J. Cull, David Culbert, and David Welch (Santa Barbara, CA: ABC-CLIO, Inc., 2003), 129.

3

AMERICAN PROPAGANDA
AND THE PRESS

THE AMERICAN RIGHT TO NO

I became a newspaperman . . . I couldn't find honest employment.

—Mark Twain

The term Fourth Estate refers to the press role in society, often in a context as advocate for educating the masses, protecting democracy, and forging the public interest outside the domains of the media owners or privileged classes. During the French Revolution period, the First Estate referred to the clergy who owned a considerable portion of the land tax-free, served as arbiters for publication of books, and acted as the moral police. The Second Estate referred to the French nobility class, and the Third Estate constituted the remaining 98 percent of the population that ranged from the peasantry and working class to the wealthy bourgeoisie. The origin of the term "Fourth Estate" is often attributed to British philosopher Edmund Burke who referred to the Three Estates of British Parliament that represented the clergy, aristocracy, and the commons, but in the upper gallery sat the reporters, members of the Fourth Estate, whom Burke thought held their own political power to sway public opinion. Nineteenth-century Scottish historian Thomas Carlyle credited Burke with the term and explained the noble and persuasive purpose of the reporter's role:

> Burke said there were Three Estates in Parliament; but, in the Reporters'
> Gallery yonder, there sat a Fourth Estate more important than then all. It is
> not a figure of speech, or a witty saying; it is a literal fact. . . . Printing, which
> comes necessarily out of Writing, I say often, is equivalent to Democracy:
> invent Writing, Democracy is inevitable. . . . Whoever can speak, speaking
> now to the whole nation, becomes a power, a branch of government, with
> inalienable weight in law-making, in all acts of authority. It matters not what
> rank he has, what revenues or garnitures: the requisite thing is that he have
> a tongue which others will listen to; this and nothing more is requisite.[1]

In the American context, some refer to the Fourth Estate as a fourth
branch of government, outside the three main branches of the executive,
legislative, and judicial. Whether the reporters' gallery or a fourth branch,
the American media system as a whole has come under enormous scrutiny
from both the Right and Left ends of the political spectrum. Since the
1980s, many Americans view the media as either serving primarily the interests of corporate America or acting as enemies of the state and thereby
being un-American (unpatriotic) in attitude or story selection. Certain
prominent media personalities like Dan Rather, the longtime anchor on
the CBS Evening News, have been accused of having a liberal bias against
the Republican Party in general and the Bush dynasty in particular, as
documented by CBS reporter, Bernard Goldberg in his 2002 book, *Bias*.
Based on a 1996 editorial in the *Wall Street Journal*, Goldberg became
an overnight sinner to some and saint to others for speaking out of turn
and violating what he referred to as the code of *omerta* in American news
reporting: "I said out loud what millions of TV viewers all over America
know and have been complaining about for years: that too often, Dan and
Peter [Jennings] and Tom [Brokaw] and a lot of their foot soldiers don't
deliver the news straight, that they have a liberal bias, and that no matter
how often the network stars deny it, it is true."[2] More recently, the so-
called Rathergate scandal of 2004, in which Dan Rather was charged with
reporting a damning story about President Bush's service in the National
Guard using false documents that weren't checked out in advance, el-
evated the liberal bias tendencies of the American press to presidential campaign frenzied levels. Liberal, perhaps. Sloppy journalism and
arrogant attitude, most definitely. In early 2005, CBS News released a

lengthy document holding a number of producers accountable and thus expendable, though Rather was able to more gently go into that good night from his anchor perch by leaving its post in March.

Dan Rather's departure from CBS News wasn't the big news about the news in 2005, nor was the retirement of NBC's Tom Brokaw or even the sad death of Peter Jennings of ABC News. The story of the American press in 2005 was not even a liberal elite media, the newspaper triumvirate of the *New York Times*, *Washington Post*, and *Los Angeles Times*, for that's an old story. No, the real story was the continued cozy interrelationship between government and media, an old story of its own, but one not often revealed. The poster children for this inbreeding come from a liberal and conservative wing of the American media landscape. Judith Miller, reporter for the *New York Times*, was revealed to be stenographer to power in her almost total reliance on official unnamed government sources to promote the missing weapons of mass destruction narrative of 2002–2003. Miller spent 85 days in jail in 2005 for refusing to reveal her sources related to a government leak of a CIA covert operative, but what emerged during her jail tenure was closer scrutiny of Miller's subservience to the government media frame(up)—that the main reason for going to war with Iraq in the first place was because Saddam Hussein had weapons of mass destruction that he was imminently preparing to use against the United States, thus requiring a preemptive attack on Iraq. Miller is, like former Watergate investigative reporter Bob Woodward, too close to government power for her own good. Neither can see clearly because access has destroyed the objectivity lens.

The other side of the ideological coin comes in the personage of Kenneth Tomlinson, former editor-in-chief of *Reader's Digest* magazine and former Reagan administration official who sits on the Bush Administration's Broadcasting Board of Governors overseeing U.S. government international broadcasting efforts. Until recently, Tomlinson served as chairman of the board at the Corporation for Public Broadcasting. The neoconservative Tomlinson went on his own personal crusade against former press secretary to Lyndon B. Johnson, Bill Moyers, whose sin was telling underreported stories on his public affairs program, "Now," stories that were, to Tomlinson, not friendly enough toward the administration and frankly, too hard-hitting and critical of the power elite (aka Republican leadership) in Washington. In a speech at the National Conference on Media Reform gathering in St. Louis, Missouri, Moyers indicted the American media establishment from Miller to Tomlinson for not doing their duty as current and former members of the Fourth Estate, promoting the official government line without scrutiny:

> Judith Miller of The New York Times, among others, relied on that credibility, relied on that credibility of official but unnamed sources when she served essentially as the government stenographer for claims that Iraq possessed weapons of mass destruction. So the rules of the game permit Washington officials to set the agenda for journalism, leaving the press all too simply to recount what officials say instead of subjecting their words and deeds to critical scrutiny. Instead of acting as filters for readers and viewers sifting the truth from the propaganda, reporters and anchors attentively transcribe both sides of the spin invariably failing to provide context, background or any sense of which claims hold up and which are misleading. I decided long ago that this wasn't healthy for democracy.[3]

For his McCarthyist efforts, Tomlinson made the Worst TV list of 2005 as reported by *Time* magazine's James Poniewozik: "This clumsy partisan meddling—from the head of the very body meant to shield public broadcasting from political influence—put the BS in PBS."[4]

Tomlinson and Miller are just the tip of an all too big iceberg. The danger for the rest of us is that we rely disproportionately on the reliability of those who present and represent the news. The communications revolution involved a transition from interpersonal to mediated communication. Today this mediated communication is on steroids as information gets presented to us in such a rapid pace that most of us have little time to check out its accuracy. Walter Lippmann famously told us in 1922 that our world is mostly a pseudo-environment of stories told second-hand and through the prism of others' realities. Because of this limitation, the public held a distorted picture of truth, shaped more by propaganda and stereotypes. This was a world before faxes, instant messaging, global satellites, television, email, iPods, and podcasts. Today we believe that we are closer to the truth but it's a false belief. Our fingertips may be closer to information these days, but we are no closer to deeper meaning so long as stenographers-to-power dominate our media landscape. The more that we remain dependent on those who seek to close us off from meaning than disclosing its inner core, the more vivid the pseudo-environment remains.

JOURNALISM, PUBLIC RELATIONS, AND
GOVERNMENT PROPAGANDA

> Imagine that you manage a small-market TV station. You are pressed
> for time, understaffed and face the usual gaping holes of several news-
> casts to fill. What do you slap on the air, another minor local crime
> story that will take staff time, or a ready-made, professionally pack-
> aged treatment of a timely issue? The White House spin doctors have
> made your life easy. They've provided a one-sided but slick-looking
> report on the new Medicare law, something nobody in-house has time
> to cover.
>
> —Joanne Ostrow, TV and radio reporter for *The Denver Post*[5]

Andrew Gumbell, Los Angeles-based correspondent for *The Independent*, a London newspaper, says that the controversy depends on point
of view, though it "is deeply troubling in a country that prides itself on
the media's independence."[6] To broadcast public relations (PR) executives whose business falls or rises based on how many video news releases
(VNRs) are produced for corporate and government clients, this is nothing
like propaganda, which in their definition is anything misleading or hidden, but rather, paid advocacy, where contact information is provided and
broadcast media affiliates are left to their own devices to decide whether
or not to disclose the sponsors.

To many critics of the Bush Administration still reeling from the 2004
election, the war in Iraq, and the Bush Doctrine with its preventive war
strategy, the news-as-propaganda charge is not overreaching. It plays right
into the post-election political gamesmanship. The phenomenon—known
to its detractors as "covert propaganda" and to its advocates as the harmless
business of putting out video news releases—is deeply troubling in a
country that prides itself on the media's independence from government
censors.

In a General Accounting Office (GAO) report issued February 2005,
the U.S. comptroller David Walker said, "Prepackaged news stories can
be utilized without violating the law so long as there is clear disclosure to
the television viewing audience that this material was prepared by, or in
co-operation with, the government department or agency."

There is no "smoking gun" evidence, but plenty of speculation that the
Bush Administration has strong-armed network affiliates or forced news

directors to play the administration-produced videos. Many news reports include editorializing comments to that effect such as when Gumbell began the body of his article with the following charge: "The Bush administration has produced look-alike news propaganda clips and then persuaded television stations across the country to air them uncritically and, often, uncut." "As many as 20 government departments have produced fake news which stations broadcast as though they had produced the segments themselves," according to *The New York Times*.

Broadcast media in smaller markets are likely more susceptible to media manipulation. *The State of the News Media 2004* report by the Project for Excellence in Journalism cites a seller's media marketplace along with an overworked, under-staffed news room. This creates conditions whereby a news staff is more likely to take a ready-made video news release package and put it on the air without comment or context. Think of it as the news media business answer to Meals Ready to Eat (MREs) that are fast and efficient ways to feed a lot of soldiers, but not satisfying or nutritionally complete. The VNRs are prepackaged, slickly-produced editorials posing as news segments with hired communication professionals like Karen Ryan who appear to be legitimate journalists.

Would it have made any difference to us as viewers if Karen Ryan had said the following: "On behalf of your government, this is Karen Ryan reporting." William Pierce, a spokesman for the Department of Health and Human Services that hired PR professional and former news producer/reporter Ryan to appear in two VNRs said, "We're trying to influence you. It's nothing new. I'm at a loss as to why the media is coming down on this. This is frankly a problem for the media." In fact, administrations do work with the technology available and the Clinton Administration prepared VNRs to promote its own Medicare policy. The difference now is that we're living in an even more polarizing media environment than the days of Monica Lewinsky, Vince Foster, and Whitewater. With the exception of the Lewinsky scandal that broke on the then new Drudge Report website in early 1998, most of the public relations operations in previous administrations were closed door. Even the expensive White House coffees with President Clinton or the overnight stays in the Lincoln Bedroom were reported first by the mainstream broadcast and print media, not by the online media community. Today, it is much more likely that a news scandal will "break" online and then get picked up by the traditional media. In this case, while the liberal/left blogosphere has been leading the

"Bush uses propaganda" charge, it does seem to have merit and not be just politically motivated.

What the Left in America seemed to jump onto to balance the liberal charges of bias in mainstream media from the Right were the press-as-propaganda scandals of 2005 involving a number of conservative journalists who were paid to serve as cheerleaders for various Bush Administration causes. This time left-wing media advocacy groups and Democrats in Congress were charging some members of the press as acting as stenographers to power, in particular, the powerful in the Oval Office. These included newspaper columnist and prominent African American radio host Armstrong Williams, hired for $240,000 through his own PR firm, the Graham Williams Group, by Ketchum PR, a Washington, D.C.-based public relations firm. Ketchum was under direct contract with the Department of Education to find those who would tout the best qualities of the Bush Administration's No Child Left Behind legislation. Williams was initially unapologetic, arguing that he wore many hats, as it were, and that his Ketchum contract was for his public relations consultancy and not in his capacity as independent journalist. As part of his contract, Williams was asked to interview the outgoing Secretary of Education Rod Paige on his radio show in a cheerful give-and-take about NCLB. At no time during the interview did Williams acknowledge his public relations role with Paige's agency, which Williams deemed an oversight since his Ketchum contract was "for advertising time." The 4,000 member National Association of Black Journalists, of which Williams was not a member, called on all media outlets to drop Williams as a paid print or broadcast commentator. Bryan Monroe, a vice president of the NABJ said, "I thought we in the media were supposed to be watchdogs, not lapdogs. I thought we had an administration headed by a president who took an oath to uphold the First Amendment, not try to rent it."[7] Another NABJ vice president, Barbara Ciara, called Williams "tainted fruit." "He's lost his credibility. . . . he's unfairly indicted all commentators who have their own independent opinion, don't need a script from the administration and don't need to be paid off." Tribune Media Services, the distributor of Williams's weekly column, quickly dropped him and released a statement: "Accepting compensation in any form from an entity that serves as a subject of his weekly newspaper columns creates, at the very least, the appearance of a conflict of interest. Under these circumstances, readers may well ask themselves if the views expressed in his columns are his own, or whether they have been purchased by a third party."[8]

Another journalist-for-hire was marriage expert and syndicated columnist Maggie Gallagher, who in exchange for $21,500 from the Department of Health and Human Services, advised the agency on marriage policy and wrote columns that defended the Bush marriage initiative. Gallagher defended her government contract in a column, stating that "I've been a marriage expert, researcher and advocate for nearly 20 years. It is not uncommon for researchers, scholars, and experts to get paid by the government to do work relating to their field of expertise."[9] She was soon joined by another "pay to sway" journalist, Michael McManus, who pens a column, "Ethics & Religion," but whose nonprofit advocacy firm, Marriage Savers, received nearly $60,000 from the same government agency, HHS, to train marriage counselors in support of the $300 million White House marriage promotion program. Like Gallagher, McManus defended his relationship with the White House, this time by saying that he didn't personally pocket the government funds nor allow his firm's consultancy to sway his journalistic integrity. Coincidentally or not, he did state full support for the White House marriage initiative.[10] Their defense was indefensible even to the President, who in a news conference said that the Department of Education contract paying Williams to represent the administration's policy was "a mistake," and that the practice of using taxpayer funds to hire commentators to represent administration policies would end. Bush told reporters, "There needs to be a nice, independent relationship between the White House and the press, the administration and the press . . . We will not be paying commentators to advance our agenda. Our agenda ought to be able to stand on its own two feet."[11]

In light of the scandals, the Democrats were quick to gain some political capital and sponsor legislation in Congress, including the "Stop Government Propaganda Act" to end the practice of using public relations tactics and fake news such as prepackaged video news releases with actors posing as journalists. The investigative arm of Congress, the Government Accountability Office, had twice acted in 2004 to rule that the administration violated federal law against "covert propaganda," and reported that its own investigation showed a dramatic increase in Bush Administration spending on public relations services from $64 million in 2003 to $88 million in election year 2004. According to the Associated Press, government-funding

PR in 2004 jumped 128 percent over 2000 expenditures and *USA Today*, in a follow-up to its first revealing the Williams' controversy, said that the $250 million the Bush Administration spent for PR services in its first term was double the amount that the Clinton Administration spent from 1997–2000. This would probably surprise *Washington Post* media critic Howard Kurtz, whose 1998 book, *Spin Cycle*, said that the Clinton White House was in its first term the most well-oiled propaganda doctoring operation in history. Kurtz reports a typical White House press corps seduction by the Democratic salesman-in-chief when *Washington Post* columnist Courtland Milloy says of his presidential meetings, "I could feel the wool being pulled over my eyes. And it felt good, too."[12]

WHEN TRUTH IS A DANGEROUS THING

It is said that when a country goes to war, the press follows. That same press doesn't always stay to the bitter end, especially when it thinks nobody cares. In May 2005, ABC News political editor Mark Halperin and his associate editors at the network released a memorandum that explained press coverage of the war in Iraq:

> We say with all the genuine apolitical and non-partisan human concern that we can muster that the death and carnage in Iraq is truly staggering. And/but we are sort of resigned to the notion that it simply isn't going to break through to American news organizations, or, for the most part, Americans.... Democrats are so thoroughly spooked by John Kerry's loss— and Republicans so inspired by their stay-the-course Commander in Chief— that what is hands down the biggest story every day in the world will get almost no coverage. No conflict at home = no coverage.[13]

As former Green Party presidential candidate Ralph Nader wondered,

> Is ABC's excuse wholly understandable?... These same networks certainly did not show such inhibitions when they went out of their way day after day to hoopla the coming invasion of Iraq and not question the unsupported claims for going to war by Bush, Cheney, Rice, Rumsfeld and Powell. The networks in varying decrees were either cheerleaders or ditto machines. Passing the buck can be very costly to the American people's right to know—in time.[14]

What may be astonishing to think in the age of the Internet and hundreds of channels on the cable or dish, is that so many Americans, or at least those not wholly involved with the war in Iraq or Afghanistan, are far too oblivious to what's really happening on the ground. And when one of our Big Three network television news bureaus says that they will not cover the truth because the political landscape isn't up for it, then America isn't in any position to represent what a free press looks like to the rest of the world. It reminds me that the search for truth in times of war and global conflict is a truly dangerous thing. I recall the intrepid journalist, Elizabeth Neuffer of the *Boston Globe*, whom I had the chance to briefly meet but whose work continues to inspire. In the fall of 2002, I attended a small intimate dinner for eight women on the luxurious Westside of Los Angeles who came together to honor Elizabeth's work as a war correspondent. We were a few miles away from Hollywood and thousands of miles from the realities of war. As a journalism professor, I was admittedly awestruck by a chance dinner with the globe-trotting Neuffer, whom I knew had covered the world's most dangerous hot spots over the last 10 years, including Bosnia and Rwanda, where genocide was the favored means of settling disputes. Her book, *The Key to My Neighbor's House: Seeking Justice in Bosnia and Rwanda*, explored the aftermath of war and the war crimes tribunals that often go unreported in favor of the next big story. The book's narrative is told through extensive interviews with victims and their perpetrators, whose views of justice range from the legal, to the passive, to the bloodiest forms of revenge.

Our dinner with Elizabeth Neuffer was not focused on war and foreign policy. We established our common ground by talking about the unique demands that professional lives place upon women, the trade-offs between work and family, singlehood versus motherhood, and the (sigh) single woman's dilemma of trying to date while trying to write. To hear the bullet-dodging reporter express her own struggles over life choices versus professional pursuits made her seem all the more approachable and human. She ultimately shared her excitement for getting back into the action, this time the Middle East, where the Iraq war was looming. One woman asked about her workplace hazards and Elizabeth said that covering wars and conflict was something exceedingly interesting and exciting. It was in her blood to do what she did.

I learned in May 2003 that Elizabeth Neuffer was killed in a car accident, along with her translator Waleed, while on assignment covering the aftermath of the Iraqi war. Her last story for the *Boston Globe*, due to be published Sunday, May 11, was about efforts underway to rid Iraq of the influence of Saddam Hussein's Ba'ath Party. Elizabeth Neuffer was a rare breed in journalism, according to Globe Publisher Richard Gilman, "among that cadre of reporters who are at their best when the danger is greatest. With virtually no regard for their personal safety, they feel compelled to be wherever in the world that news may be occurring." She was also a reporter who cared deeply about the people behind war crime statistics. This connection with war victims did not put her in the good graces of their willing executioners. In 1996, while interviewing a Bosnian Serb commander about the slaughtering of Bosnian Muslim men in Sre-brenica, the commander cautioned her that she was "asking too many dangerous questions." He added, "Truth is a dangerous thing." When she won the 1998 Courage in Journalism Award from the International Women's Media Foundation, she explained her own philosophy of truth: "The truth may be hazardous to those who tell it, but truth is not danger-ous, disinformation is. As I saw in Bosnia and Rwanda, it is propaganda that fans the flames of hatred."

On March 20, 2003, the day after the bombs began to fall over Baghdad, Elizabeth Neuffer was interviewed by Fresh Air's Terry Gross about her weeks spent in Baghdad before the start of the war. When asked by Gross whether or not Iraqis looked at the war as liberation or occupation, Neuffer responded, "Absolutely occupation, not liberation. And every time I hear the Bush Administration use the word 'liberation,' I must admit I wince because that is not the sense—that is not how they're perceived on the ground in Baghdad even by the Iraqis, as I said, who I got to know who are very critical of the regime. This is a very proud nation that looks to its past civilization, that looks to the fact that it invented handwriting. It sees itself as a historical player and does not want to be ruled by anyone else. And it's very important to remember that."

She added, "I think that people in some quarters will be ecstatic to see Saddam Hussein removed from power, but I think they are deeply worried that those American troops are there to stay. They want to rule their own country. They're proud in the same way that Americans are, and you can imagine how we would react if a foreign country came here and said they were going to liberate us."

Too often in our haste to excoriate the media for going after the man bites dog story or the drippy celebrity news, we forget that there are journalists like Elizabeth Neuffer, who died en route to Baghdad from Tikrit, doing what was her calling, exemplifying the best that American journalism has to offer us. Those of us committed to bettering the world owe a debt of gratitude to those journalists on the frontlines who provide the stories we use to strengthen our case for social justice and human rights.[15]

BEYOND POLITICAL BIAS

Many Americans love to hate the media for either its right-wing or left-wing bias, but another phenomenon stirring antipathy is the rising influence of business parameters and the profit-driven bottom line in the American press. This deregulated and privatized model of the press free of government intervention in turn becomes the preferred model propagated by the United States throughout the world, most recently in the Americanization of the Iraqi press. Alternative and much more idealized visions for the press and its role in society do exist. German philosopher Juergen Habermas is famous for coining the term, "the public sphere," to refer to that important space between state and society reserved for an informed and reasoned discussion of public debate. It is neither sanctioned by the government nor driven primarily by economics. It is in the public sphere where public opinion is formed, free and unfettered from the official power restraints of government power and the economic power of the private sector. Why public opinion is so important is because it serves as a mediating function between official power and society as a whole. Where would we be without public opinion on government policies as diverse as Iraq, the war on terror, special interest lobbying in Washington, propaganda media like Al Hurra, Radio Sawa, and Radio Farda, or even privately-financed health security accounts. Without it, there is no potential check on power; with it, there is, ideally, a chorus of voices that can register its opinion outside officialdom.[16]

Over time, Habermas and other critical theory media scholars like Robert McChesney have observed a media industry emerge into an extension of economic and state interests and become more of a manipulator of public opinion that transforms citizens into consumers and active participants in public opinion shaping into passive recipients of information. As a result, the face of the press takes on a cosmetic look. News stories become product placements. That serendipitous one-on-one interview with a new book author is really part of a marketing plan by the public relations firm hired by the publisher that is a corporate subsidiary of the network doing the interview. The audience is there to act as peanut gallery approver.

Want to learn about the press in society? You are more likely to learn about changes in the media today by reading the business and finance sections of the newspaper rather than the front pages. You may in turn find people who are able to tell you whether or not AOL Time Warner's chairman is stepping down, but you do not necessarily get a well-informed citizenry that is able to carry on an intellectual discussion of the day on all civil matters. Syndicated columnist and author Richard Reeves says "were it a person, journalism would be diagnosed as depressed."[17] Why? Because Reeves sees a press system that no longer inspires free and open debate but a defeated passivity. Even anger, shaking your head and saying you hate the media, doesn't help, he argues:

> I've always been surprised by the relative immunity readers grant to newspa-
> pers and television stations. If you think we're making quotes up or distort-
> ing discussion and action, organize against us. What is the point of moaning
> about the anonymous "they" supposedly saying and doing these things? It's
> us! The press. We are the source, and we should be accountable for every
> single word. Bang on our windows. Picket our doors. Cancel subscriptions.
> Boycott our advertisers. Organize! If you don't believe us, make us tell you
> where we are getting the stuff![18]

To paraphrase Santayana, those of who don't learn from the mistakes of past journalism are doomed to repeat them. We need to go back to the modern age of propaganda in the early 20th century that put in place the foundations of our modern media system today in order to grasp why the public has been relegated the back seat in civic discourse. At the time of World War I, public relations and advertising were becoming the engines of democratic discourse. The U.S. government established its first propaganda agency, the Committee on Public Information, which happened to be run by a journalist and F.O.W. (Friend of Wilson), George Creel. Creel wrote an account of his efforts to propagandize the American people by saying that it had been turned into a "white hot mass" of subservience to the government's information program.[19]

Following the war, two intellectuals set out on a debate about the relationship between the press and public opinion, one more optimistic and idealistic than the other. Walter Lippmann authored the book *Public Opinion* in 1922, which to this day still serves as the classic text on the subject and a mandatory graduate school reading. Lippmann, who had served as a P.O.W. interrogator in World War I and close confidant to the Creel Committee, became disillusioned with the idea that the masses could be fully informed about the complex issues of public policy: "Under the impact of propaganda, not necessarily in the sinister meaning of the word alone, the old constraints of our thinking have become variables. It is no longer possible, for example, to believe in the original dogma of democracy; that the knowledge needed for the management of human affairs comes up spontaneously from the human heart...It has been demonstrated that we cannot rely upon intuition, conscience, or the accidents of casual opinion if we are to deal with the world beyond our reach."[20]

He believed people were too easily malleable and gullible, and that we were better off leaving the masses out of the most important matters of the day. Lippmann envisioned a core group of well-trained, best-educated experts who would drive public opinion in American society. He himself became a major league elite opinion shaper, much like *New York Times* columnist Thomas Friedman is on foreign policy today. Lippmann consulted with the top bureaucrats in government, sat with presidents, and penned his "Today and Tomorrow" syndicated column for over forty years.

Lippmann's intellectual sparring partner and more senior opponent was Vermont-born Columbia University professor John Dewey. Unlike Lippmann, Dewey held that the press had a certain public interest responsibility to educate the masses, even if the process were chaotic, inefficient, and not quite attainable. Dewey thought that Lippmann was too quick to blame the public for its ignorance, indifference, or even outright anger toward all things political. I agree with Dewey and think that Mark Halperin at ABC News should be reminded of the Dewey tradition in America.

CREDIBILITY AND THE AMERICAN PRESS

Our U.S. media institutions, arguably proxies for our knowledge-gathering and information brokering, lack credibility, a 20-year low, according to *The State of the News Media 2004*, sponsored by the Project for Excellence in Journalism in Washington, D.C. that is affiliated with the Columbia University Graduate School of Journalism. The March 2004 report says, "Americans think journalists are sloppier, less professional, less moral, less caring, more biased and less honest about their mistakes and generally harmful to democracy than they did in the 1980s."[21]

A June 2004 poll by the Pew Research Center for the People and the Press showed the same: whatever credibility journalists may have had is slowly eroding. According to the Pew poll, from 1996–2002, Cable News Network (CNN) founded by media mogul, Ted Turner, was viewed as the most believable broadcast or cable outlet and 42% of those surveyed said that they could believe all or most of what was reported. Today CNN's credibility rating is 33%. CBS News' longstanding investigative journalism show, *60 Minutes*, is rated highly credible by about one-third (33%) of the public. Pew attributes some of the falloff in credibility to a growing partisan tilt in the ratings game. Republicans are traditionally more skeptical toward media credibility overall than Democrats but now Republicans are even more skeptical. In the current survey, CNN's credibility rating among Dems is 45% while it is only 26% among Republicans. Republicans rank Fox News Channel as their most trusted news source (29%) while Independents rank *60 Minutes* (29%) and Dems rank CNN (45%).

Another survey by the Pew Center of 547 national and local reporters, producers, editors, and executives across the United States addresses current issues facing journalism and updates trends from earlier surveys conducted in 1995 and 1999. The greatest differences between journalists and the public are philosophical. Many more journalists do identify themselves as liberals than as conservatives, while for the population as a whole the reverse is true. The survey's findings show the percentage of national journalists who say they were political liberals increased from 22 percent in 1995 to 34 percent today. The trend among local journalists has been similar; 23 percent say they are liberals, compared with 14 percent in 1995. Only 7 percent of national journalists, and 12 percent of local journalists, think of themselves as politically conservative. Majorities of national (54 percent) and local (61 percent) journalists continue to describe themselves as moderate. The survey also revealed differences in moral values. About 60 percent of the public believes it is necessary to believe in God to be a truly moral person. But fewer than 15 percent of journalists believe that. About half of the public thinks society should accept homosexuality, while 80 percent of news people think so. This may explain the media credibility divide among American media consumers who choose their news based on their political preferences so that Fox News Channel gets the most Republicans and independents while CNN and MSNBC garner more Democratic Party viewers. I know many a Democrat who refuses to ever watch Fox News Channel, a phenomenon that sparked a website, Newshounds.us, whose tag line is "we watch Fox so you won't have to." The News Hound "team" consists of "eight middle-aged citizens who believe a viable democracy depends upon viable media."

By more than three-to-one, journalists in the survey said they believe it is a bad thing if some news organizations have a "decidedly ideological point of view." Yet, more than four in ten of them say they too often let their ideological views show in their reporting. A confessional rate of 40 percent indicates an epidemic afflicts journalism today. It shows that rather than being merely reporters of fact, many journalists have become purveyors of propaganda.

We need to put credibility and the press in context. While public confidence in journalism fell by half in the 1965–1995 period, so did public confidence in universities, major companies, and medicine. We should not pick on the news media alone. Most all institutions have slipped on the credibility slope. The press can build its credibility by correcting mistakes early and often. By being more accurate, this does not refer just to typographical mistakes. The public is increasingly turned off by an institutional bias in a news organization, which can include a tendency to rely too much on big media news wires (*New York Times*, Associated Press) and not enough on old-fashioned style original reporting. Newspaper readers are beginning to demand the sources of stories and where they can turn for additional reading, which is why some news organizations are spending more of their revenue now on online sources. If a newspaper reader wants more of the story, then it's just a click away.

In spring 2005, I participated as a faculty consultant with editors and managers of the *Orange County Register* in a roundtable meeting sponsored by the Associated Press Managing Editors (APME) organization that was sponsoring credibility roundtables at newspapers across the country. The *OC Register* is the leading daily newspaper in Orange County, California, and has a reputation as a more conservative newspaper compared to that of the liberal *Los Angeles Times*, some thirty miles up the road. Our chosen topic was the provocative subject of media bias. The newspaper invited a cross-section of older and younger readers, some left-leaning, most right-leaning, who had various grievances with the paper on the subject of bias. A young man whose brother was serving in Iraq thought the paper wasn't doing enough positive war stories. Most complained that bias amounted to leaving out too much valuable information. The consensus, whether one was Republican, Democrat, independent, or non-political, was that all media were out of touch with their communities and needed to work harder to rebuild the loss of trust between news consumer and news producer.

American media credibility overall is particularly low because too many reporters and anchors are interested in generating the heat of scandal and sensation over the light of perspective and context. Too many media sources are unnamed, nonexistent, or confidential. After *USA Today* reporter Jack Kelly was found to have fabricated parts of at least 20 stories and stolen 100 passages from other news organizations, *USA Today* initiated a new policy that anonymous sources cannot be used in any news story unless the source's identity is known to the managing editor. Finally, increasing numbers of people are relying on new forms of media such as the blogosphere and Internet sites to supplement or even replace newspapers, magazines, radio stations, broadcast networks, and cable TV channels. The result is a nation in which old style news consumers are developing news myopia, believing what they see, hear, or read on the preferred outlets—and labeling as biased or false the information that doesn't reinforce their points of view. The more partisan your outlook, the more likely you are to believe that the press system as a whole has no credibility and seek out a press outlet that reflects and sustains your ideology. What we develop then is a world in which the Michael Moore film fans fail to connect or dialogue with the Fox News Channel viewers and we stay in our own mind boxes that do not challenge but confirm our point of view.

If the use of propaganda as a joint venture of U.S. government and commercial media is now so routine and pervasive, how can we believe the validity of the news we consume? It has always been a common cultural heritage in a free society that keeping up with the news is important to upholding our democratic traditions. The elite commercial media may think that they can help us distinguish between the objective truth, subjective opinion, and downright deception, but history shows us that they are now as much part of the problem as they are the part of the solution. As the citizens did with *Pravda* in the former Soviet Union, so too can Americans learn to read between the lines of the official story.

If we want the full story, we may have to turn to our own *samizdat*[22] literature online and in alternative and independent media. *The State of the News Media 2004*, from the Project for Excellence in Journalism in Washington, D.C., indicated some major trends in American media that impact international information campaigns. These include a loss in so-called mainstream media (MSM) users over a rise in ethnic, online, and alternative media usage. This loss of consumers to the mainstream media means a loss to advertisers, which forces newsrooms to cut corners and cut staffs, hurting news quality. Media overall emphasizes distribution of information through various outlets over traditional news gathering. Increasingly, online readers and TV viewers are getting a steady supply of "insta-news" but the rapid-fire approach to news doesn't always translate into accuracy or trust-building. The public still believes that news organizations are in the news business to turn a profit and not to promote the public interest. The report's findings make one conclude that we're living in a journalism landscape dominated by a U.S. President who admits he has no time for reading the newspaper. In December 2003, President George Bush told ABC's Diane Sawyer that he preferred getting his news from people he trusted, not journalists, who, according to this president, tend to editorialize (so unlike his advisers!). The Project for Excellence in Journalism concludes that "the journalists' role as intermediary, editor, verifier, and synthesizer is weakening, and citizens do have more power to be proactive with the news. But most people will likely do so episodically. And the proliferation of the false and misleading makes the demand for the journalist as referee, watchdog and interpreter all the greater."[23] But what can any one journalist do when we're all journalists now, interpreting facts as we see them?

Two journalism events of spring 2004 illustrate this point. The first concerns the firing of a married couple employed as cargo staff for a U.S. military contractor. The couple violated Pentagon prohibition of photographing returning war dead by snapping a few photos as both were assisting in loading dead American soldiers at Kuwait International Airport for transport home. The employer, Maytag Aircraft Corp., fired them immediately after the photos were published on the front page of the *Seattle Times*. The photo depicted 20 U.S.-flag draped coffins being secured for transport to Dover Air Force Base in Delaware. This followed a Freedom of Information Act request from an Internet entrepreneurial man of thirty-four, who received over 300 images from the Pentagon that he later posted on his website, Memoryhole.com. The Pentagon later announced that it would no longer release any additional war dead pictures to protect the privacy of the families concerned to which the White House concurred. A second event concerned the censoring of a popular comic strip, Doonesbury, after Gary Trudeau dared to show one of his original characters in the comic strip, B.D., missing a leg as a result of being sent to Iraq by his creator. One northeastern Colorado newspaper wrote: "The Journal-Advocate has chosen not to publish this week's Doonesbury in the paper because of the graphic, violent battlefield depictions of Iraq in this week's installment. The Doonesbury comic strip for this week is available to our subscribers at the front counter, or by fax, mail or e-mail, if requested. Call 522–1990. We will resume printing Doonesbury in the paper when the content is deemed suitable for publication in the Journal-Advocate."[24]

In the July/August 2003 issue of the *Columbia Journalism Review*, managing editor Brent Cunningham questioned whether the American tradition of objectivity in news (promoting fairness and balance) has turned U.S. journalists into passive recipients of news, particularly from official sources like government and corporation elites. One case cited is the October 2001 memo from then CNN chairman Walter Isaacson while the war in Afghanistan was under way. Isaacson sent a memo to all CNN foreign correspondents telling them to seek "balance" in all their reports of Afghan casualties by reminding their audience that such hardship or death came in response to the terrorist attacks of September 11. Cunningham reports that an intern called newspaper editors during the war in Iraq to see whether letters to the editor were running for or against the war and was told by the editor of *The Tennessean* that although letters were 70 percent against the war, the editor chose to run more pro-war letters so they wouldn't be accused of being biased by some of their readers.

Consider also the case of U.S. Marine Corps reservist in Iraq, Lance Corporal Ted Boudreaux, whose photo of himself and two Iraqi children smiling widely shows one child holding up a sign that reads: "Lcpl Boudreaux killed my Dad th(en) knocked up my sister!" In early April 2004, the photo that had been circling all over the Internet reached the inbox of Ibrahim Hooper, communications director for the American-Islamic Relations (CAIR) in Washington, D.C. Assuming the photo was real, Nihad Awad, CAIR's executive director, issued an immediate press release that said: "If the United States Army is seeking to win the hearts and minds of the Iraqi people, this is the wrong way to accomplish that goal."[25] The CAIR release was picked up and reprinted in a number of global online newspapers, including Paknews.com, with no questioning of whether or not the photo may have been altered. A *Salon* magazine reporter said that in an age of Photoshop, we must always question the authenticity of any picture circulating the Internet. Farhad Manjoo writes:

> There was a time when photographs were synonymous with truth—when you could be sure that what you saw in a picture actually occurred. In today's Photoshop world, all that has changed. Pictures are endlessly pliable. Photographs (and even videos) are now merely as good as words—approximations of reality at best, subtle (or outright) distortions of truth at worst. Is that Jane Fonda next to John Kerry at an antiwar rally? No, it isn't; if you thought so, you're a fool for trusting your own eyes. Some photographers welcome the new skepticism toward images; it's good that people are learning not to automatically believe what they see, they say. But many fear that we're losing an important foothold on reality. Without trustworthy photographs, how will we ever know what in our world is real?[26]

The U.S. military conducted its own internal investigation and found no evidence of any wrongdoing and Ted Boudreaux, returned from Iraq in September 2003, is denying the authenticity of the photo. Other versions of the photo have now popped up all over the Internet with cardboard signs that read "We wanna see Jessica Simpson!" or inject a more positive message that says the soldier "saved" the dad and "rescued" the sister. No one really knows what the truth is, but in an age when we allow our own narrative pictures in our heads to determine the facts for us, the truth is almost irrelevant to the damage that has already been done. CAIR, for its own part, has no more reason to deny the authenticity of such a photo than anyone else, but the negative version certainly fit the prediction CAIR made before war with Iraq that such an invasion would hurt the Muslim image in the world. This is something that the United States has in common, for certainly the U.S. invasion and occupation of Iraq continues to hurt the American image in the world.

KILL YOUR TV!

The first media Monday of the New Year 2004 started like any other in America—full of cliché, celebrity, weather with Al, and this: "It was—it was like late—it was real early Saturday morning, we was—we was just chillin' at the room and, you know, we're in Las Vegas, and we were sitting in the room, let's go do something, you know. Let's go—let's go get married."

Our mind space invaded by ABC's *Good Morning America* and CBS's *Morning Show* millionaire hosts revealed the eloquence-challenged 55-hour groom of pop singer Britney Spears, one Jason Allen Alexander, who purportedly was now shopping around for the right Hollywood agent. No word on what the administration at Southeastern Louisiana University had to say about enrolled student Jason's command of the English language. Maybe they was still chillin' with the news.

Not to be outdone, the highest-paid morning anchor on broadcast television, "perky" Katie Couric (she purportedly hates that description) of *The Today Show* had this to say to America as we prepared to send the kids off to school and drank our mourning, er, morning coffee:

> Katie Couric: *Well, if you thought it wouldn't last, you were right. Britney Spears got hitched this weekend to a childhood friend at a Las Vegas wedding chapel, but the groom is already back home without the bride. NBC's Natalie Allen is in the couple's hometown of Kentwood, Louisiana. Natalie, good morning.*
> Natalie Allen: *Good morning to you, Katie. Yes, the honeymoon is over. The groom arrived back here in Kentwood yesterday. His marriage to a pop star princess apparently will not have a fairy tale ending.*

Katie probably received about $10,000 in salary for that exchange.

Lucky for us, now addicted to all Britney (or, for that matter, Jen, Angelina, or Brad) all the time, we got this from Matt Lauer, Katie's co-host, who one-upped his co-host with this reportage the next morning:

> Matt Lauer: *Oops, we're doing it again. Unless you've been hanging out in a cave, you probably know by now that Britney Spears got hitched this weekend in a quickie Las Vegas wedding. And just as quickly, she got the marriage annulled. So, just who is Britney's ex? Well, Access Hollywood's Billy Bush went to Britney's hometown of Kentwood, Louisiana, for an exclusive interview with Jason Allen Alexander.*

Thank you, Matt and Billy. In fact, that cave was sounding just fine to me. 2004 broadcast television in America was getting off to its routine self, full of gossip, trivial pursuit data, and news that you can throw away. Gaskell Media, a media buying service, reported record-setting upfront buys in 2004 for broadcast television, assuring the media business sectors of even more profit and the public of more drivel: "The good news keeps on coming for the broadcast television networks. Record setting upfronts brought in $9.3 billion for the 2003–2004 season, and there is every indication that next year will be even more profitable."[27]

British author Aldous Huxley may have predicted America's present when he wrote that a society like ours that spends more time "in the irrelevant worlds of sport and soap opera, of mythology and metaphysical fantasy, will find it hard to resist the encroachments of those who manipulate and control it."[28]

Unlike some of my recovering TV-addicted friends, I do indulge in the American media experience, including television. I do harbor thoughts of telecide and have imagined throwing my TV out of my second-floor window. My excuse is that I'm a media professor and am required to keep up with current events. Nevertheless, I'm absolutely apoplectic about the American media system's search for the latest lowest-common denominator offering and the BIG LIE that American broadcasters keep throwing at us with their "we're just giving the public what it wants" First Amendment cover. That's just what they say in public gatherings to wrench themselves of any responsibility for Britney, Michael Jackson, and Laci Peterson (latest murder victim) wall-to-wall coverage. Behind the scenes and in advertising revenue reports they speak in different tongues: entertainment is king, pulp fiction is profit, and quality be damned if it affects the bottom line.

Perhaps we should borrow a page from ACT-UP, whose memorable slogan for the AIDS crisis in the 1980s, "Silence Equals Consent," was united with a shaming campaign at public gatherings. Why don't we in America publicly shame those broadcasters who keep throwing us junk food for the mind? The next time you hear a broadcast executive in public try to explain the decline in broadcast news with a people's choice lament, stand up, point your finger (something other than the middle, unless you are ambitious), and say, "Shame on you."

And while you are it, ask why—as reported by The Tyndall Report, which tracks television news—the three major U.S. television networks' evening news broadcasts devoted just 39 minutes to AIDS coverage in 2003 when the disease killed more than 3 million people, 2 million in Africa alone. We shouldn't hold our collective breaths for *Entertainment Tonight* to cover that story, unless Britney has something to say about those poor suffering people. Even the Asian tsunami disaster, which received unprecedented media coverage in the United States, was driven by ethnocentrism of the highest magnitude. The disaster became a media event for many reasons to be sure—the magnitude in death and destruction and overall shock value of a rogue wave (instead of, for once, a rogue nation). Media technology allowed instantaneous and 'round-the-clock news coverage, assisted by the availability of so many tourists' home-made movies that amped up the shock value and gave the story a "you are there" feel. Mostly though, the event garnered the world's eyes because so many of the victims were Western tourists, such as the fair-haired, blue-eyed Swedish children, or a gorgeous supermodel from the Czech Republic and her missing handsome fashion photographer boyfriend from London. Wolfgang Donsbach, president of the International Communication Association, asks, "Who of us, however, remembers today that in 1991, 140,000 people died in a flood at the coast of Bangladesh—or that, in 1971, 700,000 Chinese lost their lives in an earthquake? The news value of the tsunami at the end of 2004 has also been affected by the fact that so many people from the industrialized world were among the victims—which was not the case in the other Asian disasters just mentioned."[29]

In his book, *Propaganda*, the French propaganda scholar Jacques Ellul said that modern forms of communication, including mass media, are instruments of propaganda. At the time of the English-language publication of his book in 1965, he described three major propaganda blocs of the day—the Soviet Union, China, and the United States. Only one of these countries was democratic, but to Ellul, in a democracy propaganda still thrives. Most often it is through the mass media, which are anything but mass in ownership and distribution. To Ellul, without the monopoly concentration of mass media, there can be no modern propaganda. For propaganda to thrive, the media must remain concentrated, news agencies and services must be limited, the press must be under central command, and radio, film, and television monopolies must pervade. In other words, in a democracy and among a so-called free media, propaganda still thrives.[30]

MARRYING PRESS AND PROPAGANDA IN AMERICA

Modern propaganda began in the United States in the early 20th century. During World War I, the mass media were integrated with public relations and advertising methods to advocate and maintain support for war.

The Creel Committee established the first American publicity campaign to spread and disseminate the gospel of the American way to all corners of the globe. In the United States today, private commercial propaganda is as important to our notions of American democracy as any governmental propaganda. Commercial appeals to the people through advertising, which plays on irrational fantasies and impulses, are some of the most pervasive forms of propaganda in existence today. But there are fantasies perpetrated not just by the advertising industry but often by its handmaidens in the top levels of government who "sell" a war when they know the public is in the mood to buy. In the foreword to my co-edited volume, *War, Media and Propaganda*, Dean *emeritus* of the Graduate School of Journalism at the University of Berkeley and former *Washington Post* executive editor Ben Bagdikian writes, "The absence of Iraqi weapons of mass destruction and the fraudulence of the uranium importation were known and knowable to the standard news media of the country at the time. But there has been a reflex throughout the history of modern news: when the country goes to war, so do the major news organizations. They consider it 'patriotic.' But it is dubious patriotism that abandons citizens in unnecessary ignorance of political information."[31]

Bagdikian is the author of *The Media Monopoly*, which, when it was first published in 1984, was attacked for being exaggerated in its forewarning that the U.S. media system was heading toward monopoly control. Bagdikian predicted that just a handful of corporations would control all media by the year 2000 and for that he was accused of being the chicken little of media criticism. Nowadays he's seen as just one among a crowd of media reform scholars who criticize the conglomerization of news when he should be credited for daring to predict the obvious trend in news media toward concentration at a time when no one else was looking at the media system as a whole.

Propaganda in a democracy establishes truth in the sense that it creates "true believers" who are as ideologically committed to democratic progress as others are ideologically committed to its control. The perpetuation of democratic ideals and beliefs in the face of concentrated power in propaganda institutions (media, political institutions) is a triumph of propaganda in modern American society. What makes the study of propaganda so problematic in America is that it is still generally regarded as the study of the darker side of our nature; the study of their evil versus our good. Those whom we consider evil thrive in propaganda, while we spread only the truth. The best way to study propaganda is to separate one's ethical judgments from the phenomenon itself. Propaganda thrives and exists, for ethical and unethical purposes. Propaganda connotes something sinister (brainwashing, lies, deceit) and it is still widely believed that propaganda is what others do to us, i.e., they lie and mislead; they attempt to brainwash our thinking, while we tell the truth. The origins of the word extend back to medieval Rome, when the papacy sought a need to strengthen its influence vis-à-vis the rise of the Protestant faith in Europe. Pope Gregory XV established a permanent Congregation for the Propagation of the Faith to manage foreign missions. Thereafter, propaganda came to mean any organized, institutional effort to spread a doctrine or set of ideas in order to support the mission of that institution.

When attached to what governments do, there is no nation on earth that does not seek to influence the way in which its subjects view that government. If propaganda sounds a lot like public relations, human relations, marketing, or even advertising, it's because in a global modern context the term is often used interchangeably with these persuasion industries. If we don't think of advertising or PR as inherently evil, we shouldn't think the same evil thoughts about propaganda.

In the United States, we have a particularly negative response to propaganda in part because of its association with WWII Nazi Germany or Stalinist Russia. The social influence literature credits the United States with being the greatest purveyor and consumer of propaganda in the world. We are the world's leader in the propaganda industries, whether you want to cite Washington, the center for government propaganda, Hollywood, the center for broadcast propaganda, or Madison Avenue, the center for advertising propaganda.

Propaganda has always been associated with the press. First, modern propaganda is virtually nonexistent without a medium by which the information gets distributed (film, pamphlets, broadcasting, books, and speeches). Two, when nations go off to war, the press tends to follow along quite blindly and makes itself institutionally vulnerable to propaganda campaigns. As California Senator Hiram Johnson is credited with saying in 1917, "the first casualty when war comes is truth." In late 2004, both the *New York Times* and the *Washington Post* printed mea culpa editorials asking the public's forgiveness for their lack of vigilant watch over the U.S. government's PR campaign in favor of intervention in Iraq. It is generally the tendency for media to first go to war and then ask for forgiveness from the public after the fact, as the two newspapers of record did by waiting until nearly two years after the start of the war in Iraq. In this case, both the *Post* and *Times* were undoubtedly worried that a loss in newspaper credibility could spell a loss in newspaper sponsorship, namely advertising, and decided to do what they could to re-build that credibility, however slipping it may be. Were it more about maintaining credibility than restoring it, the two great papers would have had ongoing internal investigations throughout the buildup and beginning of the war with Iraq and asked themselves what they knew, from whom, and to whose advantage did that information most benefit? Any person on the street doing a quick mental examination would have told himself that the government was telling us that Saddam Hussein had weapons of mass destruction but without any credible proof.

Because we all, mainstream media included, lulled ourselves into believing our own government leaders over what our critical mindset was telling us, we accepted the truth of the government's claims without any verification. We wanted to believe the truth of the government's claims because the alternative, that the government was lying, was too difficult for us to accept. A government that lies, we thought, fit in more with a totalitarian society, not an open society. Even President Ronald Reagan was famous for saying about his dealings with the Soviets over nuclear arms reduction talks, "Trust, then verify." We should have heeded the words of this former American president in our reaction to words of the present.

Third, we tend to link propaganda to the press because like the press, propaganda campaigns focus public attention on only certain facts, processes, and necessities of a story or event. In mass communications research, we refer to this process as media framing, priming, and news values. Ever since the publication of Walter Lippmann's *Public Opinion*, it is generally accepted that that news media can only tell part of the story, not the whole story. This raises critical questions about what gets left out, whose voices aren't being heard, and what is being taken away from the context of the story. When we criticize the news media in our society, we often use a critique that associates it with a propaganda campaign. We tell ourselves there has got to be more to the story. It's too simple. They just talk about a few facts associated with the case, repeat those facts, and leave out everything else. Because of this parallel universe between press and propaganda, many worry that the modern media are serving the interests of government and corporate propaganda rather than the needs of the public. Think about this when you analyze your next news program. Propaganda research tells us that the most effective propaganda is the simplest argument that concentrates your attention on a few points that are often repeated, and usually wrapped in emotional dualities like love/hatred.

MEDIA AND DEMOCRACY: THAT WOULD BE NICE!

> When asked by a journalist what he thought of Western Civilization, Mohatmas Ghandi replied, "I think it would be a good idea."

In the spring of 2004, I was asked to speak at a fundraiser for the American Civil Liberties Association (ACLU) Los Angeles Chapter. I was introduced by longtime ACLU member and actor James Whitmore, most famous for portraying Harry Truman, Will Rogers, and writer John Griffin in the film *Black Like Me*. I was specifically asked to comment on the media landscape and its impact on democracy. In April 2005, I gave an updated version of the speech to the League of Women Voters of Orange County, California. The news then wasn't good, nor is it now. In fact, spin, public relations, and propaganda still dominate the media landscape and only seem to be getting thicker in their layering. But to paraphrase Ghandi, I think media and democracy are still a very good idea. Here I share some of my observations that still persist.

In the twenty-first century, the state of the media reminds me of that modern American political communications philosopher and pop singer, Sheryl Crow, and her hit song of 2002, "Soak Up the Sun," that seemed to pull together a nation still reeling from 9/11. When it comes to American democracy and the press, to paraphrase Crow, it's not having what we want, it's wanting what we've got.

Unlike our fellow global citizens in Iraq who aspire to democratic institutions, rule of law, transparency, accountability, and representation, we've already got it in America through our Constitution, Bill of Rights, and Congressional legislation. How much of what we already have do we take for granted? How much do we allow our political proxies in the White House, Pentagon, and Capitol Hill, or our communication executives at Sony Pictures, AOL Time Warner, and Disney to direct us like sheep, corral our thinking and freedom of speech? In spring 2004, the Walt Disney Corporation announced that it would not allow its subsidiary Miramax to be the distributor of the Michael Moore documentary, *Fahrenheit 911*, a film highly critical of the Bush Administration, allegedly because the film was a politically divisive hot potato, which no family-friendly corporation that promotes a very small world has an interest in involving itself. Michael Moore said of the controversy on his website (www.michaelmoore.com): "At some point the question has to be asked, should this be happening in a free and open society where the monied interests essentially call the shots regarding the information that the public is allowed to see?"

The Disney media executive's statement seems to contradict the politically partisan actions of the Baltimore-based Sinclair Broadcast Group, known as the Clear Channel of local news and a 98% Republic campaign contributor, which pulled the ABC flagship news program *Nightline* from eight of its affiliates for daring to recite the name, rank, and age of the U.S. war dead in Iraq on its April 30, 2004 broadcast. Its decision was based on the news as propaganda charge as published by Sinclair Broadcasting in a press statement:

> Despite the denials [of *Nightline*], the show appears to be motivated by a political agenda designed to undermine the efforts of the United States in Iraq. . . . Before you judge our decision, however, we would ask that you first question Mr. Koppel as to why he chose to read the names of the 523 troops killed in combat in Iraq, rather than the names of the thousands of private citizens killed in terrorists' attacks since and including the events of Sept. 11, 2001.

Media bias is often cast as being too liberal, when there are other biases not often discussed. How about bias toward the source? How often do we not get the information we need because of national security concerns, USA Patriot Act restrictions? This is censorship without officially appointed censors or censorship at source. And what of the censorship by omission so often practiced by the media oligopolies that carpet-bomb our thinking with the truly irrelevant, the truly insubstantive. The American Civil Liberties Union in the 1930s worked with other socially conscious organizations to try to promote the public interest against the rise of the chain newspaper owners and media concentration in the young radio industry. It was that progressive zeal that led to the Federal Communications Act of 1934, which mentions over 100 times the need for broadcast media to promote the "public interest, convenience, and necessity." And over 60 years later, we got Colin Powell's son Michael to lead the cause of free speech as the chair of the FCC, sometimes now referred to as the "Failure to Communicate Commission."

We need to be concerned with the propagandistic tendencies associated with the manipulation of the press today, a trend that makes the United States less of a beacon of free press and more of a shadow of its former self. *The State of the News Media 2004* report said, "Those who manipulate the press and public appear to be gaining leverage over the journalists who cover them."[32] It is a seller's market for information, as more news outlets compete for information with each other. The typical journalist is overworked and increasingly must rely on sources that may not get checked out thoroughly. If you were to conduct a content analysis of one twenty-four news cycle, you'd find fewer sources for the news you consume than ever. We live in an age in which we want our news and we want it yesterday. What is emerging is a new form of checkbook journalism in which anybody's story is open for grabs in the marketplace. Army Private Jessica Lynch's "war heroism" of 2003 became a press blemish when it was discovered months after the fact that a lot of exaggerated heroic deeds were implanted in the news coverage of Jessica. The Pentagon didn't deny and the press didn't question. The petite blonde young gal from West Virginia who wanted to become a kindergarten teacher captured the hearts and minds of a nation at war that needed some good news.

The State of the News Media 2004 report came on the heels of the U.S. government's establishment of Al Hurra ("The Free One"), a Middle East TV Network funded entirely by the American people for the service of democracy promotion in the Middle East. Since its establishment on Valentine's Day 2004, Al Hurra received funding of $62 million its first year and so far has been mostly rejected as a credible media institution. When President Bush appeared on Al Hurra to address Iraqi prisoner abuse in Abu Ghraib, he promised that there would a "full investigation," but as of yet, no such investigation has taken place.

Bush's attempt at damage control was probably too little, too late, in shifting attitudes and opinions among Arabs and Muslims, much less in global public opinion. By contrast, on the domestic front there has never been an administration like the one at 1600 Pennsylvania Avenue so skilled at harboring information and able to work with its proxies in the conservative press to chastise those who would like to shine a little sunlight onto the U.S. Constitution. *U.S. News and World Report* said that the Bush Administration has "quietly but efficiently dropped a shroud of secrecy across many critical operations of the federal government—cloaking its own affairs from scrutiny and removing from the public domain important information on health, safety, and environmental matters. The result has been a reversal of a decades-long trend of openness in government. . . ."[33]

In that same vein of control, the White House was able to make Abu Ghraib a non-story during Election 2004. We watched as some in the Grand Old Party (GOP) went quickly on the attack against the "liberal" bias in the press and against the "Bush haters" who perpetuated the scandal story. Those liberals and haters were in turn charged with increasing the vulnerability of our fighting troops in Afghanistan and Iraq, thereby enhancing the terrorists' efforts to attack us here at home and abroad.

Helen Thomas, the longest serving White House correspondent who has covered eight presidential administrations since the days of Kennedy, is now a Hearst White House columnist. She thinks that the current trend toward control of the press went into overdrive after 9/11. "I think that the media really went into a coma and rolled over and played dead, just as Congress did. It was a politics of fear after 9/11. Everybody, even reporters, started wearing flags after 9/11. At these White House briefings there was an atmosphere among the reporters that you would be considered unpatriotic or un-American if you were asking any tough questions."[34] Thomas directly challenges the words of *New Yorker* writer, A. J. Liebling, who said, "Freedom of the press belongs to the man who owns one." To her, a free press is free to those who hold it accountable and only the public can do that by putting pressure on journalists to ask the right questions.

Like propaganda, sometimes a good press story is just that, a story, with a strong narrative that may not be the whole truth, but even devoid of the truth, isn't enough to cause much stirring among readers. Freedom of the press may not be as sacred anymore as it once was, especially among our young people. Perhaps the students are lulled into a false sense of optimism about American free press. Most Americans, if asked, would argue that the American press is the freest in the world, thanks to our First Amendment and Bill of Rights that support a free press unrestricted from government censors. A report by Freedom House, a civil liberties advocacy group based in New York City, would challenge that standing. Their report, "Freedom of the Press 2005: A Global Survey of Media Independence," revealed that the U.S. score of 17 (out of 100) was tied for twenty-fourth place out of 194 countries in press freedom. Each country receives a rating from 0–100 based on three measures: "the legal environment within which media operate; political influences on reporting and access to information; and economic pressures on content and the dissemination of news."[35] The U.S. score still placed it within the "free" range, just lower than the previous year when it was a 15. The United States shared its new position in 2004 with Barbados, Canada, Dominica, Estonia and Latvia, while the freest nations in 2004 were Finland, Iceland, and Sweden, each with a score of 9. Overall, 75 countries or territories out of 194 were labeled free, just 39 percent of the global media landscape. The brightest spot on the map was Western Europe with 92 percent free press countries while a low spot was Asia, a region where just 7 percent of its population enjoys a free press.

According to the Freedom House survey, the U.S. score for press freedom declined due to "a number of legal cases in which prosecutors sought to compel journalists to reveal sources or turn over notes or other material they had gathered in the course of investigations." It wasn't just the sacred pledge to protect sources, which is universal among journalists. Turns out, the United States media system is more propagandistic than ever. The report revealed that press freedom slipped further down the scale in America where "doubts concerning official influence over media content emerged with the disclosure that several political commentators received grants from federal agencies, and that the Bush administration had significantly increased the practice of distributing government-produced news segments."[36] While press gains outnumbered press setbacks in 2004, the Freedom House study reveals that press freedom worldwide declined. Freedom House Executive Director Jennifer Windsor said, "Even in established democracies, press freedom should not be taken for granted."[37]

The future of American democracy and the press must not rely strictly on presidential promises of results to Arab language media, but rather on results themselves. The challenge is to remain vigilant when we live in an environment of war and a declared war on terrorism, both of which tend to stifle public participation and dissent.

WE BECOME PROPAGANDISTS (AGAIN!)

I feel partly nostalgic and somewhat chilled as I re-read "We Are All Americans," a column by Jean-Marie Colombani that was published in the liberal daily, *Le Monde* on September 12, 2001:

> In this tragic moment, when words seem so inadequate to express the shock people feel, the first thing that comes to mind is this: We are all Americans! We are all New Yorkers, just as surely as John F. Kennedy

declared himself a Berliner in 1962 when he visited Berlin. Indeed, just as in the gravest moments of our own history, how can we not feel profound solidarity with those people, that country, the United States, to whom we are so close and to whom we owe our freedom, and therefore our solidarity?[38]

Where did this "profound solidarity" with the American people go? And if we still had it, would the United States government under the auspices of the Pentagon feel so compelled to engage in such intense media propaganda campaigns in Iraq? Was Iraq the tipping point that caused such a fissure between the United States and Europe, between those who supported the invasion and deposition of Saddam Hussein and those who did not? I do know that Iraq has become the battleground for much more than lives, votes, and resources. It is also a battleground for free speech and free ideas. This is something the American president has reminded all too often. So how can we explain this love of freedom and free press when our very own Pentagon elects to plant "false positives" in Iraqi media. A *Miami Herald* editorial said such a decision "insults the intelligence of the Iraqi people, undermines the U.S. war effort and delivers a black eye to the purported U.S. campaign to promote democracy throughout the Middle East."[39] Other than that, it must have been a good idea, or seemed so at the time. Here's the rub. Planting such stories puts us in the same company as those we are purportedly fighting against—those who hate freedom, tyrants, jihadists, despots, evil-doers, etc. A free and independent media is as fundamental an American value as, well, recreation, apple pie, the Fourth of July, Thomas Jefferson, CNN, Fox News, and dare I say it, public broadcasting. Why we aren't pumping millions of dollars into establishing a truly free press or teaching media and training journalists in Iraq is beyond me.

It seems the Pentagon disliked the bad news and overall negative news coverage that the real free media were bringing so they decided to tweak the news a bit. Problem is, word gets around eventually and everything came to light with the revelation that the planted news stories were brought to Iraq by an organization with a politically ironic name, Lincoln Group, which was hired by the U.S. Special Operations Command in Tampa, Florida for a sweetheart deal of $100 million over five years. Talk about your Emancipation Proclamation. They could have hired me for millions less. Not that I would have actually been clear in my head about propagating friendly stories in the Iraqi press, but inevitably there are plenty of groups out there who helped to reelect the President who are very comfortable with that mission. Its CEO is Christian Bailey, a 30-year old FOG (Friend of George Bush). All the work at Lincoln is "classified," which means that the rest of us, the people, the tired, hungry, yearning to be free, are not privy to its propaganda management style. Jonathan Alter of *Newsweek* said, "Bailey has put a bunch of Bush campaign hacks on the gravy train, finagled security clearances, then assigned them to corrupt the Iraqi media. Democracy in action!"[40]

No one can expect the Pentagon not to use its information resources to promote sunnier stories than all the doom and gloom that insurgency and integrated explosive devices bring. The problem isn't with the effort to promote the Pentagon version of the war. You can do that with honest reporting that reveals your sources. That was not done here. By not disclosing the origins of such reporting, the fact that they were bought and paid for by a subsidiary group contracted with the U.S. military, all goodwill, much less, global solidarity, was lost. We quickly moved the needle from "we are all Americans" to "it's those Americans." As Alter wrote, "the cold war taught us that propaganda works best when it's served straight up—by Radio Free Europe (a hugely positive influence) or by the commercial broadcasters who hawked capitalism behind the Iron Curtain. . . . It's the culture of secrecy, self-dealing, and subversion of truth that's killing us."[41] Of course, I might quibble with even Alter on that one, for Radio Free Europe, though successful, lost credibility during the Cold War for not disclosing its secret CIA funding and using third-party front organizations to present itself as a grassroots-supported radio broadcast.[42] Nevertheless, now the world has to wonder if the U.S. military, known historically for airing (at least eventually) its dirty as well as clean laundry, has elected to pay for just clean. The dirt is always within the details and unfortunately, in this case, the details were omitted. As the *Herald* concluded: "The hubris inherent in the propaganda campaign presumes that Iraqis cannot properly judge the war's effect on their lives in all that they see around them. The campaign undercuts the credibility of the military's erstwhile efforts to win the hearts and minds of the Iraqi people."[43] On that last effort, I think it's fair to say that unless and until we present our message of freedom and democracy with clean hands, hearts and minds in the Middle East region are going to remain up for grabs.

NOTES

1. Thomas Carlyle, *On Heroes: Hero Worship and the Heroic in History.* (London: H.R. Allenson, 1905), 349–350.

2. Bernard Goldberg, *Bias: A CBS Insider Exposes How the Media Distort the News* (Washington, D.C.: Regnery, 2002), 12.

3. Bill Moyers, "Bill Moyers Responds to CPB's Tomlinson Charges of Liberal Bias: 'We Were Getting it Right, But Not Right Wing,'" National Conference on Media Reform, May 15, 2005, St. Louis, Missouri.

4. James Poniewozik, "The Worst TV of 2005," *Time* web exclusive, December 28, 2005.

5. Joanne Ostrow, "Bush Crew Feeds 'News,' TV Swallows," *Denver Post*, March 18, 2004.

6. Andrew Gumbell, "Bush Turns Us On to Fake Television News," *The Independent*, March 14, 2005.

7. CNN.com, "Columnist Axed After Taking Cash to Promote Bush Plan," January 8, 2005, www.cnn.com/2005/ALLPOLITICS/01/08/bush.journalist/index.html.

8. CNN.

9. Anne E. Kornblut, "Bush Bars Use of Paid Commentators," *New York Times*, January 27, 2005, A18.

10. Susan Campbell, "Propaganda, Journalism, and Knowing the Difference," *Hartford Courant*, February 2, 2005.

11. George W. Bush Press Conference, White House, January 26, 2005. Available at www.whitehouse.gov/news/releases/2005/01/20050126-3.html.

12. Howard Kurtz, *Spin Cycle: Inside the Clinton Propaganda Machine* (New York: The Free Press, 1998), 7.

13. Ralph Nader, "America's Right to Know War News," Common Dreams, May 15, 2005.

14. Nader, Common Dreams.

15. Read my original essay on Neuffer's death along with articles she wrote that are posted on Common Dreams, www.commondreams.org/views03/0511-07.htm.

16. Juergen Habermas, *The Structural Transformation of the Public Sphere: An Inquiry into a Category of Bourgeois Society.* Translated by Thomas Burger. (London: Polity Press, 1989). Originally published in German in 1962.

17. Richard Reeves, *What the People Know* (Cambridge, MA: Harvard University Press, 1998), 114.

18. Reeves, *People Know*, 24–25.

19. George Creel, *How We Advertised America* (New York: Harper & Row), 1920.

20. Walter Lippmann, *Public Opinion* (New York: Free Press, 1997), 158. Originally published in 1922 by Macmillan.

21. www.stateofthemedia.org/2004/narrative_overview_publicattitudes.asp? media=1.

22. *Samizdat* is a term for the secret publication and distribution of officially-banned literature in the former Soviet Union but has also come to mean any underground, alternative, or unofficial press.

23. The Pew Center for Excellence in Journalism, State of the News Media 2004, 2.

24. *The Journal Advocate*, editorial, April 20, 2004.

25. "U.S. Muslims Seek Pentagon probe on Iraq Photo: Soldier's Sign says He Killed Boy's Father, Impregnated Sister," Council of American-Islamic Relations, April 2, 2004. Available online at www.cair-net.org/asp/article.asp?id=1058&page=NR.

26. Farhad Manjoo, "A Picture is No Longer Worth a Thousand Words," *Salon*, April 22, 2004.

27. Gaskell Media, January 2004. www.gaskellmedia.com.

28. Aldous Huxley, *Brave New World Revisited*, New York: Perennial Classics, 2000, 36. Originally published in 1958 by Harper & Row publishers.

29. Wolfgang Donsbach, "Communication and Natural Disasters: What the Tsunami Tells Us," International Communication Association newsletter, Message from the President, 2005.

30. Jacques Ellul, *Propaganda* (New York: Vintage Books, 1973), 236–237.

31. Ben Bagdikian, *War, Media and Propaganda: A Global Perspective*, ed. Yahya R. Kamalipour and Nancy Snow (Lanham, MD: Rowman & Littlefield, 2004), xii.

32. The Pew Center for Excellence in Journalism, State of the News Media 2004.

33. William Fisher, "How Free is the US Press?" *Inter Press Service*, May 6, 2005.

34. Gael Murphy, "The Guards Are Sleeping," *AlterNet*, May 2, 2005.

35. Mark Fitzgerald, "Freedom House: Press Liberty Declined Worldwide in 2004," *Editor & Publisher*, April 29, 2005.

36. Freedom House, "Freedom of the Press 2005: A Global Survey of Media Independence," available online at freedomhouse.org/research/pressurvey/pfs2005.pdf.

37. Fitzgerald, *Editor and Publisher*.

38. Jean-Marie Colombani, "We Are All Americans," *Le Monde*, September 12, 2001.

39. The *Miami Herald* staff editorial, "All the Good News that Money Can Buy," Our opinion: Iraq Propaganda Campaign is Counterproductive, December 5, 2005.

40. Jonathan Alter, "The Real Price of Propaganda," *Newsweek*, December 12, 2005.

41. Alter, "The Real Price of Propaganda," December 12, 2005.

42. Martin Manning, *Historical Dictionary of American Propaganda* (Westport, CT: Greenwood Press, 2004), 238–240.

43. The *Miami Herald*, "Propaganda Campaign is Counterproductive," December 5, 2005.

4

INFORMATION WARS

BRANDING AMERICA, VISION 4.1

Ever since 9/11, I'm surely not alone in wondering if America has lost its attractiveness edge. We are still the number one country with the most powerful military and economy in the world, but whatever happened to our image in the world? Did the war in Iraq change everything or is it more complex than that? Is the American culture, so technologically and humanly diverse, helping or hurting America's image in the world? The way we view America generally and the American culture is an ambivalent concept of attraction and repulsion. You love it. You hate it. Sometimes you don't quite understand it. Everyone seems to hold both a positive or negative mental image of what constitutes the American culture. And this picture is shared by many who live here in it. To some people, if you even just utter the word "America," it's immediately seen as a threat, a monster that will overpower the indigenous culture. This picture of America has a push-away factor. Particularly threatening are American cultural values exemplified in the most propagated image of the American culture, Hollywood, which conjures up amoral, illicit, anything goes behavior. Many of us just don't think family values or the family hour on television when we picture Hollywood. We might picture glamour, luxury, and beautiful people in multimillion-dollar homes, but we don't think of Mom and Dad and the kids praying at church or sitting around the dinner table in conversation.

The other picture of America is an exciting, commercially driven, market-friendly adjunct global culture to one's native culture that symbolizes openness, trend-setting, and the latest "in" thing in fashion, music, film, and television. Here American cultural attributes are viewed as easily adaptable to one's own usage and there isn't a fear that a dominant culture will overrun or dilute the less powerful culture. This America has a pull factor, "give us your *Baywatch*, *Dallas*, *Dynasty*, and now *Desperate Housewives*, and we can see for ourselves what the American dream looks like."

There's no question that the picture of America today is the face of our age of globalization, even though it is a simplification, too. American culture as the symbol of economic globalization is more of a threatening concept than American culture alone. When used interchangeably, both come across as the *McWorld* we fear is taking over, where no matter what town or city you inhabit, there will be a convenient American-based corporation like Starbucks or McDonald's close by to fulfill your consumer impulse needs. From Public Square to Mega Mall, the picture of America as the land of the brand logo is illustrated in *Abusters* magazine corporate America flag, which dons the second edition cover of my first book, *Propaganda, Inc.: Selling America's Culture to the World*. *Adbusters*, based in Vancouver, B.C., has a two-thirds U.S. reader circulation and presents itself as an magazine concerned with economical and ecological balance. The *Adbusters* reader is asked to step outside his comfortable box and confront the commercial clutter that invades our mind space. To replace the stars with corporate symbols in one of America's most sacred symbols, the Stars and Stripes, is an attempt to show the interrelationship between government and corporation, and particularly the power that American corporate power and influence has over the decisions made by the American government. Further, the *Adbusters* corporate America flag, which we see at many anti-war and anti-globalization demonstrations, is a way to re-present or reflect America back onto itself.

To the anti-globalist activists, America espouses a consumerist ideology that is harmful to the physical and mental environment, and this toxicity needs exposing so that other countries won't adopt this consumerist ideology as their own. Ironically, one of the *Adbusters* designs that included the phrase, "America: Open for Business" along with the image of an American flag with shopping handles, was duplicated on shopping bags

by the office of San Francisco Mayor Willie Brown shortly after 9/11. The
Mayor wanted to encourage San Franciscans and tourists to the city to
follow the advice of President George W. Bush who told non-combatant
Americans that the best way to fight the terrorists was to continue going
about our business and doing the patriotic duty of shopping.

Shortly after 9/11, the Advertising Council initiated its own branding
campaign to remind Americans of our cultural heritage. In a series of
public service advertisements (PSAs), the picture of the American culture was one of diversity that unites a nation in crisis as reflected in one
of the most memorable ads, "I am an American." The Council's rationale
was that September 11th had so shaken the core of how we see ourselves
as a nation and citizenry and that it needed to return to its "wartime
footing" as the former War Advertising Council to provide inspirational
messages that could help the country remain strong in wartime. The Advertising Council's origins are not of war, however, but of business. In the
early 1940s, American corporate executives were greatly concerned that
the American people were losing faith in the economic credo, "the business of America is business." Advertising in particular came under public scrutiny and criticism as American citizens and government officials
were beginning to question the truth of its claims. Advertising executives
were fearful that an erosion of their industry's credibility might lead to
more government scrutiny and regulation, both in content and taxation.
It would take the speech of J. Walter Thompson executive James Webb
Young at a gathering of advertising executives in fall 1941 to light the fire
that created the Ad Council vision that continues today. Of advertising,
Young spoke poetically and with a vision few imagined advertising could
achieve: "It ought to be used for open propaganda in international relations, to create understanding and reduce friction. It ought to be used
to wipe out such diseases of ignorance as childbed fever. It ought to do
the nutritional job this country needs to have done. It ought to be the
servant of music, of art, of literature and of all the forces of righteousness,
even more than it is."[1] Within three weeks, Japanese kamikaze pilots
attacked the military base Pearl Harbor in Honolulu, Hawaii, America
declared war on Germany and Japan, and by January 1942, the War
Advertising Council (1942–1945) was underway. Raymond Rubicam of
Young and Rubicam said at that time that "if advertising and advertising people play the part they are capable of playing, then fewer men
will die."[2]

This background may help explain the Bush Administration enthusiasm for an advertising person to jumpstart the post-9/11 public diplomacy efforts in the war on terror. When Charlotte Beers was confirmed in October 2001 as Under Secretary of State for Public Diplomacy, she jumped at the chance to rebrand the United States of America, in her words the most "sophisticated" branding assignment she'd ever been asked to manage. A woman who had a legendary reputation in American advertising, Beers quickly pointed to two senior administration officials, then Secretary of State Colin Powell, and the sitting forty-third president of the United States, George Bush, as the faces or leading men in this new Branding Uncle Sam global venture. Powell eventually lost much of his marquee luster when he appeared before the U.N. Security Council in February 2003 to back the U.S.-war in Iraq, and President Bush continues to spark anger and dismay among global publics who perceive him incapable of listening to American criticism. Just a week after Bush delivered his Second Inaugural Address and days before the elections in Iraq, Thomas Friedman, foreign affairs writer at the *New York Times*, wrote a column from Europe titled "Read My Ears," in which he said, "Let me put this as bluntly as I can: There is nothing that the Europeans want to hear from George Bush, there is nothing that they will listen to from George Bush that will change their minds about him or the Iraq war or U.S. foreign policy. Mr. Bush is more widely and deeply disliked in Europe than any U.S. President in history."[3]

Friedman, whose columns often praise Bush administration policies, had just returned from 10 days of travel in Europe where he encountered snickers and sneers at the very mention of George Bush. Why the strong emotion? Friedman's theory, which he lays out in his usual 750 word op-ed fashion, is that Bush doesn't listen to the world and the world is offended by the self-satisfied manner in which the American president manages his country. "The only thing that Mr. Bush could do to change people's minds about him would be to travel across Europe and not say a single word—but just listen."[4]

If it's true that President Bush, for all his famous malapropisms, is really worse at listening then talking, then this does not bode well for an American branding campaign that seeks to "make its case" to the world, as President Bush once told the country in response to a question about anti-Americanism. Case making is when an audience is receptive to your message. Listening is when an audience wants to take turns holding the conversation. As one German bar owner told Friedman, "Bush took away our America. I mean, we love America. . . . We believe in America and American values, but not in Bush. And it makes us angry that he distorted our image of the country which is so important to us . . . America lost so much in its reputation worldwide."[5]

One of the most daunting challenges for the United States, exclusive of the polarizing president at its top, is that the U.S. position as a sole superpower makes it more difficult to exercise one's active listening skills. It's like asking billionaire Donald Trump to just sit down and listen to what you have to say. There aren't too many of us in an equivalent position of authority who measure up to the powerful CEO or to one who answers to Leader of the Free World. This brings me back full circle to Beers's vision for Branding Uncle Sam. Perhaps it is precisely because the U.S. president so preoccupies the anxieties and concerns of the rest of the world that any effective public diplomacy must extend its reach beyond the beltway of Washington, D.C. It should involve a more broad-based network of American students, grassroots activists, nongovernmental and private sector organizations equally concerned as is Thom Friedman that America isn't listening and learning.

IT'S ALL ABOUT THE BENJAMINS

If one were to draw a picture of America, what would first come to mind? It might be a book about one of the Founding Fathers like Thomas Jefferson or Benjamin Franklin, a photo of President Bush, an oversize American flag flying over a car dealership, the flag-draped coffin of former President Ronald Reagan lying in state in the Rotunda of the U.S. Capitol. It could be a thousand things, you might say, because our country's very cultural core rests on difference, variety, and choice. Simon Anholt, a national brand expert based in London, wrote a book along with Jeremy Hildreth, entitled *Brand America: The Mother of All Brands*.[6] The London publisher, Cyan Books, chose an interesting cover for the book that got a lot of us American-by-birth types talking about it in terms of both accuracy and message.

On the book cover of *Brand America* is a gapped-tooth smiling sweet face of an Asian American little girl in pigtails, dressed in a bright red cowboy hat and red bandanna. She has a play horse by her side, the one with the horse's head on a stick for the child to pretend to be riding, and an orange bag with pumpkin heads pasted on to indicate that she's likely dressing up as a little cowgirl for Halloween. Many of my students who saw the cover found it a bit puzzling because the book's title, *Brand America*, implied to them something political or commercial, while the image of the little girl seemed to be about innocence and child's play. They completely understood why the face of an Asian American was used. We are the most ethnically and racially diverse country on the planet, a fact that was used most recently by New York City in its 2012 Olympic-hopeful branding campaign, "The World's Second Home," trademark-pending.[7] Of course, I always thought such a phrase should be trademarked for post-9/11 U.S. public diplomacy campaigns since it would seem sensible that no one would want to attack his or her own home, second or not.

The cowboy image is itself a ubiquitous symbol for the United States, not just in terms of our ruggedness and open country, which people love, but also in our foreign policy assertiveness, which many don't always like. Intercultural communicator scholar Senko Maynard contrasts the collective "samurai" society epitomized in Japan and the individualized "cowboy" society of the United States driven by the American cultural myth of the rugged individualist cowboy. The cowboy bucks the establishment "and yet cannot completely deny his society. He is an independent individual secretly seeking social approval. . . . As symbolized by the image of the American cowboy, American individualism calls for the hero who must leave society in order to realize the moral good on his own terms. This connection between moral courage and a lonely individualism seems to be at the root of the American ethos."[8]

Donald Gilbert Y. Chavez writes, "If Hollywood is to be credited with anything correct in documenting who the American cowboy was to evolve into, it was that indomitable, intrepid, persevering genetic stock which separated the weak from the strong. Indeed, it was the strongest that survived and those very survival instincts greatly contributed to the strength of American character which has made the USA the most powerful country on earth."[9]

Cowboy-style presidents from Teddy Roosevelt to Ronald Reagan and now George Bush are much beloved at home and more mixed in reputation abroad. Having a cowboy attitude is to exude a strong demeanor and swift and simple justice like John Wayne in *Rio Bravo* and *The Man Who Shot Liberty Valance*. So is the picture of the little girl dressed up as our cultural symbol, the cowboy (or cowgirl), America? Halloween is

certainly a uniquely American holiday with some very non-American religious origins not known for young children ringing neighbor's doors and
asking for candy, or else. But even Halloween, though very American, is
today not the Halloween that it was in my childhood. There was a time
in the 60s and 70s when the door wouldn't stop ringing with streams of
children offering that perilous choice, trick or treat. Today, the more common experience for young children at Halloween is private house parties
or school functions because it is considered too dangerous for children to
be wandering our neighborhoods at night.

Even with our cultural icons from cowboy hats to carved pumpkins,
these artifacts are likely to change over time. What endures, according
to the U.S. State Department and echoed by our own American president, are American cultural values. The experience may vary, but we still
treasure certain sacrosanct values that serve to support a secular religious
fervor. It is thought that these values—Freedom, Equality, Egalitarianism, Democracy, and Liberty have so well fed our own culture that they
must be shared with the rest of the world. Listen to any speech about
Iraq by President Bush and he'll use a reference to one or all of these
concepts to provide rationale for why our nation had to go to war. In his
Second Inaugural Address in January 2005, President Bush used the word
"freedom" or "liberty" twenty-nine times. On the White House website,
the following excerpt from that speech is highlighted: "America has need
of idealism and courage, because we have essential work at home—the
unfinished work of American freedom. In a world moving toward liberty,
we are determined to show the meaning and promise of liberty."[10] It
wasn't just Bush, however, who started this hat-tipping to American cultural values in times of war. American presidents from Lincoln to Wilson
to Roosevelt and Truman to Bush Senior and Clinton have been doing it
for decades. The difference now is that this nation is engaged in the most
costly and public effort ever to combat anti-Americanism by marketing
these enduring values to the rest of the world.

A past experience stands out as the first time I realized what America
and Americanism meant to me. It was my first trip overseas as a young
college student at Clemson University in South Carolina, two years before
my Fulbright study in Germany. It was somewhat atypical in that a single
digit percentage of American students will travel abroad as exchange students at some point in their undergraduate studies. What made my study
trip a little different is that it included travel to Eastern Europe, which at

that time in the early 1980s was quite rare for Americans. I was majoring in political science and minoring in German and philosophy. When two of my German professors announced a three-week travel to German-speaking countries, I jumped at the chance to practice my Deutsch. I especially liked the opportunity we had to visit the Communist states, East Germany and Czechoslovakia, since those countries were part of the larger Soviet Bloc and located behind the "Iron Curtain," the phrase made famous by Winston Churchill in his address at Westminster College in Fulton, Missouri, March 5, 1946. We were going to meet college students our age in Leipzig, Germany, and get a chance to discuss our different systems, as well as travel to cities like East Berlin and Prague, that Churchill said were "subject, in one form or another, not only to Soviet influence but to a very high and in some cases increasing measure of control from Moscow."[11]

What America represented for me just before leaving on that trip was freedom. I wasn't particularly politically astute at that time (that would come later!) about every economic and political theory that gave rise to our nation's development, but I did know that my country represented freedom, the free market, and free speech. We were leaving the world's number one name brand for freedom, the United States of America, and flying out of Atlanta's Hartsfield International Airport to some Communist countries that represented the very antithesis of freedom. Ironically, Communist East Germany had chosen to brand itself as the German Democratic Republic, which made me wonder if the East German citizens thought that their government had a sense of humor. They did. They also told me that inside the GDR, Communist propaganda was quite obvious, but the people did not have the political power to challenge it. They read newspapers that towed the Communist Party line and made Moscow look like a Holy Mother of perfection. As citizens, they were not free to carry on a regular conversation if it included politics because the fear was that this conversation held with a neighbor would be reported to state authorities and might end up with a knock on the door from the *Ministerium für Staatssicherheit* (Ministry for State Security), commonly known as the "Stasi" East German secret police. The Soviet Bloc countries utilized extensive spy networks to punish dissident speech and organization and keep the population suspicious and fatalistic. The more I learned from my conversations with students and from our East German guides, the more I treasured the freedoms that America gifted me.

My East German counterparts told us Americans that they thought we suffered from propaganda too, but in a very different form, and perhaps less obvious to us. Our propaganda was the love of money, a market economy that helped the rich and hurt the poor, and a democracy that allowed racial discrimination and an aggressive foreign policy. What they did love the most about America was our popular culture, including music and movies. I'll never forget dancing the night away in Leipzig to the Western music so familiar to me at home.

Two decades removed from my amateur ethnography project in East Germany, I can see why brand experts Simon Anholt and Jeremy Hildreth would say about the mother of all marketing brands, "In international cultural activity and cultural influence, no other country comes close to America's dominance—some would say its stranglehold—over global television, cinema, music, book and magazine publishing and internet presence" (p. 17). It is this stranglehold that is America that dominates the picture that the rest of the world has of us—both good and bad. Michael Moore, before he was the Oscar-winning documentary filmmaker of *Bowling for Columbine* and *Fahrenheit 9/11*, shot a lesser-known film called *The Big One*, the nickname Canada often refers to the United States. Anholt and Hildreth call the United States a strong brand, but misunderstood, implying that we're like the big oaf who has enormous strength but no sophistication in projecting it. We are the mother of all brands because the United States invented all the industries associated with branding, including marketing, public relations, and advertising. America "has done more to control its reputation than any other place in history... today, there is no person, place, or thing that has managed to achieve a recognition as that of the United States of America."[12] It is precisely because we seem to be everywhere and that our image and reputation precedes us that people have such strong opinions and attitudes about the United States, both positive and negative, never neutral.

As Anholt and Hildreth observe, there is no other nation outside ours that has two brand names, the United States of America, and just plain old America, a point not lost on our North American continental neighbors to the north in Canada or to our Latin American and South American continental neighbors to the south. Like a party goer who never leaves, we seem to suck up all the oxygen in the room by assuming that America stands first and foremost for the U.S.A. I recall while living in West Germany as a Fulbright exchange student that my German interlocutors, particularly the young students I interacted with on campus, were reluctant to designate me anything but USA in origin. They rightly chose to separate the people, culture, and government of the United States of America from South America and Latin America, so they wouldn't like me to use the shorter word for nationality, *Amerikanerin* (American), which could mean that I might be from anywhere on the American continent like Canada or Mexico, but rather preferred that I said my country of origin was the *Vereinigte Staaten* (United States).

THE HARD SELL AND SOFT POWER

Part of our unique position as both "big one" and brand central is that, as Anholt and Hildreth point out, and as I learned working at the U.S. Information Agency in Washington, D.C., branding, like selling and marketing, is considered propaganda in most of the world. It's not held in the highest favor, more like a necessary evil that most people don't like to admit they are involved in, but not an evil in and of itself. While in the United States we have a rich and proud history of entrepreneurs who made their name in self- and organization promotion, in other parts of the world, including Europe, propaganda industries are seen more like the poorer stepchildren to legitimate business ventures. *Brand America* provides examples where world leaders have insulted in the name of commercial enterprise, as when Napoleon referred to the British as "a nation of shopkeepers," and the title of an autobiography by French advertiser, Jacques Seguela, that reveals the distrust levied at a particular persuasion industry that is perhaps less respectable than even the world's oldest profession: *Don't Tell My Mother I Work in Advertising: She Thinks That I Play Piano in a Brothel.*[13]

Hilary Swank, when accepting the best actress Oscar for her role in *Million Dollar Baby*, included a thank you to her publicist, even though the music was by then playing for her to stop talking. There's no other country I know of where I could imagine an actress even wanting to admit she had a publicist before hundreds of millions of people. Swank, being the ueber American actress who's now in that extra special category of two wins for best actress, was reflecting what the rest of the world already knows to be so true—we are a nation that sells itself and most everyone who wants to succeed here thinks nothing of marketing one's image in an effort to rise above the celebrity clutter.

Hilary Swank has her publicist and America has its own global publicity machine to control image, reputation, and character. For film, it's located in Hollywood and for advertising, it's on Madison Avenue. Throughout much of our history, the political process of how to wage a fight in support of Brand America has been located in Washington, D.C. Recall the nation's reeling after 9/11. A *U.S. News and World Report* cover story, "Waging the spin war," bemoaned the measly efforts underway at that time to counter negative spin from not just the other side, namely Al Qaeda and Osama "Spin" Laden, but also among the 1.3 billion Muslims in the world who undoubtedly were waiting to hear the United States speak in one voice.[14] The first attempt to utilize one American voice by President Bush after 9/11 was to paint its story in stark black and white hues and good and evil judgments with statements like this:

> Now, the American people have got to go about their business. We cannot let the terrorists achieve the objective of frightening our nation to the point where we don't—where we don't conduct business, where people don't shop. That's their intention. Their intention was not only to kill and maim and destroy. Their intention was to frighten to the point where our nation would not act. Their intention was to so frighten our government that we wouldn't seek justice; that somehow we would cower in the face of their threats and not respond, abroad or at home.[15]

Such action-driven tough talk in which Bush referred to evil twelve times worked very effectively on a domestic audience that was rallying 'round the flag and taking rhetorical comfort cues from the president. There's no question that the American people wanted redemption for being blindsided and some wanted swifter revenge than even the president was willing to deliver. But as a public diplomacy and branding tactic for an overseas audience, the tone and content of this and other presidential remarks was questionable. To outside observers, it seemed as if President Bush were taking very complex problems such as terrorism, national security, international relations, and U.S. foreign policy in the world, and simplifying them into one frame: "Don't worry your pretty little heads, Americans. You keep buying those Kate Spades and we'll take care of those murderous thugs who won't know what's going to hit them." Terrorism experts said that terror attacks on the United States were classic in nature in that they worked to garner a predicted reaction on the part of the United States to show a more vengeful side. Meanwhile, the domestic population was being told to keep shopping in order to distract and dull the pain.

Critics like the Vancouver-based *Adbusters* magazine created a graphic arts image based on the phrase from Bush's speech, "We cannot let the terrorists achieve the objective of frightening our nation to the point...where people don't shop." They updated their Corporate America Flag, a design that featured corporate logos instead of stars and that first appeared during the December 1999 World Trade Organization protests in Seattle, Washington.[16] After 9/11 and Bush's declaration of freedom from shopping avoidance, the Corporate Flag started reappearing with shopping handles. What was intended to be an anti-American and anti-Bush graphic quickly morphed into an accepted representation of the president's imperative. Mayor Willie Brown of San Francisco, working with poster artist Craig Frazier, replicated the image of the American flag with shopping handles to let tourists to the famed city know that their hearts could still be left there, as well as their credit slips. The week of November 11–17, 2001 was declared "San Francisco: Open for Business Week," in order to "let the world know that this city, and this nation, will rise from the ashes of the national tragedy and get this economy moving again."[17] Writer Heather Havrilesky observed one year later that "in America, we grieve by buying stuff. Shopping soothes us, reassures us that we're coping, that we're moving on." The Open for Business campaign was "calling upon citizens to seek revenge and healing through retail."[18]

America is indeed a place associated with success through money and shopping is seen as the American way of keeping the economy humming along. Anholt and Hildreth say that the America = success association is so strong that in Italy, America is used interchangeably with a sense of utopia or paradise. Something that "isn't America" may translate into "it's not paradise," while "he thinks he's found America" translates into "he's found a way to make his money."[19] Think of the most famous America-branded TV programs globally. They are *Dallas*, *Dynasty*, and *Baywatch*, all about the good life, beautiful people, no one living in poverty.

So how do we go about branding America after 9/11? In his floor statement for the Freedom Promotion Act of 2002, Representative Henry Hyde of Illinois laid out the paradoxical problem of brand America—how we see ourselves—good and selfless–versus how others see us, ending with his famous refrain:

> As Americans, we are justly proud of our country. If any nation has been a greater force for good in the long and tormented history of this world, I am unaware of it. We have guarded whole continents from conquest, showered aid on distant lands, sent thousands of youthful idealists to remote and often inhospitable areas to help the world's forgotten. Why, then, when we read or listen to descriptions of America in the foreign press, do we so often seem to be entering a fantasyland of hatred? Much of the popular press overseas, often including the government-owned media, daily depict the United States as a force for evil, accusing this country of an endless number of malevolent plots against the world. As we battle the terrorists who masterminded the murder of thousands of Americans, our actions are widely depicted in the Muslim world as a war against Islam. Our efforts at self-defense, which should be supported by every decent person on this planet, instead spark riots that threaten governments that dare to cooperate with us. How is it that the country that invented Hollywood and Madison Avenue has such trouble promoting a positive image of itself overseas?[20]

What are the main ideas behind Brand America and does the little girl on the cover with the pig tails, holding the Halloween bag portray it accurately? Politically speaking, America has a brand that I call the FED, not the U.S. Government, but rather the acronym for freedom, equality, and democracy. To that, you can add egalitarianism, liberty, and opportunity. In America, the brand is marketed as the American Dream, not something ethereal experienced only during rapid-eye-movement, but rather something very tangible and measurable, seen in the pages of the annual report of the top entrepreneurs, top billionaires, and top celebrities. It is part of the American mythos and brand to tell the rest of the world that you can come here and, unlike anywhere else, America will accept your ideas, ingenuity, and your hard work. In other words, there is nothing here to hold you back from your highest dreams and aspirations. Anholt and Hildreth say that "America may be the original aspirational brand," and that the pay-off in America is not through a fate of birth or heritage but through carrying out a dream to fruition.[21] If making it in New York means that you can make it anywhere, than making it in America means that you've made it, period. There is no higher level to achieve. A *Vanity Fair* interview with the best-known soccer player on the planet, David Beckham, whose very name was branded into a movie, *Bend It Like Beckham*, showed that even for Beckham and his wife, former Spice Girls' singer, Victoria "Posh" Beckham, making it in America is the penultimate achievement. Despite his being the highest paid soccer player in history and having multi million dollar advertising contracts, he still feels somewhat the underachiever that he hasn't broken completely into the American market.

Scholar Joseph Nye refers to the aspirational brand as soft power—the ability to attract through nonviolent coercion or force. Our aspirational attraction makes people want to do what you want them to do through attraction rather than coercion. Soft power is not something unique to the United States; all countries have the ability to attract adherents, and in fact, U.S. soft power is not more powerful than its hard power in military might and the threat or use of force. But soft power becomes a brand promise in that it attracts adherents to the American brand who wish to make their mark.

Nye tells us why the United States continues to have such a challenging time explaining and influencing in the world through a simple visual model of a three-dimensional chess board that is U.S. power in the world—military, economic, and cultural. At all three levels the United States displays power, which he describes as the ability to get the outcomes you want, but it is the third level, soft power (attractiveness of one's culture, political and social ideals), that is the most neglected by the United States.

The top level, military, is the hard power dimension displayed in Operation Shock and Awe that captured the world's attention in the first days of the Iraqi war. At this level (and consider that slogan!) the United States can act coercively using force or the threat of force. Here it has no competitor and even no close behind competition. At the middle level, economic, the United States operates among competitors from the European Union to Japan, China, and other "outsourcing" countries that have the ability to challenge the United States with cheaper labor costs.

At the bottom level, soft power, no particular individual or nation has comparative advantage. It is at this level that transnational interactions occur outside the control of military power, government infrastructure, or corporate control, and like bouncing molecules the advantage occurs to whoever or whatever can attract and persuade others to its side.

Soft power involves the ideological power struggle for attention and recruitment among thousands of non-state actors ranging from international terrorist networks to global social movements as well as the spread of environmental and public health crises that impact populations without concern for national boundaries (e.g., SARS, AIDS). Nye warns that most of the world's trouble spots are originating from this bottom level where no one is in charge.

The United States continues to focus its energies on the top level where it has sole dominion and coercive power. Nye describes the U.S. military campaign in Iraq as going along as planned in the first six weeks (which led to the hubris of "Mission Accomplished" on the U.S.S. *Lincoln*) but also opening the door wide to al-Qaeda adherents and other international terrorist networks who continue to exploit Iraq as a public relations recruiting tool in the arena of soft power. (Note that Bin Laden predicted that the United States would invade an oil-rich Arab country and use it as a staging board for remaking the Middle East in its own image.) Using his chess board calculation, a win at the top (maybe) but a loss at the bottom.

Al-Qaeda uses soft power for PR purposes that are designed to kill those it opposes. Soft power in and of itself is not necessarily morally superior to hard power. It depends on how it is applied. The United States and its allies must figure out ways to challenge the soft power advantage that Bin Laden and al-Qaeda have on extremist Muslims.

As the 2004 Global Attitudes Survey conducted by the Pew Center for People and the Press showed, Bin Laden had attractive soft power advantage over President Bush in U.S.-allied Muslim countries like Pakistan and Jordan. How can this be? It may come down to two things: legitimacy and credibility. U.S. policies are considered illegitimate in many parts of the world where populations feel taken advantage of by the economic and strategic interests of this sole superpower. Iraq has only fanned the flames of resentment. Bin Laden is able to offer an alternative vision of a just society, however illegitimate the United States may see it. And U.S. credibility, the level of trust and believability displayed, is also on decline in many eyes the world over, not just in the Arab and Muslim countries. It's not enough for President Bush to simply say that "our cause is just" or "they hate freedom." Others must believe that he's genuine in such statements and establish buy-in to the same mottos and slogans. So far, few are buying, but that can change over time.

Nye points out that soft power can ebb and flow over many years and through different sources. President Jimmy Carter was highly criticized and deemed a weak commander-in-chief for making human rights a principle of U.S. foreign policy but as an ex-President is consistently praised in public opinion polls for having helped to build a more favorable global image of the United States in the world through The Carter Center at Emory University.

You build up your soft power supply by attracting people to moral causes like Martin Luther King, Jr. did in the American South and Gandhi did in India. Had either leader shown militancy and intransigence, he would never have been able to recruit thousands to what was seen as a morally superior position. Similarly, the United States and its allies must appear morally superior to the majority of Muslim moderates who are feeling pulled by the extremist minority that is garnering so much global media attention. In that, the United States could learn a lot from other countries' soft power such as the European Union's efforts to integrate across social, political, and cultural dimensions and attract Muslim countries like Turkey to join the EU.

The United States has gotten off kilter, according to Nye, ever since the end of the Cold War when the conventional wisdom was that we had won the ideological struggle and didn't need the foundation of soft power like cultural diplomacy programs, international educational exchanges, to promote U.S. values. Nye recommends a critical need to measure a nation's security and defense through a soft power persuasive dimension. Just a one percent replacement of the current military budget for public diplomacy campaigns would quadruple efforts.

Hollywood-style soft power is the alleged discovery of actress Lana Turner at Schwab's Drugstore on Sunset Boulevard. (Her official website lists the discovery location as the lesser-known Top Hat Café across from Hollywood High School.) In other words, the American Creed of liberty and equality becomes the American Dream fulfilled. Anyone who works hard enough can make it, even if you are helped along by being born under a lucky star or like Lana Turner, know where to be at the right time. It is fulfilled economically in that America dominates the global economy. The "American way" of doing business with a direct communication style and contractual obligation is becoming the dominant global model. The dominant language on the Internet is English and will probably remain so. Even Microsoft's PowerPoint tool is the adopted worldwide standard tool in business presentations.

Despite this soft power attraction and political economy dominance, American power remains a paradox: We hear messages of how much others hate us while global demand for *Baywatch* and *Desperate House-wives* is record-breaking. We see protesters in the street with placards that say, "Down with the U.S." while around the corner people line up to apply for green cards. This is why the study of anti-Americanism and "why do they hate us" is so paradoxical.

MEDIA IS A BATTLEFIELD

Missouri morphed into the "Show Media" state as the 2005 National Conference on Media Reform was held in St. Louis in May 2005. The war in Iraq, the week's public protests and deaths in Afghanistan (remember, that is the war with the "good" ending) over the desecration of the Koran at Guantanamo Bay, are inspiring many media writers, producers, and activists to paint the media as a symbiotic cog in that wheel we call the Military Industrial Complex. This time we're not along for the ride. Those who view media as a movement (and this is not yet a critical mass) know it as (1) a political economy of cooperative capital interests that shut out public participation in deference to their sponsors; (2) a form of information apartheid that forces the masses into information servitude in the form of a mindless peanut gallery of submissives driven to distraction and/or addiction to irrelevant entertainment dribble; and (3) coated in news values that are generally pro-war (war is good for business and thus good for media), anti-humanistic, and anti-global. News media owners are genuinely scared that global civic masses will gain an awareness of how the media system operates against their public interest and health, which is why we need to approach media reform as a global public health and education campaign.

When you survey the media landscape in a holistic fashion as this conference forces one to do, you come away with only one conclusion: absolute certainty that the corporate media system is on life support and this dying patient's struggle is progressive media's opportunity to distribute alternative medicine. Consider the following "points of light" in the media landscape:

Whose media is it, anyway? Media owners are out of touch with their media consumers and this cuts across partisan lines and political ideologies. News values are top-down, eyeballs are leaving traditional media (newspaper readership is down as is network news viewership), and opportunity exists to create new media in the vacuum of profit bleeding going on presently in the corporate press. So far though, too many of us are ceding the language of media content, distribution, and policy to the elite few, not working harder to inform the discouraged and disgusted marginalized many who, given the proper tools, are ready to take up arms against a system that dis-informs and infotains more than it informs and educates. If we take back ownership by creating our own media, building alliances across political lines, and organizing our own ninja investigative journalists, then we'll look back in nostalgic bliss at a time when profit ruled over public information.

Where's the fun anymore? Mainstream media journalists are bemoaning the demise of that period in journalism history in the '60s and '70s when the profession used to be fun and informative. Now it's neither. Because the bloom is off the rose for most journalists, it is imperative that independent media journalists make alliance with their corporate media insiders who are ready to jump ship. The time to view all corporate media journalists as "the other side" or "the enemy" is over. Many journalists who got into the journalist profession for the right reasons and would like to do the right stories cannot. Investigative reporting has dried up altogether or shows up in fits and starts. It costs too much at a time when newsroom staffs are being decimated, earns too little in an era when double digit profiteering in news returns is expected by owners, and isn't in public demand, or so say media owners. The embedded media message of this conference is that this is our time, our fun, and our case to make that the public both wants and needs democratic, accountable, and critical media that genuflect to neither corporate nor government gods.

Outrage alone is futile. Robert Greenwald, Hollywood film director-turned public interest media maestro (*Outfoxed*, *Wal-Mart: The High Cost of Low Price*), told our gathering that when you see/hear/read something in the media, you shouldn't be satisfied by forwarding your email post to a friend. We all need to vent over what we object to, but what he learned from working inside the Hollywood media machine is that sponsorship is everything. He has been in meetings with bigwig sponsors who gnash their teeth over just seven letters from angry viewers. Greenwald reminds us that we need to take our media reform fight to the corporate sponsors. It can take just a handful of letters to get sponsors worried about continuing to carry a program, so continue to write your letters to the editor and voice your opposition against media coverage but more important, voice your opposition to media underwriters and advertisers. My own advice: Send a letter to a sponsor the next time you are beginning to rage against the media machine with a friend over a coffee. Brent Bozell and the Parents Television Council have done this to great effect, which is why they dominate the media content conversation in America today and note very prominently on their website that "Advertisers, along with network executives, are the key decision-makers in Hollywood, and they decide what options you'll have in television programming."[22]

Know your media history. Media democracy in America has a two-hundred-year history. The flowers of today's media reform movement bloomed from the seedling struggles of the people of the United States, many of whom were native peoples and new immigrants in search of a voice for their community. How many of us were aware that the first Chinese language newspaper began in the immigrant communities of America, not China? These media facts have been so forgotten that it inspires this writer to think we need *A People's Media History of the United States* with foreword by Howard Zinn. As one who teaches mass communications history and philosophy in the United States, I see that the students are hungry for knowing this history but don't know it because our journalism and communication schools aren't teaching it. Very few schools offer independent media or media from a populist perspective. Popular majors are public relations, advertising, and other sponsored-media approaches to communication. Many of my media major students sit in class very cynical in their attitudes toward today's corporate media landscape (who cares about Dan Rather and Memogate), but if given the proper media history they may actually see beyond Jon Stewart and *The Daily Show* and view the media system as something other than just to ridicule or to discuss in a late-night television monologue.

It's been said often that war is too serious to be left to generals alone. The same applies to the dominant corporate media system now under challenge. Media reform is too serious to leave to its present owners. These owners, like many generals, perpetuate zero-sum thinking of winners and losers, with those who own and sponsor the media viewed as winners and those who consume the media as losers. I'm convinced now that the media reform movement is not fighting a lost cause. Corporate media has lost too many battles (credibility, public trust, substance) to win this media war.

THE FOX PERSUASION

I have been interviewed over the years by Fox News Channel, the most watched cable TV network on American television that has a conservative, rightwing orientation. Despite or perhaps because of its obvious political persuasion, Rubert Murdoch's Australian parent company News Corp. that owns Fox News Channel, continues to beat its competition, the declining Cable News Network (which used to dominate cable news) or the third place MSNBC. Most liberals and left-leaning Americans love to hate Fox News for being so openly conservative in many of its primetime programming. I once saw former CNN anchor Aaron Brown speak at USC and ask rhetorically if it might be a better idea for the other networks to become more like Fox, than less. Brown thought it could be to CNN's favor to label itself as the liberal response to Fox News, but he knew that it would never happen because CNN was too afraid of the liberal moniker.

There's no question that media bias affects political awareness and knowledge. One study by the Project for International Attitudes (PIPA) of American news media consumption indicated that Fox News Channel viewers were more likely than public affairs viewers or listeners to misperceive the facts about the war in Iraq. The FNC viewer was more likely to directly connect Saddam Hussein to 9/11 as the Bush Administration had directed and were more likely to believe that the U.S. military actually found missing weapons of mass destruction, which was never the case in 2003 and remains false today. Those listeners to National Public Radio (NPR), often characterized by conservative Republicans as too liberal, were less likely to reach the wrong conclusions of the FNC viewers. The survey, "Misperceptions Vary Widely Depending on News Source," concluded that "Those who primarily watch Fox News are significantly more likely to have misperceptions, while those who primarily listen to NPR or watch PBS are significantly less likely."[23]

Fox News Channel prides itself on its copyrighted "Fair and Balanced" approach to American journalism, which is more tongue-in-cheek and wink-and-nod than truly balanced. The network wears its pro-American bias on its shirtsleeve, one directed by America first, and my America, right or wrong. My liberal friends consider my appearances on Fox to be somewhat traitorous to their cause, but I have found the experience every time to be very enlightening. I do not ascribe to the philosophy of either the Democrat or Republican Party and consider myself a political independent, so I'm open to the Fox persuasion and believe that without the existence of a Fox News Channel, many Americans would be less aware of how media impacts partisan policy and opinion. News Corporation is actually an "equal opportunity" campaign contributor to the two dominant political parties in America. According to *Networks of Influence: The Political Power of the Communications Industry*, an investigative report compiled by the nonpartisan Center for Public Integrity, found that News Corp. "whose Fox cable-news operation is often criticized for its perceived right wing bias, has actually given 64 percent of its contributions to Democrats since 1998 and 36 percent to Republicans."[24] Money that buys access knows no ideology!

In fall 2004, Fox News Channel interviewed me for a primetime news special called "Hating America" that aired the weekend before Thanksgiving and several weeks after the presidential election of 2004. The Fox News producers told me after the fact that the program's content was too provocative for its initial airing before Election Day, November 2, 2004, which made me wonder if they thought that in the wrong hands (perhaps my own) Americans might actually link a rise in hating America with the war in Iraq. The host of the program, John Gibson, who authored a book on the subject, spent most of his time gauging how silly and extreme any anti-American sentiment is and at one point seemed to blame the former Soviet Union for cooking up the whole "hating America" phenomenon as part of a Cold War secret mission. I have no doubt that the Soviets promoted anti-Americanism and took every advantage to point out America's shortcomings at every turn. Their misbehavior and ill ways alone cannot be blamed for our present-day situation. Gibson focused his rage on two international authors in particular whom he identified quickly as America haters, a Canadian and Frenchman. I must say, they were easy targets since both countries have some of the highest anti-American attitudes in the post-September 11 and post-war era.

Both authors were far left in their claims that the United States was responsible for the events of 9/11. The Canadian author, Barrie Zwicker, holds some extreme views with which I take issue, particularly his notion that the U.S. was more than just negligent in its prevention of 9/11. Nevertheless, I've known Barrie Zwicker for many years and think he has a right to express his doubts about U.S. government malfeasance just as I have rights to express my doubts about his thesis. It was Barrie after all who posed the question about American complicity in 9/11 and now leads a citizens' movement to continue investigating who is responsible for 9/11. I so firmly believe in representing a variety of viewpoints that I included his controversial essay called "America and the Fourth Reich" in an edited volume of essays about war, media, and propaganda in global perspective. I did this in order to enlighten both Americans and non-Americans about how some view the United States. The Internet is especially rife with a lot of global conspiracies surrounding 9/11 and we who educate and teach need to inform others as well as remain informed about a continuum of theories and perspectives about American foreign and military policy. It also wouldn't satisfy me or any reader to present just a rah-rah perspective about how great the United States is and how wrong the rest of the world is about my home country.

I had been interviewed live on John Gibson's show, "The Big Story," a number of times since the start of war in Iraq, but this time the Fox News crew came to my home campus of California State University, Fullerton to do a taped interview. For anyone who has the opportunity, or in some cases, misfortune of being interviewed by the press (depending on the outcome!), take it from me. If given the option, you always want to request a live interview. Sometimes you have no choice, but if the news media request offers an option, go live. It may sound more nerve-wracking than being taped, but it will produce generally better results that reflect what you want to get across. A live interview allows you, the expert, to have more control over an almost out-of-control situation. You have some semblance of a back-and-forth with the host, which will come across as more intelligent and thoughtful than just words on tape. A taped interview is heavily edited. I have spent an hour or two being interviewed by broadcast media only to see my mug utter a few words for an hour-long news special. Yikes! If you make a mistake in a live interview, you can sometimes correct what you mean, and you can challenge the host not to put words in your mouth. A live interview in itself must be handled carefully, however, especially in the American news environment, because for the most part you are there as wall decoration to fill up news airtime between sponsors' ads and commercial movie tie-ins. I doubt this experience will put me in the good graces of some news media, but I share this as a metaphor for the entire dialogue surrounding anti-Americanism. For the most part, we heavily self-edit our thoughts on the subject and seek to fill in the blanks with accusations and blame. Consider John Gibson's book, *Hating America*. A list of the book's chapter headings reveals his defensive posture toward the subject: (1) France's War on America, (2) The Arabs' Mindless Hatred for America, (3) The Brits' Annoying Tendency to Hate Themselves for Not Hating America Quite Viciously Enough, (4) Germans Delighted: At Last Someone Else is Hitler, (5) The Axis of Envy: Belgium, South Korea, and Canada, (6) All the World Despises George W. Bush, and (7) They're Wrong. We're Right. Get Used to It.

Publishers Weekly referred to Gibson's book as a "rancerous manifesto" whose "main charge, leveled through a rehash of UN wranglings during the run-up to the war in Iraq, is simply that other countries didn't understand our feelings after 9/11 and didn't support the American invasion. By lumping this reluctance under the rubric of hatred, Gibson reduces serious policy differences to emotional animus, mostly motivated either by the fear and envy the rest of the globe—including the 'soft-life Europaradise'—feels towards America's 'hard power,' or by the sort of irrational tribal antagonisms characteristic of the sports world."

Perhaps most telling was Gibson's last paragraph—a prescription for challenging the America haters: "We must let the events of September 11 show us the way. The world would like us to forget 9/11, just as they would prefer to forget it, too. They'd like us to forget that those who hate us may eventually try to kill us—because they now know that we will never allow that to happen without exacting a price on those who would attempt it. The war on Iraq put the world on notice. America will fight."[25]

Imagine my delight at having the opportunity to serve as an on-air expert for John Gibson's primetime news special on the subject. Surely I'd be a featured expert since the news crew took so much time and bother to come to my campus. The results were a bit different. I was included in the "Hating America" special, but only with a few comments here and there. One of my sound bites was about the common tendency to blame all the country's ills on whoever's in charge, which means that the "leader of the free world" like the American president is often viewed as corrupt and blameworthy when things aren't going well. The masses in a democracy are often seen as mere pawns in the process. In this case, it is very common to blame President George W. Bush for all the world's problems and America's declining reputation. But this didn't start with Bush, as much as his critics would like to credit him for America's ugly image in the world. During the Carter, Reagan, and Clinton administrations there was a steady drumbeat of articles in elite foreign policy journals like *Foreign Policy*, *Foreign Affairs*, and *The Economist* about America's

declining reputation in the world. The Pew Center confirmed this reality: "The numbers paint a sobering picture. Just a quarter of the French
approve of U.S. policies, and the situation is only slightly better in Japan
and Germany. Most people around the world worry that U.S. global influence is expanding, and majorities in many countries say America's strong
military presence actually increases the chances for war. The latest survey on America's tarnished global image? No, those findings are from a
poll conducted by *Newsweek*—in 1983."[26] The same report revealed the
shift in degree and intensity of anti-Americanism over twenty years later,
following the attacks on September 11, 2001 and the war in Iraq:

> But anti-Americanism is deeper and broader now than at any time in modern
> history. It is most acute in the Muslim world, but it spans the globe—from
> Europe to Asia, from South America to Africa. And while much of the
> animus is aimed directly at President Bush and his policies, especially the
> war in Iraq, this new global hardening of attitudes amounts to something
> larger than a thumbs down on the current occupant of the White House.
> Simply put, the rest of the world both fears and resents the unrivaled power
> that the United States has amassed since the Cold War ended. In the eyes of
> others, the U.S. is a worrisome colossus: It is too quick to act unilaterally, it
> doesn't do a good job of addressing the world's problems, and it widens the
> global gulf between rich and poor. On matters of international security, the
> rest of the world has become deeply suspicious of U.S. motives and openly
> skeptical of its word. People abroad are more likely to believe that the U.S.-
> led war on terror has been about controlling Mideast oil and dominating
> the world than they are to take at face value America's stated objectives of
> self-defense and global democratization.[27]

Further, the Pew Center reports that, while historically anti-American
sentiment was tied primarily with the ruling regime, this changed in 2004.
"Now that the American people have awarded Bush a second term in a
high-turnout election that focused to an unusual degree on foreign policy,
it may be more difficult for the rest of the world to separate the presidential policies and leadership style it dislikes from the American people
and values it admires."[28] The Pew Center study was not all doom and
gloom, however. Many throughout the world continue to admire America's democratic values, even if they question America's leadership in the
war on terror and war in Iraq and the American public's support for a highly
unpopular global leader. This contradictory sentiment between values and

actions is characteristic of a nation that has a consistent global credibility gap between its democratic ideals and international practices. We are often criticized for being global hypocrites because our rhetoric doesn't match our reality. One would have to go back to John F. Kennedy's administration to find an American president who was able to reduce the global credibility gap through a combination of personal charisma, press management, and "what could have been" promise. Beloved for his worldly "Ich bin ein Berliner" sophistication, his assassination on November 22, 1963 preserved in time the image of a benevolent American president more interested in global change and human betterment (e.g., Peace Corps) than just national security interests.

Kennedy received high praise following his June 1963 commencement speech at American University where he called on a new initiative to build global mutual trust, especially with the U.S. Cold War nemesis, the Soviet Union: "While we proceed to safeguard our national interests, let us also safeguard human interests . . . The United States, as the world knows, will never start a war. We do not want a war. We do not now expect a war. This generation of Americans has already had enough—more than enough—of war and hate and oppression."[29]

Although Kennedy's administration initiated greater troop build-up in Vietnam, his untimely death removed the foreign entanglement criticism. It was Lyndon B. Johnson's administration that signified a shift in global and national perception of America's troop presence in Vietnam. By the mid-1960s, American foreign policy was perceived displaying an aggressive posture in international relations, an "arrogance of power" that survives to this day. American news media began to refer to daily press briefings by top military brass in Vietnam as the "Five O'clock Follies" in reference to the growing credibility gap between on-the-record briefings of battle briefings and what reporters were finding.[30] Progress on the ground was challenged by daily body counts in American living rooms. America, the beautiful was now viewed more consistently as putting its own security over human rights and humanitarian needs. Even President Johnson's noble efforts on poverty and civil rights were subsumed by America's foreign policy focus in Vietnam.

This history of growing anti-Americanism over the last forty years was of little concern to the Fox News Channel crew setting up its cameras in our College of Communications building. The Fox crew seemed to be most interested in which foreign entity to blame for America's bad image, not how America's own actions in the world may have exacerbated its growth.

The Fox News Crew and I spent several hours addressing all manner of questions, most of which were, not unsurprisingly, leading questions. An example of a leading question would be, "Which of the French media are most responsible for promoting anti-Americanism?" First of all, I'm not an expert on which French media are the most anti-American. I hadn't said anything about the French in general, much less their co-defendant media or suspect left-leaning intellectuals, but nevertheless, the focus was immediately on what countries and which institutions to blame for all our undeserved ill will in the world. Our dialogue was directed away from the United States, U.S. foreign policy, the last three years since 9/11, and any published opinion polls that showed a global community that had lost faith in the American tradition and reputation for "fairness and balance" in foreign affairs. All the Fox crew wanted to know was which country originated anti-Americanism, as if negative sentiment toward the United States were purely the fault of foreigners who hate us. There were the usual suspects, not surprisingly reflected in those chapter headings. I was asked about Europe in general, the two most strongly anti-Iraq war powers in the region, France and Germany, and specific broadcast networks like Al-Jazeera and the BBC, which were seen as anti-American in tone and war coverage. The Canadians weren't overlooked either for having a strongly anti-American slant. I was waiting for the Dixie Chicks and Barbra Streisand to emerge in the conversation, but they never surfaced. Perhaps that would come in a Part II special, "Enemies Among Us."

Curiously missing from our conversation was a sophisticated analysis of cause and effect, perception and misperception. In other words, could it be possible that what the United States government did in the world had a negative effect on how it was perceived? Logically, yes, since the most rudimentary foreign affairs analysis tells us that state behavior shapes public attitudes. The Pew Global Attitudes Surveys since 9/11 have laid out a conceptual map showing that a strong dip in goodwill toward the United States coincided with the build-up and invasion of Iraq in 2002 and 2003, coupled with a general perception that the United States holds too much power (particularly military) in relation to the rest of the world.[31] Negative sentiment did not coincide with the invasion of Afghanistan, although there was some global dissent against the U.S. action. What seemed to really draw the ire of the global community was an elective invasion that violated the United Nations Charter and that held no backing from the UN Security Council. The U.S. seemed to be willing and able to defy global opinion and go its own way (with a few backers) in order to promote its own vision of the world. To the world, the United States aggressively attacked a nation that had not declared war on the United States and had never been identified by our U.S. intelligence or global partners as a secret partner in the 9/11 attacks. Nevertheless, a narrative of imminent threat defined by Iraqi weapons of mass destruction poised to hit us spurred the U.S. decision to attack Iraq in March 2003. Very few global partners joined the U.S. effort; even some partners who did join, like Spain, were quick to pull out when they came under their own retaliatory terrorist attacks. Nothing came close to the U.N.-endorsed global coalition that responded to the Iraqi invasion of Kuwait in 1990.

Despite these realities, I found myself uncomfortable with a Fox News conversation that was directed to how extreme and nutty one's point of view must be to hate the United States. I could already envision what the Fox News Special was going to look like—Islamic mullahs denouncing the United States and Israel, the most virulent anti-American French writer available who authored a book about the lies behind 9/11, and a Canadian media critic driven by the inconsistencies surrounding 9/11. For good measure, there would be interviews with anti-BBC critics and efforts by well-meaning Americans to get "them" to stop hating "us." Fox did not disappoint. This is exactly what materialized in the November post-presidential special, in which I had a mere cameo appearance because I wasn't either nutty or extreme or wholly critical of anti-American views. My greatest surprise was that the one-hour primetime news special managed to find the "smoking gun" for anti-American origins. The Soviets were credited with having hatched the original conspiracy with a secret meeting in New York's Waldorf Astoria hotel in 1949. Of course. I knew it all along. The Reds did it.

Not once during our conversation did we address the possibility that there are legitimate criticisms of United States policy in the world often dismissively labeled as anti-American. Nor did we address a question about the value and necessity of criticism and dissent, even if such criticism comes down to name-calling play of pro- versus anti-American. I wanted to tell the Fox crew that anti-Americanism, like terrorism, is a contested concept. It is not strictly the creation of what non-Americans like the French, British, or Canadians think of America. Any "ism" is rooted in the past and holds a strongly ideological content. Before there is anti-Americanism, there must be an understanding of what Americanism is. Americanism is a belief in the values, culture and political economy of the United States of America, often framed in a spirit of uniqueness and moral superiority. This belief is generally unquestioned and upholds the superiority of capitalism (sometimes referred to as neoclassical liberalism) while denouncing market socialist economic policies. Americanism places a high premium on success through hard work, an entrepreneurial, risk-taking attitude in business, and a reliance on individual over collective effort.[32] Americanism is promoted and protected through a strong national defense; at least this has been the case in the last sixty years since the end of World War II. No American presidential candidate could even think of winning the U.S. presidency were s/he to question how much we spend on military expenditures, so intertwined our sense of ourselves— our Americanism—is to national defense and security. This may explain why when it comes to national defense and security, American competitiveness and the free market are in short supply, despite our quasi-religious faith in such economic structures in principle.

While we do have Constitutional support for freedom of religion and the separation of church and state, Americanism is infused with religiosity, which is reflected in the general population's belief system. Atheism in America is in the single digits and more often than not, in public discourse one is more likely to hear "I'm agnostic," a user-friendly, socially acceptable way of saying one isn't sure that God exists but is open to the idea. It is impossible to imagine an espoused atheist getting elected to any high office in the United States. Some Americans were suspicious of the Catholic John F. Kennedy's presidential election bid in 1960, so imagine how far a non-believer would advance even today in such a contest. A relatively new political lobbying organization, Godless Americans or GAMPAC, exerts its will on Capitol Hill in Washington, D.C. by leveraging non-endorsement of candidates into its public policies. In other words, if GAMPAC doesn't endorse you, then it expects something in return! Most lobbying groups seek endorsement, but the Godless Americans know that they are generally seen as the skunks at the party, Democrat or Republican, so religiously-identified and faith-based the American national psyche is. All of this is not to criticize America's religion identity but rather point it out as intimately tied to how we view ourselves and, in turn, our relationship to the rest of the world. For all our rhetorical defense of the First Amendment separation of church and state, in reality, we are a nation of believers.

Americanism supports freedom and democracy in a general rhetorical sense, but in practice, there is limited leeway for points of view outside the mainstream of two dominant political parties, Democrat and Republican. This is reflected in a mainstream media system that substitutes ping-pong style alleged "hardball" political discussion between partisans for true debate and dissent. Nonpartisans generally do not even make the cut to appear on broadcast television. Nevertheless, our view of ourselves manifests its own destiny into a staunch feeling of goodness, good intentions, and good practice, both nationally and globally. This is why we are often bewildered, befuddled, and defensive when others would question our behavior in the world, driven as it is by our self-defined good intentions.

The Americanism drive and spirit is a product of an over two-hundred-year-old Puritan heritage that originated with the earliest New England settlers who saw this new land in the context of a "City on the Hill," shining a beacon of light, prosperity, and hope for the rest of the world. John Winthrop, the English-born elected governor of the Massachusetts Bay Colony, expressed a spirit of the new American uniqueness and exceptionalism that still guides how we view ourselves in relationship to the rest of the world. The following words of Winthrop echo those of President Reagan in his Farewell Address and seem to have guided much of Bush Administration speechwriting following 9/11: "For we must consider that we shall be as a city upon a hill. The eyes of all people are upon us. So that if we shall deal falsely with our God in this work we have undertaken . . . we shall be made a story and a by-word throughout the world. We shall open the mouths of enemies to speak evil of the ways of God . . . We shall shame the faces of many of God's worthy servants, and cause their prayers to be turned into curses upon us til we be consumed out of the good land whither we are going."[33]

Karen Hughes, close Bush confidante and the Under Secretary of State for Public Diplomacy and Public Affairs, articulated the same messianic vision in a November 2005 address to the Women's Foreign Policy Group:

America must continue to serve as a beacon of hope in the world, as that city on a hill. There is no more powerful instrument of American diplomacy than our commitment to freedom, rights and opportunities for all people everywhere. We're committed to expanding freedom not because we seek carbon copies of our own democracy, but because we believe it is our common birthright, and because we welcome new members to the community of nations who protect the rights of free speech and assembly, the right to worship freely, the rule of law, and individual opportunity.[34]

The sense that all the world is watching the blessed city on the hill leaves many Americans feeling weary when we don't measure up in the eyes of others the way we view ourselves and our own actions. We tell ourselves, if we must go to war, it's because we are driven to it. We act aggressively only when provoked. We are not imperialists, but ask only that we be given a swatch of foreign land on which to bury our dead. This lack of critical introspection, an almost innate inability to even consider the world as others might see it, leads to a predictable response in times of war and crisis. Consider the American mindset following the 9/11 attacks. Instead of asking ourselves, "Why did this happen?" we asked the less introspective, outwardly-directed question, "Why do they hate us?" This is an Americanism that is altogether unimaginable for others to use in a similar context. I could not fathom the Spanish asking themselves the same on March 11, 2004 or the British on July 7, 2005. Having lived in Europe in the mid-1980s at a time when terrorist attacks were happening at a regular rate, I know that the European mentality is to view terrorism within a prism of international and state crime and not as a precept for war on those who hate.

Despite my having registered my own misgivings about how we in the United States tend to use mental shortcuts when considering how others see us, this is not to say that I do not think that the rise in anti-Americanism is entirely justified by any means. Fox News Channel, more than any other cable news network, seems particularly engaged with the topic of how or why others would hate America. The only problem is that the subject is cast often in terms of us versus them dichotomies and enemy images.

On April 12, 2005, I was invited by John Gibson to appear live on "The Big Story" and address the hating America theme from the angle of a new fall 2005 course, "Anti-Americanism at Home and Abroad," which Gibson and Fox News heard I would be teaching. It was the first course of its kind taught at the University of Southern California and in conjunction with the new Center on Public Diplomacy. John Gibson was particularly curious why I was interested in teaching a group of undergraduates about anti-Americanism. Why teach such a course four years after September 2001? My answer was based on my own experience speaking at an international media conference on the campus of the University of British Columbia in Vancouver, Canada. The speaker before me, Barrie Zwicker—featured in the FNC special "Hating America" and founder of the International Inquiry into 9/11—had polled the audience members in attendance about their beliefs surrounding the 9/11 attacks on the United States. To my amazement as a U.S. citizen, in answer to the question of how many thought the U.S. government had something to do with the attacks, over half the audience raised its hands. These were mostly Canadians, and there was a strong anti-American sentiment or at least suspicion that the government could not have been a victim as advertised, but rather a perpetrator. These were suspicions based in sentiment and rumor, not fact, but they startled me. At that moment, I felt strongly as an educator that young people in America needed to pay closer attention to this rise in anti-American sentiment, care about it, and look back in history to some periods when America was seen as truly great: the Marshall Plan era, World War II, Greatest Generation, the world of my veteran and Depression-era father who was part of that generation. It deserved a revisit. Far too few young people have any inkling about when America was seen in a different and much more positive light.

This skepticism around U.S. state behavior didn't begin with the war in Iraq. I know that it's been around for decades, but as an educator, I told Gibson that I felt strongly that young people need to pay more attention to this topic now and really care about its consequences and repercussions. I assured Gibson that examining anti-American sentiment was a patriotic act that must be looked at from many angles and across the political spectrum. To this, Gibson said, "Some people say, as you well know, that this is all America's fault. The hating America, the anti-Americanism, is the fault of America's international bullying, its unilateralism, its failure to cooperate in international agreements . . . are those people right?" I did not believe that hating America is all our fault. Every nation has its problems, but in our case, we are the sole superpower and with that comes an image and a reputation where everybody has something to say on the subject, whether it's hot or cold, positive or negative. Nobody's neutral about the United States, so there will always be a measure of antipathy toward us, while at other times, strong praise. We in the United States do have an enormous responsibility to present a more balanced image of ourselves in the world and no one else is going to do this for us but the United States. That's why, I told him, I wanted to teach this course. It was not designed to be a "how to" but a "how come." Additionally, I shared with Gibson the fact that the University of Southern California has the largest number of international students in the country, so I was hoping to have a mix of international and American students. Gibson pressed on: "You're talking about anti-Americanism among our 'friends'—Canada is supposedly our friend, Britain, France, Germany, Italy, Jordan, Saudi Arabia, Egypt . . . right?" I told him that my course would try to distinguish between the predictable nations where you expect their governments to always hate the United States (Iran, North Korea), but my equal concern was with those traditional allied nations that aren't really there as our partners. In Canada, I didn't expect such strong negative sentiment, although it did seem directed more at the government than the people of the United States. The people were viewed more as victims of their own government than active co-conspirators.

Finally, John Gibson wanted to know again, whose fault this really was. Is it America's fault or just bad attitudes on the part of our "so-called friends"? I didn't take his "Blame America First" bait, which he might have expected of an alleged "Left Coast" social science professor. Rather, I said that it is no one person's fault but everyone's collective responsibility and should be part of Karen Hughes's new undertaking as Under Secretary of State for Public Diplomacy.

Our live exchange did merit comment on the anti-Fox News website, "News Hounds," that posted this comment: "Ms. Snow came this close to noting that many of our detractors dislike the Bush administration but still like the American people. I think Ms. Snow may try to take an honest look at our past to discover where/when things went wrong. Although she reinforced Gibson's favorite whine, she did not support his childish notions of 'jealousy' and 'freedom-hating.' "[35]

What I wish that I'd said is that many detractors or dissenters, often labeled as America haters, dislike something very specific about the United States in the new century—the Bush Administration policies—and still like the American people. As was obvious following the reelection of President George W. Bush in November 2004, many of the world's press I monitored responded with "What were they thinking?" Given the nadir level of America's reputation and credibility in the world since Bush's reign began, the global media expressed a collective perplexity at what they viewed as a lack of sensitivity to how the world sees us, not the terrorists or usual America haters, but America's longtime friends. Of course, this disconnect between government policy and people is not being discussed too often because we are living in a time of war in which criticizing the government too openly can be misinterpreted that the critic does not love the country.

What my Fox News Channel experiences with the subject of hating America have taught me is that this subject is a political hot potato that generates more dramatic heat than enlighted light. Most of us would rather toss the hot subject onto the next set of hands. We rarely get to the arena where cooler heads prevail and rational discourse embarks. There is something almost inherent in our psyche that we must continue to fixate on those who hate us and how we must annihilate or eliminate the haters.

NOTES

1. "Matters of Choice: Advertising in the Public Interest," (The Advertising Council 1942–2002), 2002, 3.

2. "Matters of Choice," 4.

3. Thomas L. Friedman, "Read My Ears," *New York Times*, January 27, 2005, A27.

4. Friedman, "Read My Ears."

5. Friedman, "Read My Ears."

6. Simon Anholt and Jeremy Hildreth, *Brand America: The Mother of All Brands* (London: Cyan Books, 2004.)

7. Mike McIntire, "New York Wants to Be 2nd Home™ To the World," *New York Times*, February 17, 2005, A25.

8. Senko K. Maynard, *Japanese Communication: Language and Thought in Context* (Honolulu: University of Hawaii Press, 1997), 12, 42.

9. Online source available at www.unm.edu/~gabbriel/chap3.html.

10. www.whitehouse.gov/inaugural/index.html.

11. Winston S. Churchill, Speech at Westminster College, Fulton, Missouri, March 5, 1946.

12. Anholt and Hildreth, *Brand America*, 21.

13. Anholt and Hildreth, *Brand America*, p. 25.

14. Roger Simon, "Waging the Spin War," *U.S. News and World Report*, October 22, 2001.

15. George W. Bush, Prime Time News Conference, October 11, 2001.

16. For more about the corporate America flag designed by Canadian-based *Adbusters* magazine and its involvement in anti-economic globalization and anti-war social movements, see adbusters.org/metas/politico/unbrandamerica/unbrandamerica.html.

17. www.sfvirtualshop.com/mayor_brown.htm.

18. Heather Havrilesky, "The Selling of 9/11," *Salon*, September 7, 2002.

19. Anholot and Hildreth, *Brand America*, p. 22.

20. Floor Statement, Representative Henry J. Hyde, H.R. 3969, the Freedom Promotion Act of 2002, July 22, 2002.

21. See a longer discussion in *Brand America*, p. 39.

22. www.parentstv.org/PTC/advertisers/main.asp.

23. www.pipa.org/OnlineReports/Iraq/Media_10_02_03_Press.pdf.

24. The Center for Public Integrity, "Networks of Influence: The Political Power of the Communications Industry," Washington, D.C.: May 2005, 11.

25. John Gibson, *Hating America: The New World Sport* (New York: Regan Books, 2005), 273.

26. Pew Center, Trends 2005, "The Spread of Anti-Americanism" at pewresearch.org/trends/trends2005-global.pdf, p. 105.

27. Pew Center, "The Spread of Anti-Americanism."

28. Pew Center, 113.

29. John F. Kennedy, "American University Commencement Address," June 10, 1963.

30. Richard Pyle, "From Tonkin Gulf to Persian Gulf: Veteran AP correspondent considers how war reporting has changed; www.cnn.com/SPECIALS/cold.war/episodes/11/then.now/.

31. See the Pew Center Trends 2005 chapter on "The Spread of Anti-Americanism" and "America's Place in the World," a November 2005 report of the Pew Center for People & the Press in collaboration with the Council on Foreign Relations, available online at people-press.org/reports/display.php3?ReportID=263.

32. For more in-depth analysis of Americanism and American Exceptionalism see these works: Anonymous, *Through Our Enemies' Eyes* (New York: Brassey's Inc., 2002); Lipset, Seymour Martin, *American Exceptionalism: A Double-Edged Sword* (New York: W.W. Norton & Company, 1997); Dworkin, Ronald W., *The Rise of the Imperial Self* (Lanham, MD: Rowman & Littlefield Publishers, 1996); and Madsen, Deborah L., *American Exceptionalism* (Oxford, MS: University Press of Mississippi, 1998).

33. John Winthrop, "A Model of Christian Charity," 1630. It is said to have been written aboard the *Arabella* while crossing the Atlantic ocean. Available in its Olde English original at http://history.hanover.edu/texts/winthmod.html.

34. As quoted by Donna Marie Oglesby, CIEE Luncheon Address, Miami, Florida, November 18, 2005. www.ciee.org/annual_conference.aspx.

35. www.newshounds.us/2005/04/12/a_new_twist_on_hating_america_on_big_story.php.

5

IMAGE WARS

FACING THE ENEMY AND OURSELVES

One of my favorite books in graduate school was Sam Keen's *Faces of the Enemy*. Now, sadly, out of print, the book is a picture book and long essay that instructs on the meaning behind the UNESCO Charter: "Since wars begin in the minds of men, it is in the minds of men that we have to erect the ramparts of peace." Keen wrote the book in the mid-1980s at the top trajectory of the Cold War when made-for-TV movies like *The Day After* and *Amerika* had us thinking about mutual assured nuclear destruction. Keen called then on cooler heads to prevail and said our call to action must be an internal examination of our own deepest fears and anxieties about "The Other." He wrote:

> Our best hope for survival is to change the way we think about enemies and warfare. Instead of being hypnotized by the enemy we need to begin looking at the eyes with which we see the enemy. Now it is time to explore the mind of *Homo hostilis* ("hostile human"); we need to examine in detail how we manufacture the image of the enemy, how we create surplus evil, how we turn the world into a killing ground. It seems unlikely that we will have any considerable success in controlling warfare unless we come to understand the logic of political paranoia, and the process of creating propaganda that justifies our hostility... The heroes and leaders toward peace in our time will be those men and women who have the courage to plunge into the darkness at the bottom of the personal and the corporate psyche and face the enemy within. Therefore, the radical comment, "Love your enemy as

yourself," points the way toward both self-knowledge and peace. We do, in fact, love or hate our enemies to the same degree that we love or hate ourselves. In the image of the enemy, we will find the mirror in which we may see our own face most clearly.[1]

Were as I as eloquent as Sam Keen, a man whose vision for peace twenty years ago is as much needed, if not more, today, I would have told John Gibson that there are times when it is a gift to know what others, our professed enemies, are teaching us about ourselves. Whether or not we think they are right isn't always the point. Perceptions and misperceptions become truth in international relations. As American social psychologists Oskamp and Schultz say, "in the field of foreign affairs, the gap between perception and reality is apt to be especially large."[2] We need not always be on the defensive or name-call entire nations of people. We certainly shouldn't expect that other non-Americans feel the same about 9/11 as we do or expect that others will see us as equally victimized. If we cannot open up our eyes to how others view us, warts and all, then we cannot hope to become as truly great a people and nation as we would like to see ourselves now. Steve Allen, creator and original host of *The Tonight Show*, was also a popular comedian and author who was greatly influenced by the world's philosophers. He authored two books on the Bible, religion and morality. Based on his "Meeting of Minds" series on St. Thomas Aquinas, Allen once said, "Almost all religions teach that love is the supreme virtue, and a few spiritual teachers, perceiving that we are all gifted at loving what pleases us, teach that the highest, the most edifying forms, which might ultimately save the world, involve our regard for those who are difficult to love, some of whom are our enemies."[3] Enemies may not be right or accurate, but their perceptions and opinions allow us to dig deeper into our own self- and outward projections. Probably the most well-known teaching of Jesus is in Matthew 5:44, in the New Testament of the *Bible*: "But I tell you, love your enemies, bless those who curse you, do good to those who hate you, and pray for those who mistreat you and persecute you."

It may seem rather naïve on my part to address negative attitudes toward the United States in the context of loving one's enemies, but indeed, not all "anti" U.S. sentiments are dangerous or will self-prophesize to murder and killing, as John Gibson might have us fear. There will always be those among us who hate what they perceive the United States stands for. Some see us as a rogue nation responsible for a global military presence that enforces our rules and values onto the world through the threat of or use of force. Since the U.S. declaration of a War on Terror (WOT), many of our own allies do not see us as peacemakers or global humanitarians. Others may want to do our country harm, while others may harbor a lifetime of resentment but take no further action. Our responsibility to ourselves, if not to them, is to understand and pay attention to these detractors, not all of whom are evildoers and terrorists.

The study of international attitudes and opinions is very important if we believe that wars begin in our minds. While our most vile beliefs and attitudes may turn us into would-be killers, a better understanding of how others—mostly enemies and some former friends–see us may prevent some wars from every occurring. What the world spends in aggregate on international polling or public diplomacy programs to prevent wars and increase mutual understanding pales in comparison to the military expenditures we lay out each year to prepare for war. It is like a teardrop in the water compared to an ocean of militarism. If we ascribe to the belief that attitudes determine behavior, then our positive attitude toward military costs must determine somewhat our willingness to engage in protracted wars to "win" the peace. It is estimated that the world now spends over $950 billion each year on military expenses. In Fiscal Year 2005, the U.S. share in the global pot was over $400 billion, and the Pentagon now projects that total annual funding for the Defense Department alone will grow to $502.3 billion by Fiscal Year 2011. The United States spends 6 times more on its military than the world's second biggest spender, Russia. The U.S. military budget is more than 30 times as large as the combined spending of the seven "Rogue" or "Axis of Evil" nation-states (Cuba, Iran, Iraq, Libya, North Korea, Sudan, and Syria).[4] The Stockholm International Peace Research Institute estimated in 2003 that the United States spent approximately 47% of the world's total military spending. Granted, because the U.S. economy and gross domestic product is so significant, we can certainly afford a higher discretionary outlay for a globally-based military than most countries in the world. The U.S. national consensus is that we must maintain a U.S. military presence across the globe in order to protect our national defense and to protect open sea lanes to global trade. What's not often discussed in the same breath as a strong defense is how this same defense projects a picture of America to the rest of the world. A global U.S. military projects a picture of the United States as aggressive and threatening. While we may see ourselves as defensive in posture, global public opinion views us as over-reaching our hard power status. A June 2005 Global Attitudes Survey by the Pew Research Center for People and the Press indicated the following gap in global perception: "Majorities in every other country surveyed, aside from the U.S., favor another country challenging America's global military supremacy. Americans strongly reject this idea, by 63%-26%."[5]

In comparison, consider the United Nations, arguably an imperfect international body that seems to regularly come under harsh criticism in the United States for fiscal mismanagment, waste, fraud, and abuse. While the UN is in need of reform, it is also responsible through its 191 member countries for global peace, security, and development issues. The UN annual budget is roughly 1.5% of the annual global budget on military expenditures. In 1995, the United Nation Children's Fund (UNICEF) estimated that just $34 billion per year could provide child health and nutrition, primary school education, safe drinking water and sanitation, and family planning.[6] What is missing is the motivation to meet those needs. Every American politician almost without exception is for maintaining a strong national defense that is second to none in the world. It would be political suicide to call for a rollback in U.S. military expenditures because we have come to associate patriotic attitudes (duty, honor, country) with military spending. But what if we were reminded every day about what our overwhelming emphasis on military operations brought us? What if we called it the Military Department instead of the Department of Defense? As the Center for Defense Information observed,

> The lion's share of this money is not spent by the Pentagon on protecting American citizens. It goes to supporting U.S. military activities, including interventions, throughout the world. Were this budget and the organization it finances called the "Military Department," then attitudes might be quite different. Americans are willing to pay for defense, but they would probably be much less willing to spend billions of dollars if the money were labeled "Foreign Military Operations."[7]

CLOSING THE PERCEPTION GAP

> American philanthropy is extraordinary by any world standard, and the reason is that America herself is exceptional.[8]

> The truth is that Americans are living in a dream world. Not only do others not share America's self-regard, they no longer aspire to emulate the country's social and economic achievements.[9]

On Thursday, September 20, 2001, just a little over a week after the attacks on the Pentagon and World Trade Center twin towers, America's eyes were on the president as he addressed a joint session of Congress. In part of his speech, he spoke for the nation when he said, "Americans are asking, why do they hate us?" and immediately provided the answer: "They hate what they see right here in this chamber—a democratically elected government. They hate our freedoms: our freedom of religion, our freedom of speech, our freedom to vote and assemble and disagree with each other."[10]

This well-turned phrase, "They hate our freedoms," likely comforted a nation still reeling from shocking imagery it experienced vicariously on television that was so traumatic it seemed to demand easy explanations. In hindsight, such a rhetorical simplification of anti-American sentiment was a missed opportunity to explore the complexities of the American culture and government that engender a continuum of attitudes and emotions from the most hateful to the most effusive. Who really knows what was in the minds of the 19 hijackers who commandeered American commercial aircraft. Yes, they originated from a part of the world that is historically undemocratic, Saudi Arabia in particular, the country of Osama Bin Laden's birth as well as many of his devotees. And yet the United States is allies with Saudi Arabia, whose government has been very closely tied to many friendly British and American administrations for decades, including the Bush family. So an oversimplification that terrorism is a result of hating open societies cannot stand against the reality that tyrannical governments often ally with democratic governments.

Many scholars from the political right like Daniel Pipes to the political left like Benjamin Barber argue that hatred for America isn't about resisting democratically elected governments, which, after all, are widely shared with other countries from Asia to Europe and even now with Iraq. According to Pipes, they don't hate our freedoms but rather are a "radical, utopian and totalitarian movement. Like all such movements, be it fascism or Marxism-Leninism or this one, we are anathema in every detail and the main obstacle to the achievement of their goals. In a philosophical and a strategic sense, we are their enemy. So they have declared war on us."[11] To Barber, author of the popular mid-'90s book *Jihad vs. McWorld*, it is American-led economic globalization, with all its culturally homogenizing effects and stratified socioeconomic elements that create fissures in the psyche that lead to more violent outbursts and allegiance to the most radical alternatives. The militant jihad philosophy is to its followers the perfect antidote to all the ills of modern society as exemplified in globalization. America serves as the face of globalization and its biggest cheerleader. That's why the face took such a hit on 9/11, and at the political and economic center of this face. According to Barber, neither the economic zeal of McWorld, to which America belongs, and the retribalization and primitivization of Al Qaeda, the world of Bin Laden, can model democracy, despite presidential speechmaking. The world, like the TV viewer, plays passive observer to this violent clash of titans:

> Neither Jihad nor McWorld aspires to resecure the civic virtues undermined by its denationalizing practices; neither global markets nor blood communities services public goods or pursue equality and justice . . . Jihad pursues a bloody politics of identity, McWorld a bloodless economics of profit. Belonging by default to McWorld, everyone is a consumer; seeking a repository for identity, everyone belongs to some tribe. But no one is a citizen. Without citizens, how can there be a democracy?[12]

Shortly after the American election of 2004, conservative newspaper *The Washington Times* published a three-part series on American culture and its influence abroad. "Love it, hate it, embrace it, deny it, American power, American influence and American values are the defining features of today's interconnected world. . . . The world really is becoming more 'American.' "[13] This Americanization in ideals, Britney Spears, Hollywood, the Google search engine, Michael Jordan, and economic opportunity (the American Dream), is an amalgamation of what scholar Joseph Nye most famously calls the U.S. attractiveness as a global soft power, which we as a nation and culture don't have to force upon anyone else. People can't seem to get enough of American sports, entertainment, and ingenuity. These soft power features act as a positive magnetic pull and counterweight to a negative push factor measured in our military hard power backed up by the diplomatic forceful persuasion to tell the world, "Take It or Leave It."

The soft power attraction qualities of the United States seem to be in constant competition with our equally famous and often harshly criticized hard power strengths. Most critics of the United States are quick to point to our enormous military spending in comparison to other countries. Though accounting for just 4 percent of the overall GDP, the United States spends more on the military (roughly $350 billion in 2002) than the next twelve countries' military expenditures combined. To most Americans, this is worth every penny if it keeps us safe from terrorist attacks. To others, this military superiority gives the United States carte blanche license to intervene in the domestic affairs of other countries. Without such a strong military, the argument goes, the United States would not be able to make its own rules when negotiating with other countries or contemplating military invasions. The United States dominates in the economic arena as well, which is likely less threatening to the world than American military power and enhances its soft power image. Though only 6 percent of the world's population and 6 percent of its land mass, the United States produces one-third of the world's GDP and one-third of foreign direct investment. In research and development, the United States spends more than the next seven countries combined. Related to this economic prowess is the fact that the United States remains the number one nation in the world to attract the best and brightest from all over the planet who wish to attend American institutions of higher learning. Even the Al Jazeera senior producer Samir Khader who was featured in the documentary film *Control Room*, though harshly critical of the U.S. military presence in Iraq, dreamed of moving to the United States, perhaps working for the Fox News Channel and sending his children to American universities.

The November 2, 2004, election was as much an election for the world as it was for the United States, so divisive was the American figurehead of President Bush, not only in the Middle East but throughout Europe, our North American neighbor to the north, and South America. Not since my Fulbright year in Germany nearly twenty years earlier was I so aware of the enmity toward the United States government, despite a global love and affection for other American institutions, including education and higher learning.

On April 28, 2004, just a little over six months before the U.S. presidential election, I was speaking at the National Library of Valencia in an address to a group of Spanish students who had been specially invited to attend a two-day communication seminar. My talk was on the information and disinformation consequences of 9/11 in the United States. Much of my comments were excerpted from my second book, *Information War*, which addressed what I saw as a chilling effect that the global war on terror and subsequent wars in Afghanistan and Iraq had on American dissent and free speech. I was the only American in attendance or speaking, and somewhat surprisingly, during the question and answer period following my formal presentation, the students were only interested in knowing if I were working to defeat Bush or elect Kerry. They also seemed perplexed and even angry as to how the American people could even consider re-electing Bush. At no point in my presentation had I announced that I was working for Kerry (which I wasn't) nor had I suggested that I was working to defeat Bush, although I'm sure that my presentation indicated that I was very critical of Bush Administration policies and would therefore not vote for his re-election. Nevertheless, the American presidential election seemed to be the only thing that concerned these Spanish students and one student even said that if he could, he would vote in our election to remove Bush from office.

At the time of my visit, the Abu Ghraib prison pictures showing American soldiers abusing and mocking Iraqi prisoners had just been released and some new pictures of British coalition soldiers urinating on Iraqi prisoners were prominently displayed on European tabloid covers at every kiosk. (The British pictures were later ruled as fakes.) The Anglo-American empire nations of the USA and Great Britain were not held in the highest esteem in many parts of Europe, even though my trip happened to coincide with the May 1st addition of fifteen new nations to the European Union. I was reminded by how engaged the world is by all things American, even if they hold disdain or gratitude toward America. In my memory, there was no other election in modern history except for the re-election of President Ronald Reagan in 1984 that garnered this much European obsession than the possible re-election of President Bush in 2004. Both Reagan and Bush exuded a plethora of confidence in America's military, spiritual, economic, and cultural power and value to the world in direct contrast to their Democratic predecessors. Both men also managed to frighten a lot of civilian populations overseas who were put off by their aggressive so-called "Cowboy" rhetoric that was used to counter the ideological attraction and power of America's enemies, which in Reagan's time was the "Evil Empire" Soviet Union and in Bush's time, global terrorists "thugs" and rogue "Axis of Evil" nations.

WE'RE NOT FREE WHEN OTHERS DON'T BUY IT

The U.S. government initiated its Valentine's Day greeting to the Middle East with the launch of the noncommercial, twenty-four hour broadcast

TV network Al Hurra on February 14, 2004. Al Hurra, which means "The Free One" in Arabic, cost U.S. taxpayers an initial start-up of $62 million in its first year. It is the brainchild of Norman J. Pattiz, a self-made radio tycoon who thirty years ago started a fledgling radio company in Los Angeles that grew to be Westwood One, the largest private radio network organization in the United States. Pattiz was appointed by President Clinton in 2000 as a Democratic member of the bipartisan Broadcasting Board of Governors that oversees all of the U.S. government's broadcast operations including the well-known and oldest, Voice of America, Radio and TV Marti (Cuba), Radio Farda (Iran), Radio Free Asia (East Asia), Radio Free Europe/Radio Liberty (Eastern Europe), and Radio Sawa (Middle East).

Al Hurra is the newest addition to the family of propaganda mass media that specifically target Arab-speaking people in a post-9/11 and war on terror context. In an interview at his Los Angeles office shortly after the launch of Radio Sawa (Arabic for "together") on March 23, 2002, Pattiz told me that he was an advocate for government-sponsored media to the Middle East long before September 11, 2001. In fact, it was his several trips to the region that convinced him that the United States had to have an official voice in the region to combat what he labeled "hate media," which he defined as anti-American and anti-Israeli in tone and content. What was needed was more balance to offset the hate speech in the Middle East and something more modern and less overtly propagandistic for the 21st century, which meant that the United States had to do more than just expand its VOA broadcasting. At the time of Al Hurra's launch, President Bush said that it would serve as a weapon in the war on terror to combat "the hateful propaganda that fills the airwaves in the Muslim world and tell people the truth about the values and policies of the United States."[14]

An NBC News review of some of the global media reaction to Al Hurra would seem to have doomed its early demise, not led to an expansion. Arab newspaper editorials were universally thumbs down on the new broadcast alternative, with the not unexpected negative reaction of "It's all American propaganda, anyway." The *Cairo Times* said that many Egyptians remain "guarded" in their reaction and are suspicious of the new station's propagandistic potential to shape news from a pro-U.S., pro-Israeli governmental perspective.[15] The most prestigious Arabic-language newspaper, *Al Ahram*, said, "It is difficult to understand how the U.S., with its advanced research centers and clever minds, explains away Arab hatred as a product of a demagogic media and not due to its biased policies and propensity to abuse Arab interests."

Arab News, the Middle East's leading English daily, reported a "cool reception" to Al Hurra, which some viewers see as "short on credibility and long on arrogance." The former minister of information in Kuwait, Dr. Saad Al Ajmi, reported a mixed review overall. In a special to the Gulf News, he said that "there is most certainly a vacuum for it [Al Hurra] to fill. Before Al Hurra, America had no satellite television voice in the Arab world . . . Al Hurra is playing catch up, and it remains to be seen if it will be successful."[16]

The private commercial broadcast network CNN dominated the Arab airwaves in the early 1990s, which led to a new research phenomenon called "the CNN effect" in international media coverage. This dominance faded after the last war in the Gulf and before Al Jazeera and Al Arabiya came along to challenge this English-language global media station that was accessible to only English-speaking elites in the region.

Against a backdrop of anti-Americanism and an unfinished roadmap to peace in the Middle East, it's still doubtful that many Arab hearts and Muslim minds will be won. For one, the United States doesn't have the freedom credibility it wants to project to the Middle East and just calling a network free doesn't make it so, especially one tied so closely to the U.S. government. Telling to some Arab viewers was that President Bush was the first guest interviewed on Al Hurra. *Al Quds Al Arabi*, a Palestinian newspaper generally critical of the United States, said that the Bush interview "brought to mind official channels broadcast by regimes mired in dictatorship, just like those of the 1960s and beginning of the '70s."[17]

The greatest hurdle to overcome seems to be in the naming of the station itself. To many, if Al Hurra represents "the free ones" then that makes "us" the unfree ones. This magic bullet theory of communication assumes that the sender's need for more free speech and more accurate information about itself in a region coincides with the receiver's needs. But many naysayers to Al Hurra say that the United States still "just doesn't get it" about what the Arab audience true needs are.

One magazine writer, Amy Moufai, told an NBC News producer in Cairo that she hadn't watched the new U.S. network, but was "very surprised they would choose a name like that which highlights the fact they don't know what they are doing in the Middle East. It reeks of the whole notion of a white man's bread. 'Let us teach you our free ways.'"[18]

The United States tends to associate better communication with more information. We think that if we can just get our message out there, make it louder, make it stronger, make it bolder, then we'll be well on our way to repairing miscommunication problems. But just maybe what is sought is more respectability and acknowledgment that U.S. geopolitical and economic interests in the region don't often match up to how the Arab people perceive freedom, particularly from despotic government intervention. A government-led free press is a harsh reminder of a region dominated by unfree governments. And no slick slogans or pretty newsroom sets are going to overcome those realities.

Before he announced his resignation from the BBG in early 2006, Pattiz was often criticized as an anti-VOA board member, which throughout its more than sixty year history, is still typecast in terms of an antiquated World War II holdover given its 1942 origins following the attack on Pearl Harbor. In the crisis communications atmosphere of 9/11 with so much rhetorical questioning of "why do they hate us," Pattiz had a ready antidote and the credibility to match his bold ideas. A successful commercial broadcaster, he convinced the BBG and Congress to use a commercial approach to start Radio Sawa, which would be set up in the style of a youth-oriented 24-hour entertainment radio format using international and American pop music play lists that limited news broadcasts to minutes on the hour. Very soon the Western and Arab media headlines were peppered with references to Britney Spears as the new weapon of mass communication in the war on terror. This skepticism was not much different from the guffawing that followed the appointment of the former Uncle Ben's Rice chief advertiser, Charlotte Beers, as Undersecretary of State for Public Diplomacy, in essence, Uncle Sam's chief advertiser.

When Al Hurra first launched, the Arab and Muslim public reaction was mostly negative. *Slate* magazine writer Ed Finn said simply, "the Middle East hates Al Hurra," and considers it "unhip."[19] At the negative end, it was received by Arab media and opinion leaders as just government business-as-usual or propaganda as news. In other words, how could viewers trust the U.S. government to be the best source and model of a free press in a region like the Middle East where all broadcast operations are controlled by undemocratic Arab governments? William Rugh, an associate of the

Institute for the Study of Diplomacy at Georgetown University, told a U.S. Senate hearing on Middle East broadcasting that Al Hurra has an even harder sell than Radio Sawa:

> The content and style of the news gave the impression that it was not an Arab channel but American. Subjects that were chosen, and the time devoted to them in newscasts, seemed determined from an American point of view rather than an Arab perspective. More attention was paid to Americans in the news than to Arabs in the news. Language also did not match that of most Arab television stations; for example, Palestinian suicide bombers were not referred to as "martyrs." Most importantly, the first impression viewers got of al Hurra—and first impressions are important—was the inaugural interview with President Bush. Arab government-owned television stations have always given prominence to statements by their heads of state, and the Bush interview seemed to stamp al Hurra as just one more government-owned channel.[20]

Within days of Rugh's testimony before Congress, President Bush appeared on two Arab media outlets, Al Hurra and Al Arabiya, to discuss the Abu Ghraib scandal that showed pictures of U.S. personnel torturing and humiliating Iraqi prisoners. He told Al Hurra that "in a democracy, everything is not perfect, that mistakes are made. But in a democracy, as well, those mistakes will be investigated and people will be brought to justice." Unlike the closed societies of the Middle East, President Bush said that "we're an open society. We're a society that is willing to investigate, fully investigate in this case, what took place in that prison. That stands in stark contrast to life under Saddam Hussein. His trained torturers were never brought to justice under his regime. There were no investigations about mistreatment of people."[21] Missing from his roundabout interviews was a sit-down with the most popular Arab satellite television in the Middle East, Al Jazeera.

In February 2005, Dr. Condoleezza Rice, who as America's chief diplomat sits on the Broadcasting Board of Governors, announced that Al Hurra would be expanded to Europe using $3.5 million of supplemental funding that were originally appropriated for Iraq, this in addition to the $62 million already allocated Al Hurra annually and $22 million annual budget for Radio Sawa. The initiative was set to launch in the fall and would focus on the Islamic Arabic-speaking communities in the "Old Europe" countries of France and Germany. Kenneth Tomlinson, the former VOA director under President Reagan, told Reuters news service that Al Hurra is needed now in Europe because "most of the hijackers that carried out the September 11 attacks came from Europe."[22] Norman Pattiz sees this European focus as just an extension of the reliable media reputation that Radio Sawa and Al Hurra have had in the Middle East.

What's missing in the debate from this extension of U.S. propaganda media in a declared war on terror is any sober real world analysis outside of the politicking and lobbying that comes with so much of the decision making in Washington. The announcement of the European Al Hurra came just as the U.S. State Department Inspector General had to acknowledge to an inquiry by *Al-Sharq Al-Awsat*, an Arab-language newspaper based in London, that it was shelving a report critical of Radio Sawa and Al Hurra. The State Department had financed an outside think tank to provide an overview of its international broadcasting and then held back the results because it didn't like what the organization had to say about its post-9/11 pet projects.[23]

ENLARGING THE AMERICAN BRAND

While I was working at the U.S. Information Agency in the early to mid-1990s, it became clear that America, minus a Cold War mission, had a much more challenging time "selling" its image abroad. Every angel needs its devil, and during the nearly 50-year showdown between East and West, communist and capitalist, the U.S. could starkly compare the lightness that was a free market economy and open society from the darkness that was state-controlled totalitarianism. Given a choice, most citizens (customers) would choose the open society. Once Bill Clinton became the first post-Cold War president in 1992, what would our propaganda agency do to tell America's story to the world? The answer, not unlike the lofty-sounding "transformational diplomacy" of Condoleezza Rice, was "enlarging markets," or, as I often referred to it, making the world safe for the American shopping mall. The conventional wisdom was that the United States had beaten the U.S.S.R. with a better brand—and that all we had to do now was package the American brand for selling by encouraging and promoting the newly emerging democracies of the former Soviet Union to accept our offer. The problem was that we had no stark alternative comparison to present our potential customers. Without a Soviet threat, many nations were becoming freed up to speak their minds, and they were quick to tell us that they didn't want to become more Americanized. They may want some of our products, but the last thing they wanted was new commercial colonization. I believe that one of the reasons USIA failed to see the twenty-first century is because the agency's messianic mission became too entangled with the commercial marketing imperative so prevalent in the foreign policy of the Clinton Administration. Without an equally strong "second mandate" to build mutual understanding between the people of the United States and people in other countries, USIA no longer had a post-Cold War mission. By 2001, when the war on terrorism was underway, many diplomats and members of Congress in Washington were bemoaning the demise of the propaganda agency in 1999. This is where advertisers stepped in, to fill a void in American advocacy that the U.S. government was either unwilling or unable to do.

In 2004, advertising executive Keith Reinhard, CEO of DDB Worldwide, joined forces with other executives to form Business for Diplomatic Action (BDA), a corporate sector answer to the anti-Americanism problem. Reinhard was struck by President Bush's post-9/11 bewilderment regarding why some throughout the world hated the United States so much to want to attack its citizens. Reinhard thought the question, "Why do they hate us?" needed more than outward speculation but a consumer research response. He asked DDB's researchers to conduct hate meter surveys in 17 client countries. The bleak findings were reported in *The Economist*: "America, and American business, was viewed as arrogant and indifferent toward others' cultures; exploitative, in that it extracted more than it provided; corrupting, in how it valued materialism above all else; and willing to sacrifice almost anything in an effort to generate profits."[24] The annual NOP World survey of "power brands" noted a slight slippage in American brand trust from 2003–2004,[25] which could in part be due to the outbreak of war in Iraq, but Reinhard does not attribute this rise in anti-Americanism as a simple cause-effect of the war in Iraq. Indeed, much of the brand slippage is happening across the globe, including in allied nations like Germany, Canada, and France. He attributes the negative sentiment to a post-Cold War sense throughout the world that American-led globalization is leaving many victims in its wake; that American culture's pervasiveness is threatening to other cultures' sense of their own national and regional identity; and finally, that the American collective personality is still the stereotypical "ugly American," one who doesn't want to listen to others, is too loud and boorish, arrogant and unwilling to learn.[26] He holds the U.S. government partially at fault for the persistent bad image because, unlike business decision making, government policy moves at a snail's pace and is overly bureaucratic. "Our experience is that when we try to do something with the government, it just turns into a pile of paper."[27] Further, he told the 9/11 Commission in summer 2004 that the U.S. government as the chief public diplomacy agent of the United States doesn't work because "the United States government is simply not a credible messenger."[28] This view is in contrast to many U.S.-government and private think tank reports after 9/11 that called for the White House to initiate a new public diplomacy czar or Special Counselor to the President for Public Diplomacy who had the ear of the U.S. president. One study, "Changing Minds, Winning Peace," endorsed by a bipartisan Advisory Group on Public Diplomacy for the Arab and Muslim World, said the following about the president's role in public diplomacy and the management of the American image:

> The President, in every word, whether addressed to domestic or international audiences, is the most important voice influencing attitudes toward the United States abroad. Just as important, the President enforces discipline and makes certain that those who carry out both official and public diplomacy speak with one voice. There can be no success without the seriousness of purpose and interagency coordination provided at the direction of the President of the United States. Public diplomacy must have his stamp of approval, enthusiastic support, and long-term commitment. In fact, he must be considered the ultimate director of public diplomacy.[29]

Perhaps a meeting in the middle is in order between Reinhard's private sector answer and the president's public sector ear. Or maybe something in between, the third sector. According to a "Trust Barometer" made public at the 2005 World Economic Forum in Davos, Switzerland, "pressure groups and charities have overtaken governments, media and big businesses to become the world's most trusted institutions."[30] The Nike Swoosh and the Golden Arches earn global recognition but not necessarily citizen trust. According to the December 2004 poll by U.S.-based public relations firm Edelman, Greenpeace and Amnesty International, two international nongovernmental organizations (INGOs) are the most trusted in the United States and Europe. Business and government trail far behind. The shift away from business and government to civil society was attributed in part to a growing "democratization of information," said Edelman, and included a move to trust more information from the Internet, local sources of news, and plain-spoken brand spokespeople over business executives.[31] American brand Coca-Cola was trusted by 69 percent of those surveyed in the United States but by only 45 percent in Europe. The poll was conducted in eight countries (Brazil, Britain, Canada, China, France, Germany, Japan, United States) among so-called "opinion leaders," 1,500 university graduates age 35 to 65, with public affairs interests, and with annual household incomes of more than $75,000. This was the sixth year of such a trustworthiness survey and the most pronounced increase in NGO trust. In the United States alone, trust ratings for NGOs skyrocketed from 36 percent in 2001 to 55 percent in 2004, likely related to the Enron and WorldCom corporate scandals that dominated headlines in the early 21st century. The Davos meeting called on business to get its trust quotient in order by playing "a much bigger role in tackling environmental overload, pervasive poverty, and pandemics."[32]

THE MORE CREDIBLE MESSENGER DEBATE

Business or government? Which is the more credible messenger to tell America's story to the world? If you ask Keith Reinhard, it's business. At a Congressional Hearing on the 9/11 Commission Recommendations in Public Diplomacy, Reinhard laid out four reasons why business is the better messenger:

> First, American companies, their representatives and their brands directly touch the lives of more people than government representatives ever could. Second, foreign representatives of U.S. companies abroad are more likely to be representative of local views and perceptions than are Americans working in embassies. Third, once corporations decide to act, for the most part, they can move forward without bureaucratic entanglement, and fourth, in a corporation, policy is not automatically up for grabs every four years. This means, if a program gets up and running, and there is senior corporate leadership behind it, there is a good chance it will be sustained in the long run.[33]

Reinhard said that American "public diplomacy is the business of business," and underscored his point with an illustration of how measly the

U.S. government is spending on improving the image of Uncle Sam in comparison to American corporate branding's advertising expenditures:

> In the private sector, we can't force people to eat McDonald's hamburgers, drink Coca-Cola or wear Nike shoes. And so we spend money to invite people to engage with our brand and try our products. In fact, both McDonald's and Coke spend more money (approximately $1.2 billion each) to make friends around the world than does the U.S. government. What's more, both companies have someone in charge of the total expenditure and at both companies, someone is held accountable for every dollar spent.[34]

Business cannot act alone, however, because the root causes of anti-Americanism include disagreements about U.S. foreign policy and U.S.-led globalization as well as a sense that the American popular culture is taking over the planet. Reinhard likens the American image to a

> montage of our foreign policy, the brands we market, and the entertainment we export. It could be referred to as a cocktail of "Rummy" [Secretary Rumsfeld] and Coke with Madonna on the side. Should there be any doubt that government and commercial actions are irrevocably linked, one need only to review the political cartoons in the foreign press the day after Saddam's statue was toppled. In at least half a dozen we saw, Saddam had been replaced by Ronald McDonald.[35]

As fascinating and accurate as Reinhard's marketing analysis is for 21st century public diplomacy approaches, it contrasts with a picture of America offered by University of Chicago historian Daniel J. Boorstin in his 1962 book, *The Image*. In it, Boorstin analyzes the mid-20th century age of the Graphic Revolution, an age in which America was becoming more concerned with pseudo-events (manufactured occurrences) than reality. The American dream and American ideals had been replaced by American illusions driven by advertising, public relations, and the managed press conference. No longer was it important to follow your dreams but rather fall for these illusory events. "I suspect we suffer abroad simply because people know America through images. While our enemies profit from the fact that they are known only, or primarily, through their ideals. That is, through their professed goals of perfection."[36] Boorstin sees a problem with an advertising campaign to improve America's image in the world. It creates a mirror effect. The more we offer something bigger, better, and more pleasing to the eye than what we now project, the more it may produce an opposite effect than what we intend. We will never be able to live up to the projected flattering image of ourselves. Keith Reinhard believes that it is "our collective personality" projection that harms. "Although Americans are still admired for their openness, their creativity and their can-do approach, we are also broadly seen as arrogant, insensitive, ignorant and loud."[37] But a question remains with our public diplomacy purpose now. Is it to change that "ugly American" image to improve our credibility in the world or offer up a reality of America that is less about image projection to the world and more about understanding ourselves from the outside world in? Boorstin offers a suggestion: "We should not try to persuade others to share our illusions. We should try to reach outside our images. We should seek new ways of letting messages reach us; from our own past, from God, from the world we may hate or think we hate. To give visas to strange and alien and outside notions . . . One of our grand illusions is the belief in a 'cure.' There is no cure. There is only the opportunity of discovery."[38]

A METHOD OR MADNESS?

Dr. Condoleezza Rice, the Secretary of State, has said that she will make "public diplomacy" a top priority in the Bush Administration's second term. She describes the U.S. government's public diplomacy mission in stark terms: "America and all free nations are facing a generational struggle against a new and deadly ideology of hatred. We must do a better job of confronting hostile propaganda, dispelling dangerous myths, and telling America's story."[39]

The United States considers weapons of mass communication to be an integral part of the post-9/11 environment and the urgency to out-communicate "a man in a cave" and his enemy followers is at Cold War levels.[40] Combating anti-Americanism is a central focus of this new priority. The Bush Administration has targeted primarily the younger generation of Muslim and Arab male youth between the ages of 18–25 who are most susceptible to the message of the man in the cave. These are the youth most likely to listen to those mullahs (Islamic teachers) or madrassas (Islamic schools) that promote a virulent anti-American agenda. In response, the United States has spent hundreds of millions to establish

24-hour radio and television networks to act as a counterbalance to the hate speech in the schools and the controlled media systems that allow the dangerous myths about the United States to spread like topsy.

Not surprisingly, the targeted approach to the Arab and Muslim regions of the world does not sit well with many on the receiving end or within earshot of this American ideological battle plan. For one, the content of the public diplomacy message that places freedom at its core is putting those designated "unfree" countries like Iran, Syria, and North Korea on high alert. They do not like to be told that their political cultures are full of hostile propaganda or that their people live in complete subjugation to an illegitimate government. Indeed, many of these countries accuse the United States of propagating its own mythos of freedom, which they translate as lofty rhetoric over reality. They look for signs of underlying control and domination agendas in the American public diplomacy campaign.

Populations such as those in Western Europe that are outside the usual suspects' sphere of hate propaganda are somewhat sympathetic to the anti-American criticism. To those anti-war activists in Spain, Germany, Britain and France, it isn't really anti-American to accuse the U.S. government of using soft power rhetoric (attraction toward free societies and popular culture) as a smokescreen for hard power priorities in Afghanistan and Iraq. In fact, having a healthy and sometimes contentious debate about U.S. power projection in the world is not seen as anti-American at all to them, but rather an illustration of Dr. Rice's "transformational diplomacy" that focuses on dialogue and not a monologue.

So how do we then separate the anti-American wheat from the chaff? We could start by separating the American government public diplomacy mission from the American story. When I worked at the U.S. Information Agency in Washington, D.C., I used to view its institutional motto, "Telling America's Story to the World" every day as I entered the lobby. It always struck me as odd that the agency chose the word "story" over "stories." There is no more diverse country in the world and yet we chose a motto that reflects an image of officialdom. Just as North Korea is not simply Kim Jong Ill, so too is the story of the United States not just George Bush. In fact, in a democratic context, he's just one of the citizens. Yes, he is the official American persuader-in-chief, but his image and message alone is insufficient to mount an effective ideological campaign. For the last several years, American public diplomacy has been centrally located and managed in Washington, D.C., the political axis of the United

States but also home to a president who has often chosen hot aggressive rhetoric over cool conciliatory words. Dr. Rice may have wooed the French in early 2005 with her decent French and fashionable duds, but once the intoxicating wool is pulled up, we still have a public diplomacy mission in the United States defined by an administration whose record of divisive, disenfranchising global diplomacy rhetoric is second to none. This is why I say, release the restraints of American public diplomacy and call on the American people to forge their own social networks with our counterparts abroad. There are literally millions of stories about this country yet to be told that could do a much more effective and efficient job in communicating a message to the world. This might help overcome the dominant image of the gun-slinging superpower that throws its heavy weight around without paying for the damage.

THE PROPAGANDA CZAR FROM PARIS AND TEXAS (A PREMONITION)

> I understand that Karen Hughes was born in Paris.
>
> —John Kerry, 2004

The Paris-born former Texas reporter Karen Hughes has reported for duty once again in Washington. After leaving the president's side full-time in 2002 for Texas to devote more time to family (her son was said to either hate Washington or miss Texas), Hughes was tapped to combat anti-Americanism in the Middle East and wherever else it might rear its ugly head. Karen Hughes is the most high-profile undersecretary of state for public diplomacy and public affairs since Charlotte Beers vacated that position two years ago right before the first shock-and-awe air strikes in Baghdad. Margaret Tutwiler, the James Baker protégé and former Ambassador to Morocco, spent less than nine months in that capacity before jumping the ship of state for the New York Stock Exchange. Now Hughes gets the job that everyone agrees is exceedingly necessary but altogether practically impossible given the ongoing credibility problems of the United States and its position of *numero uno* brand nation.

Hughes is not known for her foreign policy prowess but for guard-dog-like devotion to President George W. Bush. While a professor at New England College, I was within a ten-foot pole from her in Concord,

New Hampshire in 2000 when Bush was campaigning in the first-in-the-nation presidential primary. She made a strong impression that I just might be zapped into vapor if I got too close to then Governor Bush whenever Hughes was around as his unofficial governor-in-chief bodyguard. Luckily I kept my distance and remain intact today. She was certainly good at protecting Bush far from the madding crowds, a tactic that failed to win the hearts and minds of many New Hampshire voters as we mass exited for John McCain's straight talk and open door Town Hall policy. With some irony, Hughes is tasked now with promoting a more open dialogue between our nation and overseas publics. Let's hope she uses a softer touch this time.

Shortly after 9/11, Hughes did earn her information warfare stripes while heading the White House day-to-day duties of the Coalition Information Centers (CICs) that coordinated the message of the day from London to Washington to Islamabad during the bombing raids over Afghanistan. She was identified then as one of the main players in what the *New York Times* called the largest communications war effort since World War II. Her main task now is to undo some of the ongoing anger over the U.S. invasion of Iraq, so primary focus will remain in the Middle East with increases in exchanges, radio broadcasts, and even news appearances by her and other State Department officials on Al Jazeera. In this capacity, she has something that few, outside A-list celebrities, will ever experience at the upper echelons of power—complete access. She certainly has the heart and mind of both secretary of state and president, a position that may very well allow her free reign to rev up some bold new initiatives in public diplomacy that we could surely use. But it is this access to Washington groupthink that is exactly what may hurt that overseas effort.

American public diplomacy is presently very much an insider's and owner's box seat game where the rest of us serve as passive observers to the process, much like those targeted audiences who are presumed to shift their attitudes and opinions after marinating in pop music and low intensity news. While Karen Hughes brings much-needed F.O.G. (Friend of George) status to the public diplomacy process, as such a strong insider she may become susceptible to the programs already in place that have been politically popular in Washington but not definitively successful overseas. There are some heated discussions about the success or not of two international broadcasting initiatives, Radio Sawa and Al Hurra, post-9/11 radio and television networks designed to combat hate media and Al Jazeera's influence. While the consensus among leading Arab intellectuals and journalists (and not just Arab government-controlled media), is that both Sawa and Hurra have met tepid audience response, this is not the image projected by the politically appointed Broadcasting Board of Governors that oversees all U.S. government international broadcasting.

Although audience surveys do suggest that people have listened and tuned in to Radio Sawa and Al Hurra occasionally, there is yet any solid evidence that these programs are working to convert anyone to an American point of view, whatever that might be. A 2003 GAO report documented the failings of the U.S. government to come up with any measurable indicators that could prove success. In fall 2004 a news leak to the *Washington Post* said that data were available that Radio Sawa is, like Radio and TV Marti, more boondoggle than bonanza.[41] This report was highly criticized by members of the Broadcasting Board of Governors, including Pattiz, at the time and was released to the public. Now we must wait for another inquiry by the Congressional investigating service, General Accounting Office.

I welcome the appointment of Karen Hughes because she brings so much hot talk and public scrutiny from what had become a moribund conversation about *why they hate us*. That is so 2001. In 2006, the Bush Administration is claiming democracy victory at every turn in the Middle East as it still puzzles over why the world doesn't embrace our marketed version. Now we'll get to conduct our own market watch as Karen Hughes gets to sweat out the complexity and paradoxes associated with re-branding America.

Not since the colorful Charlotte Beers have I had so much fun poking around from my perch in the pale ivory tower, but as I learned on the steps of the State Capitol in New Hampshire, I'll try not to get too close. For us media and propaganda monitors, this one is worth a good scrutiny, even from a respectable distance.

KAREN HUGHES II AND WHAT THE WORLD REALLY THINKS OF AMERICA

On September 15, 2005, I was in Washington, D.C. just blocks away from the phallic Washington monument, symbol of America's birth and power in the world. I was in town as an invited panelist for a BBC-sponsored panel, "Does the U.S. Rule the World?"[42] The panel, part of a two-week global series called "Who Rules Your World," was held at the historic

Daughters of the American Revolution (DAR) building adjacent to the
White House. It included an eclectic mix of perspectives: The well-known
soft power scholar and Dean Joseph Nye of the Kennedy School of Government at Harvard University; Jeffrey Baxter, military consultant and ex
band member of the Doobie Brothers and Steely Dan; and Keith Reinhard. We reached no consensus, as Americans are known not to do. Baxter
said that America was simply part of the marketplace of ideas and that
if some aren't buying, then others will. He was the pragmatist patriot.
Nye said that we needed to move more in the direction of our nonviolent
persuasion capacities—soft power—so that our hard power military projections wouldn't undermine the great ideas that attract so many to our
shores. Keith Reinhard came armed with a lot of debilitating data that
said the American brand was on the decline and not measuring up as it
once did. Reinhard did not call for more advertising to market America
to the world, but rather a general investment from the private and public sectors and everyday citizens, including those who do business and/or
travel abroad, to reinvigorate the American brand in the world.

I played the disheartening role of the party pooper. I suggested that
America does indeed rule the world in terms of its culture, politics, and
military, but not at the world's asking. We were no longer the America of
Henry Luce's vision. Luce had called on the United States to donate a
measurable amount of our GDP to eradicate global poverty. That's what
made America great. When we were seen as humble providers, we were
benign leaders. As he wrote in 1941, months before America's entry into
World War II:

> We have some things in this country which are infinitely precious and espe-
> cially American—a love of freedom, a feeling for the equality of opportunity,
> a tradition of self-reliance and independence. . . . We are [also] the inheri-
> tors of all the great principles of Western civilization—above all Justice, the
> love of Truth, the ideal of Charity. . . . [This century] is now our time to be
> the powerhouse from which these ideals spread throughout the world and
> do their mysterious work of lifting the life of mankind from the level of the
> beasts to what the Psalmist called a little lower than the angels.
>
> [I envision] America as the dynamic center of ever-widening spheres of
> enterprise, America as the training center of the skillful servants of mankind,
> America as the Good Samaritan, really believing again that it is more blessed
> to give than to receive, and America as the powerhouse of the ideals of
> freedom and justice—out of these elements surely can be fashioned a vision
> of the 20th century to which we can and will devote ourselves.[43]

In the new American century after Luce, I thought that we appeared more like aggressive conquerors. So long as we continued to project hard power over soft power, we did not have the world's confidence to remain a sole superpower. The crowd was sympathetic to our criticism and less supportive of Baxter's marketplace of ideas pragmatism, since our panel was simulcast on BBC Worldnews and the D.C.-based public radio station.

The BBC has been conducting similar panels and polls on America's role in the world in the last couple of years since 9/11. In one BBC/CBC poll from June 2003 that asked 11,000 people in 11 countries what they thought of America, nearly half of all South Koreans said that the United States is more of a threat to the world peace and stability than North Korea. Generally, respondents found the United States more threatening as a superpower than China, Russia, France, Iran or Syria. More than half thought the United States was wrong to invade Iraq.[44] On all accounts, American respondents reflected an opposite point of view, suggesting that the United States and the world were living their respective realities through different prisms, undoubtedly in part shaped by media consumption. This made any public diplomacy campaign to "tell America's story to the world" altogether problematic if we were seeing the world through competing lenses.

While in Washington, I was hoping to stop by to see my former colleagues at USIA who were now part of the U.S. State Department's public diplomacy mission. I did not get that opportunity, and within a week was back at the University of Southern California to teach my class on anti-Americanism. When I walked into the Center on Public Diplomacy office suite, there was a lot of buzz about the visit of Karen Hughes to the Center the previous day. Naturally I was a bit stunned to be the last to know, but I was told she did not want her visit publicly announced and only a few select people had met with her. Hughes was interested in knowing about the current communication technologies available to promote America's message to the world. She even asked about starting her own website log ("blog"). She was leaving the following week for her first trip to the Middle East dubbed "A Listening Tour." That same week *USA Today* published two editorials about her trip. The staff editorial, "Sales pitch falls flat," was quite critical, saying that Karen Hughes "has at times come across as preachy and culturally insensitive and gotten, by charitable description, a lukewarm response... Changing the world's 'We Hate America' tone to 'We Love America' won't be easy. But the kind of ties that worked so well in the past could better bring about a genuine image makeover than a superficial PR blitz."[45]

Another very positive editorial entitled "Hughes offers steps, not spin" was presented by former Voice of America director and now Dean Geoffrey Cowan of the Annenberg School for Communication, who a week before had hosted Karen Hughes at his home in Los Angeles. He wrote, "After years of foundering, the Bush administration has put America's public diplomacy in the hands of a team of talented professionals. As the *Washington Post* noted, the selection of Karen Hughes 'is seen by many in Washington as a coup,' bringing to the job an almost unique combination of communication expertise and high-level credibility and clout, earned as a result of her close relationship with President Bush."

I presented both editorials to my class on anti-Americanism and asked the students to comment on the different perspectives. What interested them the most wasn't the critical staff editorial but the praising editorial by Dean Cowan that *USA Today* noted was written "at the State Department's invitation." Since they were aware that she had just been at the Annenberg School, they were quite curious about the ethical issues surrounding such an op-ed. Did Hughes personally ask Dean Cowan to write such a comment? Did the State Department preview the commentary? I asked Dean Cowan to meet with the students and talk about his meeting with Hughes and what led to his optimistic take on her leadership. He diplomatically agreed to meet with us and spent a good half hour explaining why he, as a lifelong Democrat, believed that Karen Hughes's close tie to President Bush was what public diplomacy exactly needed now. He wrote the column on his own and without State Department oversight. Looking back over the fall of 2005 and Hughes's first few months in office, I cannot share Cowan's sanguine outlook on her leadership or vision for American public diplomacy. I believe that she is first and foremost devoted to her longtime boss, George W. Bush, a loyal devotion that clouds her ability to engage critical and dissenting positions on Bush's foreign policy. Leon Hadar, my Ph.D. classmate at American University, a CATO Institute fellow, and author of *Sandstorm: Policy Failure in the Middle East*, wrote a funny and critical piece on Hughes for *The American Conservative* that reflects my own sentiment thus far on her first trip to the Middle East:

But you've got to give this tough lady from Texas some credit. She was trying very, very hard: blowing kisses to small groups of "fans" in the streets of Cairo selected in advance by Egyptian Mukhbarrat; giving the high-five to bewildered cute little Turkish kids and telling them how Uncle George in Washington really, really loves them; attempting to bond ("I'm a working mom") with Turkish housewives; all the while assuring Muslims that her boss is a Man of God and projecting that all-American persona of a cheerleader from the University of Houston who was on a mission to recruit veiled Muslim girls for the winning U.S. team … All you need is not to deviate from a consistent message that you repeat several times a day like a parrot on crack: Democracy! Democracy! Democracy! Eventually those guys in the Middle East will come to their senses and figure out that American intentions are good and that that the country's commitment to spreading democracy is not merely a hypocritical justification for getting rid of regimes that President Bush and *The Weekly Standard* dislike.[46]

Like Leon Hadar, Sanford Ungar—another former Voice of America director, who is president of Goucher College in Baltimore, Maryland—believes that Hughes, though certainly sophisticated in the art of messaging, is less effective abroad because she is seen at the right hand, if not the right ear of an American president and administration more adept at lecturing than listening. In her first five-day tour to the Middle East, Hughes brought up America's religiosity and claimed that the U.S. Constitution included the phrase, "one nation under God," which it does not. Her preachy approach, though well intentioned (isn't it always!) fell flat in a region where faith of another kind is in plenty supply too. As with democracy, America has no monopoly on faith. Ungar wrote in a *Baltimore Sun* editorial, "Countries, like people, that go around saying they are better than everyone else provoke resentment; others take pleasure in their woes. Claiming superiority based on religious faith never works."[47]

Ungar called for the U.S. to engage "in a long-term project to convince the rest of the world that it cares about the opinions and sensibilities of others. Difficult as this might be for a nation accustomed to behaving as a superpower, the United States might need to take those views into account in the formulation of foreign policy and in decisions to go to war." Imagine, a government that considers the opinions of its own and other citizens! Ungar highlighted the decision of Goucher College to be the first U.S. college to make study abroad a requirement for graduation. His hope is that a global citizen orientation will result among these American college students to "reverse the damage done by Ms. Hughes and other American supremacists." He offers a message of hope and optimism for public diplomacy that I share, one that will not come overnight or through a few focus group sessions: "I cannot think of a better way to improve the

American image abroad than to let others see how wonderfully diverse and free-thinking and pluralistic a people Americans are, much more able to engage in introspection and self-criticism than our official actions and statements would imply. That's bound to stir genuine admiration, but it might take a decade or two to fully imply."[48]

NOTES

1. Sam Keen, *Faces of the Enemy* (San Francisco: Harper & Row, 1986), 11.

2. Oskamp and Schultz, *Attitudes and Opinions*, 345.

3. As quoted in "S-11 Redux," a video compilation of the Guerrilla News Network, October 2001. Available online at www.gnn.tv.

4. See "U.S. Military Spending vs. the World," a report by the Center for Arms Control and Non-Proliferation, February 7, 2005, viewed online November 26, 2005 at www.armscontrolcenter.org/archives/001221.php.

5. "American Character Gets Mixed Reviews: U.S. Image Up Slightly But Still Negative," Pew Global Attitudes Project, June 23, 2005. Available in PDF format online at pewglobal.org/reports/pdf/247.pdf.

6. Oskamp and Schultz, *Attitudes and Opinions*.

7. "The Billions for 'Defense' Jeopardize Our Safety," Center for Defense Information, Issue 10, March 9, 2000.

8. Alexander C. Karp, Gary A. Tobin, and Aryeh K. Weinberg, "An Exceptional Nation," *Philanthropy* magazine, November/December 2004. Publication of The Philanthropy Roundtable.

9. Andrew Moravcsik, "Dream On America," *Newsweek International*, January 31, 2005.

10. George W. Bush, Joint Session to Congress, September 20, 2001.

11. Quoted in "Hating America," Mary H. Cooper, Congressional Quarterly Researcher, Vol. 11, No. 41, November 23, 2001, page 971.

12. Benjamin R. Barber, *Jihad vs. McWorld: How Globalism and Tribalism are Reshaping the World* (New York: Ballantine Books, 1995), 7–8.

13. David R. Sands, "America Enjoys View from the Top," *Washington Times*, National Weekly Edition, January 3–9, 2005, 1.

14. George W. Bush, 2004 State of the Union Address, January 2004.

15. "Arabs View U.S. Network with Deep Skepticism," Charlene Gubash, producer, NBC News, February 25, 2004.

16. Gubash, February 25, 2004.

17. Unsigned editorial, Al-Quds al-Arabi (Palestinian expatriate), London, England, Feb. 17, 2004.

18. Gubash, February 24, 2004.

19. Ed Finn, "Unhip, unhip Al Hurra," *Slate*, February 20, 2004.

20. William A. Rugh, Testimony to U.S. Senate Foreign Relations Committee, International Operations Subcommittee, U.S. Congress, April 29, 2004.

21. Bush Al-Hurra Text, Associated Press Online, May 5, 2004.

22. David Morgan, "U.S. Planning Arab Language TV Broadcasts to Europe," *New York Times*, February 27, 2005.

23. Munir Mawari, "Washington Plans to Counter Islamic Militancy in Europe by Extending Al Hurra Broadcasts to Europe," Washington, D.C.

24. *The Economist*, "Selling the Flag," February 26, 2004.

25. Linda Tischler, "Brand That I Love," *Fastcompany* Issue 88, November 2004.

26. See Business for Diplomatic Action at www.businessfordiplomaticaction. org/learn/index.html.

27. BDA website.

28. Kristina Sacci, "Brand That I Love," *Fast Company*, November 2004, 33.

29. "Changing Minds, Winning Peace: A New Strategic Direction for U.S. Public Diplomacy in the Arab and Muslim World," The Advisory Group on Public Diplomacy for the Arab and Muslim World, October 2003, 59.

30. Dan Roberts and Alison Maitland, "NGOs Win Greater Trust than Media and Big Business," *Financial Times*, January 24, 2005.

31. Eric Pfanner, "NGOs Gain Confidence of Public," *International Herald Tribune*, January 24, 2005.

32. Roberts and Maitland, *Financial Times*.

33. Keith Reinhard, Testimony Before the House Subcommittee on National Security, Emerging Threats, and International Relations, Hearing on the 9/11 Commission Recommendations on Public Diplomacy: Defending Ideals and Defining the Message, August 23, 2004.

34. Reinhard, Testimony, 4.

35. Reinhard, Testimony, 5.

36. Daniel J. Boorstin, *The Image: A Guide to Pseudo-Events in America* (New York: Harper & Row, 1964). First published in 1962 by Atheneum Publishers as *The Image or What Happened to the American Dream*.

37. Reinhard, Testimony, 6.

38. Boorstin, *The Image*, 261.

39. Condoleezza Rice, Prepared remarks before the U.S. Congress, Subcommittee on Foreign Operations, House Appropriations Committee, February 16, 2005.

40. David Hoffman, "Beyond Public Diplomacy," Foreign Affairs, March/April 2002. He is referring to Richard Holbrooke's question, "How can a man in a cave outcommunicate the world's leading communications society?"

41. Glenn Kessler, "The Role of Radio Sawa in Middle East Questioned," The *Washington Post*, October 13, 2004, A12.

42. For a full airing of our comments, see www.bbc.co.uk/radio/aod/events/whoruns/aod.shtml?wservice/wryw_live.

43. Henry Luce, "The American Century," *Life* magazine editorial, February 1941.

44. See CBC News, "What the World Thinks of America," June 17, 2003, available online at www.cbc.ca/news/america/poll.htm.

45. "Sales Pitch Falls Flat," *USA Today* editorial, September 28, 2005, available online at www.usatoday.com/news/opinion/editorials/2005-09-28-our-view_x.htm.

46. Leon Hadar, "Innocent Abroad: 'Karen Hughes' mission impossible," *The American Conservative*, December 19, 2005.

47. Sanford Ungar, "Preaching U.S. Supremacy Won't Help Image Abroad," *Baltimore Sun*, October 9, 2005.

48. Ungar, *Baltimore Sun* op-ed, October 9, 2005.

6

PUBLIC DIPLOMACY AND AMERICA THE BEAUTIFUL

A CAREER DIPLOMAT'S PERSPECTIVE ON PUBLIC DIPLOMACY

John Brown is a former American diplomat who resigned from the Foreign Service in opposition to the planned war in Iraq, stating in his resignation letter to Secretary of State Powell that "The president's disregard for views in other nations, borne out by his neglect of public diplomacy, is giving birth to an anti-American century." He now edits a "Public Diplomacy Press Review" that is hosted by the USC Center on Public Diplomacy. In spring 2005, Brown sent a memo to newly nominated Karen Hughes to offer his insights on American public diplomacy from a twenty-year experience working for the U.S. government. It is reprinted here with permission.

Memo to Karen Hughes

TO: Karen Hughes

FROM: John Brown, former Foreign Service officer

SUBJECT: Your New Job: Some Advice from a 20-year Public Diplomacy
          Practitioner

Ms. Hughes: The below is offered for your consideration as you think about your future position as Under Secretary for Public Diplomacy and Public Affairs.

1) Get real! Face the fact that the Bush administration's foreign policy will continue to be unpopular abroad unless major corrective actions are taken, both in substance and style. Yes, the recent U.S. "democratization" push may be viewed less negatively abroad than unilateral military strikes in the "war on terror." But foreigners are still intensely suspicious of American motivations and actions.

2) Don't assume the world is like (or likes) America, and that what worked in getting George W. Bush elected will be successful in "selling" America's policies abroad. Don't treat foreigners as just potential Republicans. Listen to what they have to say.

3) Forget about spin, focus on intelligent persuasion and bi/multilateral communications.

4) Remember that America is a country, not a product, and that it can't be "sold" to the rest of mankind like a brand to be consumed. Leave marketing to the business sector.

5) Always be present when important foreign policy decisions are made, be it in the White House or the State Department. Constantly remind other decision-makers that policy and public diplomacy are intrinsically linked and that foreign public opinion counts. You must be there on the take-off, not the crash landing, of policy—to cite the words your distinguished predecessor, Edward R. Morrow, head of the United States Information Agency (USIA) during the Kennedy administration.

6) With as little bureaucratic disruptions and endless "reorganizations" as possible, give public diplomacy an essential role at the State Department (today PD officers are second-class citizens in the foreign affairs bureaucracy).

7) Provide field public diplomacy posts greater autonomy, a larger budget, and direct lines of communications with your office at the State Department; remain in close contact with officers in the field. Visit the posts, using such occasions to inform foreign governments of the importance the USG gives to public diplomacy.

8) Remind political appointees assigned to direct public diplomacy programs in Washington that they should work with career civil servants with respect, and not micromanage them out of fear that they lack sufficient "loyalty."

9) Urgently deal with the Muslim world, but don't neglect other countries, including traditional allies. Forget about the flavor-of-the-month approach to foreign policy, when one region dominates all of Washington's attention at the exclusion of others.

10) Drop the one-size-fits-all attitude towards programs for overseas audiences; tailor outreach to individual countries and regions.

11) Increase educational exchanges worldwide and reemphasize the importance of cultural programs (e.g., exhibits, concerts).

12) Maintain funding for U.S. government electronic media directed to overseas audiences, but don't make them the be-all and end-all of public diplomacy. Provide greater support for local independent media. But do remember that people the world over do more just than look at TV and listen to the radio.

13) Bear in mind that public diplomacy can only do so much, and that it is not the solution to all our foreign policy problems.

14) Thirteen isn't a lucky number, so here's one more: Keep your sense of humor.

AN OUTSIDE-THE-BELTWAY PERSPECTIVE ON PUBLIC DIPLOMACY

When I worked inside the beltway (Washington, D.C.) at the U.S. Information Agency (1992–1994), the public diplomacy agency was clearly out of fashion and on its way out. I came into my public service position full of enthusiasm and interest in learning how the U.S. government promoted America's image and international exchanges. I also wanted to contribute to what I saw as a very worthy cause—promoting the best that America had to offer in exchanges, arts, and culture. As a former Fulbright scholar who penned a dissertation on the role of Fulbright scholars as cultural mediators, I was seen by some of my peers and superiors at the agency as a person with added value in terms of what I knew in a textbook sense about the history and theory behind U.S. public diplomacy. My boss, Addie O'Connell, who then headed the exchanges division, asked me to write some text about the Fulbright program for President Clinton's First Inaugural Address, a very heady assignment. The text was sent to the White House in the hopes that public diplomacy might get a mention, but it did not make the final cut. Nevertheless, it was clear as I observed my new co-workers that most USIA staff were very pleased to have Bill Clinton as president and thought that he would shepherd in a new era for post-Cold War public diplomacy. Government bureaucrats as a whole lean Democratic, and in fact, one day after Clinton's election in November 1992, there were spontaneous office parties celebrating the changing of the guard from Republican to Democrat. The impression was that Clinton, more than George H.W. Bush or even Ross Perot, would see the value of an agency like USIA, at least in terms of its promotion of American values in the world. Clinton did see the value of USIA, but more as a shadow to the Commerce Department in its promotion of NAFTA, market expansion, and U.S. business interests to target countries. We had discussions about the Coca-Cola Fulbright scholars that seemed a little too commercial-friendly for my tastes. USIA's second mandate, to promote mutual understanding between the people of the United States and people in other countries, was of lesser value, even to the Democratic president. The post-Cold War euphoria dictated that we no longer needed a prominent public diplomacy mission, or at least no longer needed an independent agency with a mission to "tell America's story to the world."

The United States Information Agency ceased to exist as an independent agency a mere five years after my departure. It is now part of the State Department apparatus, which offers a host of challenges and opportunities. One opportunity is the chance to elevate the status of public diplomacy. USIA was historically seen as poorer cousin to the State Department, the official agency for U.S. foreign policy production and management. I found that out from what my co-workers at USIA expressed as well as what I observed on a four-month work assignment to the State Department. The State Department was the Big Daddy to the little brother known as USIA. The DOS (Department of State) had all the heavy lifting to do in terms of making U.S. policy, while USIA simply had to carry the water buckets along the sidelines. But after 9/11 when America found itself missing a full-time agency devoted to winning hearts and minds, public diplomacy became prominent. Now everyone seemed to have an opinion about what the United States could and should do to gain influence in the world. Nobody seemed to care before 9/11, and even when I was at USIA in the mid-1990s, it was very difficult, if not impossible, to get much of any prominent press visibility for our programs. After 9/11, USIA would have a stronger voice by promoting public diplomacy to a position of Under Secretary and putting a face to the process, Charlotte Beers, who, though criticized by the press for her leadership, was nevertheless of great interest to them.

The great challenge now for any Under Secretary is to advance public diplomacy's combined mission: (1) to inform about us (people, culture, society) and tell our stories to the world, which is one-way, informational, and more aligned with propaganda efforts to win hearts and minds; and (2) to listen and learn from others, promote dialogue, international visits and exchanges in order to build mutual understanding. The second mandate, a two-way communicative, cultural mediation approach to international relations, is often at odds with policy formulation, which like it or not, is always more about us than them. Karen Hughes likely knows this all too well in her short tenure, and her predecessors, Margaret Tutwiler and Charlotte Beers, knew the same. Someone else who knows this all too well is John McDonald, Chairman and Co-Founder of the Institute for Multi-Track Diplomacy, and a 40-year U.S. diplomat. Most of us are familiar with Track One diplomacy when we watch Secretary of State Condoleezza Rice meet with her counterparts overseas. Track One diplomacy is the arena for formal, official, government-to-government interaction by designated representatives of sovereign states. It is the face of formal diplomatic relations, the publicity shot for what governments do across borders. Track Two diplomacy is much more hidden from public view, but just as important. It refers to nongovernmental, informal and unofficial ties between private citizens and groups, who interact and relate to each other outside the constraints of formal government power. Often these meetings are designed to bring people together who are in some type of conflict and require mediation. McDonald says, "Track Two aims to reduce or resolve conflict by decreasing the anger, tension and fear between peoples by improving communication and understanding of the other side's point of view. In no way is Track Two a substitute for Track One; instead, it complements and parallels the goals of Track One."[1]

While I was still at USIA, McDonald was meeting with USIA officials to promote Track Two citizen-based diplomacy and conflict resolution. Then Director Joseph Duffey approved an agency-wide Conflict Resolution Project Team in May 1994, which dissolved in a few months, but the

International Visitors Program continued to embrace the citizen diplomacy function, even if the agency didn't overall. In September 1996, McDonald led a State Department seminar, "Public Diplomacy and Conflict Resolution: Linking Track One and Track Two Diplomacy," which met with a resounding thud. Ten people attended. It is only now that the U.S. government in general and U.S. State Department in particular are beginning to see the need to expand Track Two-style diplomatic efforts. A promising development was the State Department announcement in December 2005 of a new journalism exchange program, the Edward R. Murrow Journalism Program, which brought 100 foreign journalists to leading journalism schools, including the University of Southern California's Annenberg School for Communication. From what I know about foreign journalists, they are likely to be very frank and open with their American counterparts about their impressions of the United States and U.S. foreign policy and hopefully the opportunity will exist for much interaction with students and private citizens. What makes this program so promising is that it offers extended ties across multiple sectors, including public, private, and nongovernmental and is being managed under the State Department's International Visitor Leadership Program (IVLP). My only concern is that the partner institutions will keep the journalists tied very closely to on-campus activities and the American public will have limited contact with these VIP journalists, but I hope that the program will get the publicity it deserves and that the journalists will return to their home countries with a balanced, informed, and highly diversified impression of what the United States represents.

It is evident that the world of diplomacy is no longer hidden from view and the public diplomat is becoming as much a face of a nation as its appointed secretary of state. The State Department is recognizing this more, but we still need more John McDonald types in to educate and train on the second diplomatic track. Public diplomacy is still mostly about promoting the national security interests of the United States than it is about promoting mutual understanding. It still overemphasizes an elite, top-down, official, and formal approach to international relations, with overseas visits that feature handpicked audiences, while underemphasizing the study of what citizens worldwide are doing to prevent conflict and create understanding. Why study citizen diplomacy? Because U.S. diplomats don't always get it right. McDonald points to three areas of concern in traditional U.S. international negotiation style and attitude: (1) arrogance,

(2) impatience, and (3) lack of listening. The arrogance is a result of a combination of being the world's sole superpower with an over 50-year legacy of American supremacy, and yet American negotiators don't believe that they come across as arrogant, even though McDonald states that "most diplomats from other nations believe that the United States is the most arrogant nation in the world." Because American negotiators naturally bristle at such a characterization and tend to discount it altogether, this leads to reinforcement of the arrogance of power belief. Americans are notorious for wanting change to happen almost overnight, when the world seems to operate on a much slower timeline. The American habit of not listening to global criticism "closely relates to their impatience and arrogance. 'Why should we listen carefully?' they ask. 'We already know what is good for you, and we will be pleased to tell you what your needs are and how we can fix those needs.' Because we have not developed good listening skills, which require patience, American diplomats are perceived as superficial, uninterested in other points of view, and therefore arrogant."[2]

John McDonald has much courage to write so frankly about the nature of the foreign policy process. My tenure at USIA and State included interacting with a number of Foreign Service Officers, most all of whom were extremely intelligent and very impressive to serve with, but the point is well taken that there is a tendency to see events through the prism of our cultural values, which can be perceived by others as not caring for their concerns or needs. Once again, it is the nature of our superpower status that we need to be even more sensitive to how others see us. Unlike John Brown, I did not resign my USIA position out of protest, but left at the end of my two years service required as a Presidential Management Fellow. I did leave USIA for academia, which in a sense, is a resignation that the U.S. government doesn't always welcome contrarian points of view on policy. Ever since my graduate school days, through my USIA tenure to today, I've been an outspoken critic of U.S. foreign policy and U.S. public diplomacy, not to draw attention to myself, but rather because I see some glaring insensitivities and a tendency to overplay the establishment card. Foreign policy making is still an elite-level game that expects and asks little from the general public. In turn, we are a woefully ignorant society on international relations matters, but not due to an inability to understand or even show interest in the subject. Rather, the masses are often seen in different roles as overly meddlesome, driven to distraction, or all too uninformed about international relations to be of much help anyway, so they are kept out of the conversation by and large. This is all too true when one reads dozens of reports on recommendations for U.S. public diplomacy.[3] The public has a minor supporting role, that of sidelined cheerleader, while the influentials and leaders from government, academia, and the private sector are given the heavy burden of advancing the American agenda to the world.

Washington, D.C. is still one of the most exciting places in the world to live because it is the seat of political power for the United States, but there are times when the beltway serves as a straightjacket for the truth. One has to be very careful about one's criticisms if you hope to make it as far as you'd like to go in your profession. As a tenured professor, I am much more at peace in the classroom where I am freer to lead class discussions on conventional, unconventional, global, and national perspectives, and not feel the strain of walking the line in support of U.S. foreign policies in the world. My own memo to Karen Hughes is in response to her early performance returns since taking the reigns of public diplomacy in September 2005. I do not have the breadth and depth of career foreign service officers like John Brown or John McDonald, but do offer some suggestions based on a common heritage of 20 years in the business of international exchange and cultural diplomacy.

Memo to Karen Hughes

TO: Karen Hughes

FROM: Nancy Snow, former USIA Presidential Management Fellow (PMF)

SUBJECT: Your New Job: Some Advice from a 20-year Public Diplomacy Recipient, Practitioner, and Scholar

Ms. Hughes: The below is offered for your consideration as you think about your position as Under Secretary for Public Diplomacy and Public Affairs.

1) Support active listening! Active listening is a behavioral approach to international communication that promotes mutual understanding and trust. It requires that all participants in a communication first receive and then accurately reflect the other's message before offering a response. Active listening, also known as empathic or reflective

listening, allows all partners in a communication exchange to release their emotions, reduce tension overall, and create an environment that is conducive to collaborative problem solving. It seems as if your "Listening Tour" to the Middle East in September 2005 did not live up to its billing. While emphasizing listening, the press reports of your visit were largely negative. The Washington Post's Al Kamen created his own montage of what newspapers said about the tour.[4] Among these were the following:

> "Preachy, culturally insensitive, superficial PR blitz."
>
> —USA Today

> "Non-answers, canned macabre."
>
> —Los Angeles Times

> "Fiasco, lame attempt at bonding."
>
> —Slate

> "Painfully clueless . . . pedestrian . . . vapid . . . gushy."
>
> —Arab News (The Middle East's Leading English Daily)

Active listening skills can be learned, and there is no reason that these negative headlines cannot be overcome by practice in the art of constructive dialogue.

2) Be mindful of too many references to President Bush, his love of freedom, his man of God position, for the world is at odds with him, even though it is he you have primarily served over your career. The President is the elected leader of the United States, but he is not America. In your position as Under Secretary of State for Public Diplomacy and Public Affairs, you are representing all of America, which was divided about whether or not to reelect Bush to a second term, and is now divided over war in Iraq and the President's handling of the war on terror in general. The presidential election outcome of 2004 reflects the American value of disagreement in opinion. Reflect all of America to the world, not just your boss's bidding.

3) Allow the voices of America to channel through your position as public diplomacy czar. Don't confuse your position with yourself.

You were appointed to this position because you have the ear of the president, but this position is not yours, it is ours. Public diplomacy is first and foremost, public. Please don't forget that.

4) Be careful not to vet only Bush-friendly visitors and/or U.S. speakers through your office. You will suffer from tunnel vision if your programs and directives are filtered. Allow critical perspectives on foreign policy to be reflected in international exchanges, international visitor programs, and public diplomacy meetings. It is a healthy example to the rest of the world to show it that we are not of one mind. Dissent and disagreement are what made America in the first place.

5) Make sure that public diplomacy becomes a front burner issue at the State Department and is not relegated to the status of what little old ladies do at Sunday afternoon tea.

6) Offer a picture of America that listens first, doesn't dictate, and leads by example, not rhetoric. America has no patent on democracy and freedom, but we can display our version to the world. Like the marketplace of ideas, let the world decide if it's interested in pursuing our example.

7) The world is more than the Muslim and Arab world. September 11, 2001 has overly emphasized a public diplomacy crisis in the Middle East and Muslim-majority countries to the disadvantage of other countries. Do not let the war on terror define all of our public diplomacy. It is overly self-serving and ultimately patronizing to the Middle East and Muslim majority countries if we see them only within a terror matrix.

8) Seek mutually beneficial relations with individuals and groups by raising the profile of citizen diplomacy and cultural exchanges. Advocate for as much expenditure on exchanges as we spend on international broadcasting initiatives. There is no greater opportunity to influence and potentially change a person's mind than at the interpersonal level.

9) Advocate the public in the foreign affairs process and extend the second mandate of American public diplomacy—the promotion of mutual understanding between the people of the United States and people in other countries. You can do that by studying the public diplomacy in other countries and allowing them to educate us about what works/doesn't work.

10) Increase people-to-people interaction where the government merely facilitates contact but does not dominate discussion. The Edward R. Murrow Journalism Program is just one example, but there are a thousand more opportunities to allow people to engage in open, unrestricted meetings that allow for dialogue free of government oversight and intervention.

11) Don't just work with elite institutions that tend to suck up all the oxygen in the room. America is a large living space and our international visitors need to get to know it outside of the better known cities and universities. Send them to the Blue Highways cities and towns and the lesser-known colleges and universities that may offer more publicity to the public diplomacy program than the big city that never sleeps.

12) Did I say, listen more, talk less? I know that Southern women like to talk a lot, since I am one, but we are also known for our hospitality, which means that we make our guests feel at home and allow them to direct the conversation.

13) Realize that public diplomacy is a long-term process that will continue long after your government service. Be realistic about short-term expectations.

14) Thirteen isn't an unlucky number to me!

AMERICAN PUBLIC DIPLOMACY AND THE TWO-WAY STREET

Tupac Shakur, a controversial rap singer who was gunned down in Las Vegas in 1996, shared words in his debut album, *2Pacalypse Now*, that addressed his own internal battles with self-identity as a young black male raised by a single mom who was a member of the Black Panthers, a revolutionary black nationalist party formed in the turbulent late 1960s. He shares an ongoing external battle with cultural identity, in particular with his words to conquer the enemy we know with education. Similarly, the United States in the 21st century is searching for its own internal and external compass in the declared war on terror that resulted from the attacks upon this country in 2001. As a public diplomacy advocate, I consistently monitor the rhetoric and tactics of American efforts to "win hearts and minds" in the war on terror. In particular, the rhetoric of public diplomacy is being increasingly linked directly to national security policies tied to particular administrations, a worrisome trend if a mutual understanding-driven public diplomacy is one's mission.

Battelle, a global science and technology firm headquartered in Columbus, Ohio, released a list of the top ten innovations for the war on terror in 2004.[5] Battelle's team of experts included retired generals from the U.S. Army, Air Force, and Marine Corps, as well as Ohio State University faculty. The team linked public diplomacy innovations directly to the U.S.-led war on terror that arose from the events of Sept. 11, 2001.

One innovation they predicted likely to emerge in the coming decade (2005–2014) is 21st-century public diplomacy that requires non-technical skills development in intercultural communication and advanced strategic communication. To that, I would say, touché! My worry is that intercultural communication is a bit of a strange elixir with counterterrorism efforts. We already have the problem of how to define just what we mean by terrorism. We have the problem in 2005 of the U.S. State Department deciding to no longer release annual statistics but relinquishing that role to the post-9/11-created National Counterterrorism Center (NCTC). This follows an embarrassing event in 2004 when the Bush Administration admitted "great progress" in lowering the incidents of international terrorism in 2003 to a thirty-year low as reported in the 2004 "Patterns of Global Terrorism," only to be caught later with its statistical hand in the cookie jar when it was revealed by outside reviewers that terrorist attacks that killed or injured civilians had actually increased twofold than earlier reported. Now the U.S. public has to be kept satisfied with the government's warning that global terrorism is still a threat but without real numbers to assess that threat. The lack of a gold standard in terrorism statistics is a result of the politicization of terrorism following the attacks on 9/11 and the subsequent wars in Afghanistan and Iraq where the U.S. government is reluctant to count attacks on U.S. soldiers as terroristic.[6]

The Battelle Report states that the war against terror is an ideological struggle between Western values and extremists who challenge those values. Since extremists distort the picture of the West to their advantage, "America needs to project a more balanced image of Western culture through strategic, positive communication. This could be achieved by communicating the Western message through targeted use of mass media, developing a next-generation Voice of America approach, perhaps supported with distribution of inexpensive, disposable TVs."[7] This is likely what Secretary of State Condoleezza Rice had in mind with her announcement in February 2006 that the U.S. government would request $75 million for communication efforts to promote democracy in Iran.[8]

While acknowledging the obvious strains in policy and projected images between the Middle East and the West, the Battelle definition of 21st-century public diplomacy and Dr. Rice's vision for transformational diplomacy in Iran offer primarily an asymmetric information model of public diplomacy that seeks to break down barriers in the Middle East to a Western worldview, message, and values. In contrast, the more accepted definition of intercultural communication is to seek a balance of understanding and mutuality between and across cultures in perspective, values, and norms. This is not to say that each culture cannot provide its own barometer of what's acceptable, moral, or valued by its own standard; the key is to avoid projecting a superior notion of ethnocentrism, which we know to be a nation's or people's overriding belief in its own superiority vis-à-vis others. My colleague in the College of Communications at California State University, Fullerton, Dr. Stella Ting-Toomey, is a worldwide leading scholar on intercultural communication. In her book, *Understanding Intercultural Communication*, she and Leeva Chung promote a synergistic perspective in intercultural communication, whereby problem solving in global teams "involves the core intercultural communication skills of mindful listening and careful perception checking. By mindfully listening to the diverse viewpoints articulated by members of different cultures, we can understand their cultural standpoints and expectations. Through mindful dialogue with culturally different others in a team, we can learn to 'bounce off' creative ideas that can incorporate the best of all cultural viewpoints."[9]

Further, they lay out a need for the field of intercultural communication to contribute to global peacemaking. When one thinks about 9/11, for most Americans we probably recall all the images of the Wall Street workers and the NYPD or NYFD. The killing of nearly 3,000 included people from all over the world and not just those home-grown. It is no irony that New York is now seeking to trademark an image of itself as home to the world, for indeed people from all over the world fell victim to the attacks of 9/11. This reality should make us pause when we think about making public diplomacy a nation-based phenomenon. Why not practice public diplomacy in concert with and not opposed to global peacemaking goals.

Ting-Toomey and Chung offer a different approach than the Battelle forecasters:

- To practice global peacemaking, we need to hold a firm commitment that considerations of fairness should apply to all identity groups
- We need to be willing to consider sharing economic and social resources with the underprivileged groups to level the fear and resentment factors.
- We need to start practicing win-win collaborative dialogue with individuals or groups we consider as our enemies.
- We need to display a mindful listening attitude even if we do not like the individuals or disagree with their ideas or viewpoints.
- In displaying our respect for the other nation or groups of individuals, we may open doors for more dialogues and deeper contacts.
- Human respect is a prerequisite for any type or form of intercultural or interethnic communication.[10]

Generally speaking, public diplomacy initiatives should be separated from battlefield tactics associated with counterterrorism. Otherwise you blend narrow and potentially ethnocentric national security outcomes associated with one nation or people with strategies and outcomes associated with mutual security and mutual understanding, i.e., International Visitor Program, Fulbright Program, Peace Corps.

In the definition of intercultural communication and public diplomacy provided by the Battelle forecasters, Western tension with the Middle East is causally linked to combating terrorism and overcoming oppositional cultures and values. It does not bother to address specific foreign policy disagreements with the United States that diminish public diplomacy efforts. Primary focus is on gaining understanding of another culture in order to better comprehend its motives and desires in order to combat terrorism, not to build mutual understanding that may improve the foreign relations of the United States, its people and government, with other nations and peoples.

While the Battelle definition of 21st-century public diplomacy is an accepted dimension of public diplomacy, PD, in practice and conception, uses multifaceted approaches to global communication. The Battelle version belongs to the political information side of public diplomacy that advocates the U.S. case, in particular, and the Western civilization model in general. Within this school of thought, it is most important that international publics gain a better understanding of the United States, its culture, values, and institutions, primarily for securing U.S. foreign policy ends and defending national security objectives. In other words, this approach makes public diplomacy "all about U.S." instead of "all about us" with people working together toward a common goal.

Missing altogether from the Battelle definition but included in the Ting-Toomey definition is the intercultural communication dimension of public diplomacy advocated by Senator J. William Fulbright, to foster "mutual understanding between the people of the United States and the people of other countries" as advocated in the Fulbright-Hays Act of 1961. In this framework, cultural comprehension is also sought, but not primarily for unilateral advantage and outcome (which by definition stresses fast media such as radio and television). Rather, long-term strategies for mutual benefit and mutual trust are emphasized, including slower media such as films, exhibitions, and educational and cultural exchanges (Fulbright, International Visitors Program). An intercultural communication dimension in public diplomacy should not be sidelined but separated from the more tough-minded battlefield tactics associated with counterterrorism.

WHAT THE YOUNG PEOPLE KNOW
(AND CAN TEACH US)

I have had the great privilege over the years to know thousands of students through my teaching. Anyone who doesn't love teaching should get out of the profession right away, because it is the kind of work that is almost like a calling. If I weren't teaching, I might just as well be preaching, so passionate am I about exchanging ideas with students and learning from them as often as I teach them. Teaching is a lot like that other Bully Pulpit. You have enormous powers of persuasion. There are times when I'm lecturing on a topic and I am taken aback by the rapt attention to what I have to say on a topic. I'd like to think that my life experience and book knowledge have given me a certain level of expertise, but I am never too arrogant to believe that I know better. I just probably know more, as I should. The dirty little secret about us teachers is that we have a Peter Pan Syndrome. We want to stay students forever, but since we can't, we become teachers, a close second to the perpetual student. I know that I'm younger in years because of my contact with young people and students in the classroom. Not all are so young these days. In fact, a few of my students have been much older than I, but with rich life experiences that contributed much to our class discussion. In my USC course on Anti-Americanism, I asked the students to not only study and learn about the topic, but really immerse themselves in living the questions. What can be done to overcome anti-Americanism? Has America lost its legitimacy in the world? If so, why? If not, what are we doing right and what can we do to maintain that legitimacy? I was so impressed with their diagnoses of the problem and solutions for change that I submit them here in excerpt. I first asked the students if they wouldn't mind being featured in my book and they happily obliged. To my students, thanks for your contributions, and thanks for allowing me to come along for the process. It isn't just a teacher that can change a student's life; a student can change a teacher.

Throughout the semester, we struggled with the definition of anti-Americanism. We weren't sure how legitimate the term was, given its pejorative context. No one generally aspires to become anti-American and even if one does, there is no agreed-upon definition of what the term really means. It is pretty much whatever you want it to be. I tried therefore to cover a variety of perspectives on the topic. Our first text, *Hating America: A History*, by Barry and Judith Rubin, provided a framework from which we could analyze the subject. To their credit, the Rubins spelled out how they defined the term, as I noted in chapter 2:

- an antagonism to the United States that is systemic, seeing it completely as inevitably evil
- a view that greatly exaggerates America's shortcomings
- the deliberate misrepresentation of the nature or policies of the United States for political purposes; and/or
- a misperception of American society, policies, or goals which falsely portrays them as ridiculous or malevolent.[11]

The problem with such a definition is that it doesn't acknowledge how much political manipulation and propaganda is associated with such a term. As many students observed, anti-American sentiment ala Rubin is always wrong. The blame shifts to the critic of American foreign policies who has no recourse for sentiment, views, or perceptions that are characterized as unpatriotic. They also became familiar with Daniel Flynn's interpretation of American antipathy. In his book, *Why the Left Hates America: Exposing Lies that Have Obscured our Nation's Greatness*, he writes, "While self-hating Americans make up but a fraction of the population, their influence is great. They are museum curators, journalists, college professors, librarians, and movie stars."[12] He is particularly incensed by the lack of credit these self-hating Americans give to U.S.-based contributions to the world. A book review by the media watchdog group Accuracy in Academia supports his thesis:

> The quality of life for nearly all six billion people on the planet would be unimaginably worse if not for the ingenuity of the American mind. From such basic inventions as the light bulb, to such groundbreaking ideas as the Internet, when America creates, all humanity benefits . . . John Walker Lindh once asked his mother, what "America has ever done for anybody?" Flynn mockingly asks, "apart from the telephone; the Internet; the computer; the television; air-conditioning; the laser; serving as a place of refuge for immigrants; [numerous] vaccines . . . generous allotments of foreign aid; nearly all popular entertainment; basketball; baseball; surfing; football; the lives of its own servicemen defending the freedoms of non-Americans; the example of self-government; economic prosperity; a more enlightened world order; the Panama Canal; the discovery of DNA; and other medical, scientific, and technological advances, what has America ever done for anyone?"[13]

Flynn suggests that American leftists get an anti-American flavoring from birth. These include a constant refrain that the West in general and America in particular are responsible for all the world's ills, that American power is ultimately imperialistic and greedy; that the rich in America keep getting richer to the detriment of the poor; that America is inherently sexist and racist; and finally, that American-style capitalism fails women, minorities, children, and the environment in general. Finally, the Left attacks the most prevalent religion in America, Christianity, for its intolerance to alternative values. "Every predominantly Christian nation in the West protects the freedom of conscience of practitioners of the other major faiths," Flynn responds. There is no other religion that so responds to diversity in belief than Christianity. Flynn challenges the America Left to overcome its self- and nation-hatred, but his characterization of left-leaning people as blanket promoters of neo-Nazi-like "Big Lies" didn't fulfill many students' need for a balanced perspective on a provocative topic.

The students then read British image consultant Simon Anholt's *Brand America: The Mother of All Brands*, which characterized America as the number one aspirational brand, along with noted linguist and U.S. foreign policy critic Noam Chomsky's interpretation of hating America and anti-Americanism. Chomsky sees such terms as "regularly employed to defame critics of state policy who may admire and respect the country, its culture, and its achievements, indeed think it is the greatest place on earth. Nevertheless, they 'hate America' and are 'anti-American' on the tacit assumption that the society and its people are to be identified with state power."[14] One student, Kelly, sums up her own take on the topic by referencing a controversial political activist in 2005:

> The Rubins and Chomsky illustrate how one extremely important term in American vocabulary is not only ambiguous, but also used to place blame on dissenting opinions. While the Rubins and Chomsky attempt to define an abstract term, "anti-American," the contemporary public realm holds no concrete definition. . . . Instead, individuals on both sides of the highly polarized debate assume their own stance is self-evident. . . . One example that specifically highlights the difficulty in the use of the term is the case of Cindy Sheehan. Depending on the person with the power to define, Sheehan has been heralded as both the ultimate American and the ultimate un-American. On the one hand, Sheehan has been called the ultimate American because she lost her son in the military effort to protect the U.S. In addition, after realizing what she considers to be the evils of the military [effort in Iraq], she used her First Amendment right to voice her opposition to actions she now argues are detrimental to the U.S. However, she has also been labeled "anti-American" because critics claim Sheehan uses the death of her son to criticize an operation that she initially supported. In addition, she has criticized (at times, severely), the President and government of the U.S. during a sensitive time of war. The division between the two points of view regarding the character of Sheehan revolves around the definition and subsequent perceived responsibilities of an "American." One side argues that an "American" is defined by the willingness to challenge acts which threaten to harm America and her people. The other side defines an "American" as a person who shows an unquestionable commitment to the actions of the country. While there is obviously a discrepancy in the definition of terms like "American" and "anti-American," there also remains a lack of debate over how to establish a neutral and appropriate definition for these words. . . . This abandonment of intelligent debate is the most fright ening and detrimental effect of using politically-loaded words. Variance and

dissent define America as well as any other democracy in the world. Men like Martin Luther King, Jr. added significant value to American society because they were not afraid to oppose the current societal and governmental structure. King did not achieve success through labeling or marginalizing his opponents, but instead through inspiring societal discussion to induce change. As King once said, "I criticize America because I love her. I want to stand as a moral example to the world."[15]

To underscore Kelly's analysis, criticism of America is often marginalized as anti-American extremism when it can be an opening for discussion and a revelation that other points of views must be considered, whether domestic or international. This was discovered by U.S. Ambassador to Canada, David Wilkins, who told a Canadian Broadcasting Corporation audience in December 2005 that 9/11 changed everything about national security and American self-interests. "9/11 forever changed the United States and the way we are willing to protect our citizens," including the globally unpopular U.S. war in Iraq that he linked to the post-9/11 U.S. war on terror. Wilkins said, "It may be smart election-year politics to thump your chest and criticize your friend and your No. 1 trading partner constantly, but it is a slippery slope, and all of us should hope that it doesn't have a long-term impact on the relationship. . . . It's easy to criticize the United States; we're an easy target at times, but the last time I looked, the United States was not on the ballot."[16] Wilkins implied, but did not specifically name Canadian Liberal leader Paul Martin for using American criticism to federal election advantage. Wilkins warned that Canadian anti-Americanism was detrimental to long-term goodwill between the nations. This remark, which followed the sunnier, "I've become one of the biggest fans of Canada," irked one audience member enough to respond, "Friends criticize friends, and friends pay attention to the criticism of others."[17]

So many of my students offered practical suggestions as to how to repair America's damaged reputation and image in the world. It won't happen overnight, they said, and it won't come easy. It will require listening to global public opinion with an ear toward understanding and not trying to immediately correct. Krystel writes:

In the end, we need to bolster our credibility. We should stop focusing on selling an image of America to the world and concentrate instead on understanding their criticisms. A powerful source [like the U.S.] can produce compliance, but only a credible source can produce internalization of a message. In order to regain credibility, Americans must always act in accordance to our values. Actions speak louder than words, and glittering generalities like "freedom" and "democracy" sound hollow in the face of hypocritical policies. We need to do a better job of listening to our neighbors, particularly those nations which hold the same values and commitment to democracy that we do. Public opinion matters. Political leadership cannot continue to act contrary to the wishes of its constituents. This is why world public opinion is called "the world's second superpower."[18]

Another student, Kristy, referred to U.S. foreign policy as "the dancing purple elephant in public diplomacy's living room." It simply cannot be ignored, she wrote. Anti-Americanism is bound to remain a politically contested and politically loaded term so long as the two, foreign policy and public diplomacy, are interconnected. She suggests that we abandon dangerous rhetoric like "a clash of civilizations" or "they hate us for who we are" and apply a principle of universality of values, something along the lines of the Marshall Plan's economic agenda. "The security of all nations and economic development will eventually benefit the entire world because of increased trade and security. If we believe in this simple economic concept then we should stop breaking the rules and simply help other countries, rather than impose our way of life on them, since eventually this will be in our self-interest."[19] Her classmate, Kat, agreed: "Tiptoeing around the 'elephant in the living room' of U.S. policy only increases the polarity of international opinions of America, so while Hughes' version of public diplomacy is well-intentioned, it may be simply contributing to dialogue about U.S. foreign policy that produces very negative results."[20]

Another student, Adam, describes different levels of anti-Americanism:

The United States has enemies and some of them are vicious. Enemies need to be distinguished from critics. If U.S. foreign policy changed tomorrow and a kinder and gentler U.S. developed, its enemies would not be satisfied. But, the change would take the focus off the United States. The radical Islamic world will never be satisfied unless Israel and other "devils" cease to exist. Their anti-Americanism is unique and does not fall into the patterns of anti-Americanism in the West. However, the U.S. has created more terrorism by its war on terrorism. The Iraq War has been a rallying cry for radical Islamists and a breeding ground for terrorists. The U.S. needs to befriend moderate Muslims.[21]

Finally, Catherine observes that a reduction in American antipathy must come through a two-pronged approach:

> Both the way Americans view themselves and their role in the global community and American foreign policy must change to reflect a more conciliatory position to others . . . rather than the adversarial one its projects now. As foreign policy reflects the internal feelings of the American people, both must move together down the path of reconciliation. The government must recognize the vital role the public plays in our foreign policy even if the public themselves are not the decision makers. The Bush administration needs to garner public support for a change in foreign policy and in doing so, Bush must grasp the opportunity for open debate to truly show our global community that our sincerity is not empty . . . We as a nation need to recognize that continuing to respond to terrorism with force may not be the appropriate course for us to take, but through collective action America may once again restore its legitimacy as a nation championing the rights of all citizens.[22]

I wish that I could have produced a complete distillation of these students' reflections on a semester-long course that took a long, hard look at a problematic subject like hating America at home and abroad. As learners, they were convinced that avenues of dialogue needed to increase, most readily through educational ties across cultures. Marissa noted, "As J. William Fulbright knew, the simple act of listening and sharing with each other is often the fastest route to a respectful and harmonious relationship. We must listen openly to the criticisms directed at our country and we must share our beliefs honestly and respectfully if we are to establish any sort of common understanding between our people and the people of other nations."[23] Throughout the semester, the students walked their talk and remained sensitive observers and respectful debaters, convincing me that America's best days may be yet to come.

PUBLIC DIPLOMACY, POWER ELITES, AND THE PHANTOM PUBLIC

> In the standard image of power and decision, no force is held to be as important as The Great American Public. More than merely another check and balance, this public is thought to be the seat of all legitimate power. In official life as in popular folklore, it is held to be the very balance wheel of democratic power. In the end, all liberal theorists rest

their notions of the power system upon the political role of this public; all official decisions, as well as private decisions of consequence, are justified as in the public's welfare; all formal proclamations are in its name.

—C. Wright Mills, *The Power Elite*

Throughout this book I have tussled with the concept of public diplomacy and the U.S. government efforts since September 11, 2001, to rescue America's image and reputation from further damage in global public opinion circles. I once worked the corridors of the U.S. government's effort in this process during the post-Cold War era of the early to mid-1990s. I know what the ideal of public diplomacy is: to effectively and openly communicate with global publics. What I've seen since 9/11 are efforts that, thus far, have been roundly criticized in the U.S. press and global media as ineffective media propaganda campaigns favoring broadcast television and radio, tailoring of pro-U.S. messages, and even deceptive psyops over open lines of communication. The public's input, criticism, and debate is missing in action. Rather, to paraphrase Walter Lippmann, we have engaged in public diplomacy with a phantom public. We have reduced public opinion to mass media management, a result of decades of corporatization and concentration of power in government and industry. This trend is nothing new in America.

Fifty years ago, C. Wright Mills published his classic sociological indictment of American society. Mid-'50s America had come under the throes of concentrated power. Local society had evaporated. Power had shifted to the national level and the mass media-friendly political candidate. Democracy was more myth than reality as government and corporate power were now merging into a two-headed monster. Mills identified three specific prongs of power elites emerging—corporative executives tied to the national interest; an ascendant military tied to a permanent concept of war; and a political directorate tied to both industries. By 1961, Eisenhower himself, the conservative Republican and decorated general, would echo Mills's prognosis with his reference to a military-industrial complex pervading American society. Most troubling to C. Wright Mills was the penetration and domination of the military into American foreign affairs and diplomacy:

The military ascendancy and the downfall of diplomacy have occurred precisely when, for the first time in United States history, international issues are truly at the center of the most important national decisions and increasingly relevant to virtually all decisions of consequence. With the elite's acceptance of military definitions of world reality, the professional diplomat, as we have known him or as we might imagine him, has simply lost any effective voice in the higher circles. Once war was considered the business of soldiers, international relations the concern of diplomats. But now that war has become seemingly total and seemingly permanent, the free sport of kings has become the forced and internecine business of people, and diplomatic codes of honor between nations have collapsed. Peace is no longer serious; only war is serious. Every man and every nation is either friend or foe, and the idea of enmity becomes mechanical, massive, and without genuine passion. When virtually all negotiation aimed at peaceful agreement is likely to be seen as "appeasement," if not treason, the active role of the diplomat becomes meaningless; for diplomacy becomes merely a prelude to war or an interlude between wars, and in such a context the diplomat is replaced by the warlord.[24]

In the power elite matrix, the civilian-based public, so lauded in the ideal of democratic pluralism, had been transformed into the mediated masses that were sidelined by the political process, reduced to distant endorsement of elite-managed opinion. In the present media landscape, at times such manipulation is downright deceitful at the source. C. Wright Mills bemoaned the loss of what he called a "community of publics" that he saw as necessary and fundamental to sustaining a vibrant democracy that could challenge the three prongs of power. He defined the term "public" as having essential features fundamental to good communication:

1. Virtually as many people express opinions as receive them.
2. Public communications are so organized that there is a chance immediately and effectively to answer back any opinion expressed in public.
3. Opinion formed by such discussion readily finds an outlet in effective action, even against—if necessary—the prevailing system of authority.
4. Authoritative institutions do not penetrate the public, which is thus more or less autonomous in its operations. When these conditions prevail, we have the working model of a community of publics, and this model fits closely the several assumptions of classic democratic theory.[25]

By contrast to publics and at the opposite end of good communication, we have a mass (as in mass media) that has the following characteristics:

1. Far fewer people express opinions than receive them; for the community of publics becomes an abstract collection of individuals who receive impressions from the mass media.
2. The communications that prevail are so organized that it is difficult or impossible for the individual to answer back immediately or with any effect.
3. The realization of opinion in action is controlled by authorities who organize and control the channels of such action.
4. The mass has no autonomy from institutions; on the contrary, agents of authorized institutions penetrate this mass, reducing any autonomy it may have in the formation of opinion by discussion.[26]

U.S.-led public diplomacy is geared toward the masses over the public. An informed, active public role is minimized in favor of the machinations of elites (diplomats, military men, political appointees, think tank fellows) who analyze the public diplomacy challenge from a top-down, military-media-industrial perspective. Having reviewed dozens of public diplomacy reports and hundreds of op-eds published since 9/11, few, if any, acknowledge any active, input-oriented public opinion role in public diplomacy that would model the definition of C. Wright Mills's notion of public. Whenever public opinion is acknowledged, and this is quite often, it is within a narrowly-defined context of control and management by the representatives of authority institutions (political, corporate, and military) who manipulate public opinion through mass media communications in the national interest. Global publics are viewed simply as targeted segments on the receiving end of a mediated message.

Given the absence of active publics, undue influence, and domination of the dialogue by power elites who control mediated messages, what current picture of United States' public diplomacy emerges? A widely-distributed and media-touted Pentagon-based report by the Defense Science Board Task Force on Strategic Communications said that U.S. public diplomacy "seeks through the exchange of people and ideas to build lasting relationships and receptivity to . . . [U.S.] culture, values, and policies. It seeks also to influence attitudes and mobilize publics in ways that support [U.S.]

policies and interests . . . In an age of global media . . . no major [U.S.] strategy, policy or diplomatic initiative can succeed without public support."[27] In this case, public diplomacy is an instrument of power used to advance U.S. nation-state interests. Mass public opinion plays a supporting—not a countervailing—role to existing national interest and U.S. foreign policies.

The subjugation of the public in public diplomacy is what has led to such negative outcomes so far in current methods to "win" the hearts and minds of global publics, particularly Arabs and Muslims targeted for tolerance conversion under the war on terror rubric. On December 22, 2005, the Department of State announced suspension of the print version of its Arabic language version magazine named *Hi*, a youth magazine project first launched in July 2003 at a cost of $4.5 million per year. The reason for the suspension, according to the Department, is "to develop quantitative data on how broadly *Hi* magazine is reaching its intended audience . . . part of a broader effort to develop a 'culture of measurement' and to evaluate regularly the effectiveness of the Department's public diplomacy programs."[28] This is government bureaucratese for "we're not sure what we're doing, and whatever it is, it's ineffectual." The *Hi* magazine suspension follows a short-lived advertising video portraying Muslim life in America that aired during Ramadan in December 2002, but was pulled shortly thereafter in 2003 after Arab and Muslim governments said they would not accept paid political advertising (i.e, propaganda media) from the United States on their broadcast airwaves. The U.S. media-driven public diplomacy efforts, including Al Hurra and Radio Sawa, are failing to connect with their audiences because the public is seeing through the medium to the message. The message is that the ultimate benefactor in these multimillion dollar campaigns is not global civic society but the American national security interest, which to these publics is a narrowly-defined self-interest of the power elites in the United States.

Following the release of the "Strategic Communication" report by the Defense Science Board Task Force, U.S. Representative Mac Thornberry (13-TX) filed legislation to establish a nonpartisan, nonprofit, Center for Strategic Communication. The Department of State would oversee bids for establishing such a center and earmark $250 million per fiscal year to fund the Center, which would provide assistance to federal departments involved in public diplomacy and psychological warfare campaigns, including the Departments of State, Homeland Security, Justice, and Defense: "The center's input would help government officials make decisions concerning such matters as global public opinion, media trends, and the way human behavior is shaped by culture, values, and religion . . . The center would assist the government in a variety of ways in devising communications strategies that promote diplomacy, provide a positive view of the United States, and respond to national security threats."[29]

Rep. Thornberry explained U.S. strategic communication as a much-needed improvement over traditional marketing and advertising efforts, all within the matrix of U.S. national security interests. He was introducing such legislation because military power alone could not win the global war on terror:

Strategic Communication is not marketing; it is not simplistic slogans; it is not simply looking for better ways to tell the world how good we are. Strategic Communication is deeper and more sophisticated than that. It is how we communicate with—and thus relate to—the rest of the world. It includes public diplomacy (how we communicate with people outside of the United States), public affairs (how we communicate with Americans and the media), international broadcasting, and various governmental information operations programs. It must, of course, utilize and take into account ever-evolving technologies. Any communication begins with listening and understanding, which is certainly where Strategic Communication must begin. We cannot conduct a poll or two and assume we know what the people think. We have to understand history, culture, traditions, values, and anxieties. Without that understanding, any attempt at communicating, much less influencing, will be futile. Our understanding must extend to networks of influence within societies and to the factors which influence human behavior. In addition to understanding attitudes and cultures, Strategic Communication involves engaging in a dialogue of ideas, advising policy makers of the implications of various decision choices, and developing and implementing communication strategies that can help shape attitudes and behaviors.[30]

While the idea of a strategic communication approach that emphasizes "understanding attitudes and cultures" and that involves "engaging in a dialogue of ideas" sounds like a perfectly reasonable way to engage a globally and civic-minded public, how does one reconcile this communications approach with the revelation that the U.S. military power elites are utilizing unpopular media propaganda efforts in Iraq? In November 2005, the *Los Angeles Times* reported that the Pentagon was paying journalists to write favorable stories about U.S. efforts in Iraq. Such efforts were part of a covert or black propaganda effort to plant positive stories about the American effort without revealing the source of the story or that such stories were paid for by the U.S. government. A *USA Today*/CNN/Gallup Poll published just before Christmas Day said that nearly three-quarters of Americans surveyed thought it was "wrong for the U.S. to pay Iraqi newspapers and journalists to publish and writes stories about U.S. efforts in Iraq." The Pentagon's response to such public criticism has been anything but conciliatory. Efforts to win hearts and minds of the Iraqi people will continue and even expand to other countries targeted as part of the U.S. war on terrorism with a projected budget of $60 million per year over the next five years.

Covert operations are common in wartime. Clandestine efforts to target the enemy in a conflict are warranted. The problem for the Pentagon in this context is that both the American public and Iraqi people are offended by efforts to "hide" the source of favorable news. The Pentagon brass was likely motivated to pay Iraqi journalists in order to balance good news with all the bad news the commercial media were bringing. This is no excuse for this type of media propaganda. It is expected that governments will engage in propaganda efforts; what is condemned here are efforts to patronize the public in world war era manners that were thought to have gone out of style in the twenty-first century. The Internet and global satellite have forever popped the cork on the genie that is global information and communications. We live in a world of an increasingly better informed public that is skeptical of being targeted with paternalistic information strategies that suggest the public just cannot handle the truth. It can. The power elites that dominate public diplomacy efforts need a public education themselves on how effective and meaningful a community of publics is to democracy and mutual understanding reform efforts at home and abroad. When such publics are ignored or manipulated through paid propaganda efforts, credibility of the source may be damaged forever, and no amount of public relations, marketing, strategic communications, or advertising effort is going to restore it.

A CALL FOR GLOBAL EDUCATION
IN PUBLIC DIPLOMACY

George Allen, Assistant Secretary of State for Public Affairs (the Charlotte Beers or Karen Hughes of his day), wrote in 1949, when the Cold

War was just a few years old, "I am not particularly concerned whether either gunpowder or propaganda have benefited or harmed mankind. I merely emphasize, at this point, that propaganda on an immense scale is here to stay. We Americans must become informed and adept at its use, defensively and offensively, or we may find ourselves as archaic as the belted knight who refused to take gunpowder seriously 500 years ago."[31]

Whether we call it propaganda or public diplomacy, the United States has for decades used all kinds of means to inform, influence, and engage with the world in order to market a more positive image of America to the world. Who is represented in this process? Opinion leaders, broadcasters, elites. Who is targeted? In broadcasting, mass audiences and in opinion formation, generally elites and up-and-coming influential types from academia, business, and journalism. Public diplomacy is a major aspect of nation branding. We use all kinds of means to influence, including bringing in persons of interest and position from other countries in our International Visitors Program (IVP), sending and receiving the best minds to study and lecture abroad through the Fulbright program, expanding our brand through international broadcasting endeavors that both inspire and are designed to capture reputational value. The 9/11 Commission Report issued in July 2004 recommended that the United States should strengthen its public diplomacy methods to win the hearts and minds of those in the world who may harbor resentment or misperceptions about the U.S. people, government, and culture. This recommendation emphasized the national interests of the United States in the context of a war on terrorism and protection of homeland security interests but it did not offer insight into what role or responsibility higher education institutions could offer in the realm of public diplomacy. I'd like to make a case for public diplomacy curricula in higher education, particularly those campuses that emphasize teaching and student-involved projects, and describe a prototype for a national higher education initiative in public diplomacy that would transcend nation-state boundaries and national security interests of the United States for one that embraces global security and citizen diplomacy.

Over the last four years I've taught an upper-division class in Global Media Systems. In it I've shared with my students the U.S. government's efforts in the arena of public diplomacy, most notably the radio and TV broadcasting efforts to the Middle East or new initiatives to bring high school students from the Middle East to the United States for education about a free society. I've spent twenty years either studying or being actively involved in intercultural and international communication efforts. Throughout I've become frustrated at the lack of programming on college campuses that integrate what's happening in the real world (terror, war, campaigns of hate) with the international resources on college campuses. We have a ready-made population of international students who serve as eyes and ears for intercultural understanding but how often do we engage these students outside the classroom? How many active research projects do we have that offer outlets for promoting mutual understanding, not just to serve national interests, but also the global public interest?

Why not establish a Global Dialogue Project (the "other" Gross Domestic Product), that would call on American universities and campuses to install a public diplomacy element into their international education classes. The GDP could be capped off with a proposed annual one-day GDP summit to bring together international education faculty, international students, international organizations (Fulbright, Sister City, Rotary, International Visitor Councils, Chambers of Commerce) for a diagnosis of the state of global citizenship in higher education. Such dialogue may help to internationalize college campuses to better walk the talk of global citizenship.

Public Diplomacy as defined by the U.S. Information Agency emphasizes a two-track process of informing, educating, and understanding: PD promotes the national interest and national security of the United States through understanding, informing, and influencing foreign publics abroad and broadening the dialogue between American citizens and institutions and their counterparts abroad. This second track of public diplomacy, sometimes called citizen diplomacy, is what J. William Fulbright emphasized in his vision for the Fulbright program: The Fulbright-Hays Act of 1961 incorporated provisions of Senator Fulbright's amendment in 1946 and the Smith-Mundt Act to establish a new educational and cultural exchange policy:

> To increase mutual understanding between the people of the United States and the people of other countries by means of educational and cultural exchange; to strengthen the ties which unite us with other nations by demonstrating the educational and cultural interests, developments, and achievements of the people of the United States and other nations, and the contributions being made toward a peaceful and more fruitful life for people throughout the world; to promote international cooperation for educational

and cultural advancement; and thus to assist in the development of friendly, sympathetic, and peaceful relations between the United States and the other countries of the world.

PD or "PubD," as we call it at the Center on Public Diplomacy at the University of Southern California, is not about advocating our side to foreign publics or delivering the best spun message of the day to target markets overseas; it is about what the business of public institutions of higher learning is—to understand, to inform, to educate. In the classroom, students and teachers listen to learn as much as they talk. Our campuses extol the virtues of international education and exchange, but we make far too few outlets for globally-minded students to come together. This is why Senator Fulbright wanted his namesake international exchange program to be moved away from the oversight of a U.S. government agency (USIA/State) to the Smithsonian Institution. He did not see his dream fulfilled, but his love of education in the service of public diplomacy remains my commitment.

According to Mark Leonard, director of the UK's Foreign Policy Centre, there are three dimensions in modern public diplomacy: (1) news management; (2) strategic communications; and (3) relationship building.[32] We need better measures in all three, but the third dimension of public diplomacy, relationship building, is of particular note to me as a Fulbright alumna. What has been called the Fulbright "ideal" or the Fulbright "difference" needs further analysis. There is some evidence that participants in government-sponsored exchanges are more inclined to participate in multilateral efforts to build global civic society. Over 200 former or current heads of state are Fulbrighters. Charlotte Beers once observed about the program that, "Coming from the private sector, it's hard to find anything comparable to the sheer productivity of our Fulbright and International Visitor exchanges. The $237 million spent in 2002 for about 25,000 exchanges, was magnified by the 80,000 volunteers in the U.S. and matching support from many countries like Germany and Japan. Considering that some 50 percent of the leaders of the International Coalition were once exchange visitors, this has got to be the best buy in the government."[33]

We could start out our GDP by surveying the experience and attitudes of incoming Fulbright scholars to all American university and college campuses. We need to marry two objectives—public diplomacy efforts that are clearly a national interest of any government—with vested interests in international education and create a one-day GDP summit to explore what campuses can offer in resources, perspectives, international programs, and research. Has anyone to date ever taken inventory to find out what campuses are doing to measure global attitudes, attitudes toward the United States, the ebb and flow of anti-American attitudes, how visa security problems impact higher education? There's no reason that we couldn't create an online database documenting what campuses do and see if there might be a possibility to inform local, state, and national governments about what college campuses can offer public officials in the strength and opportunities for understanding that international students bring to our respective campuses.

This is an initiative that is ripe for private-sector or foundation funding. Concerns about America's reputation and position in the world, the decline of Brand USA if you will, impact everyone from the corporate suite to Wall Street to the American campus. Keith Reinhard formed Business for Diplomatic Action in January 2004 to address disturbing trends in anti-American sentiment overseas, including toward American corporate brands. A recent NOP World annual survey of global consumer attitudes showed a declining regard and erosion in credibility for American brands, culture, products, and perceived values. World perception of America in 2004 was more about power and so-called striver values (wealth, power, status, ambition, material security). What's missing? Internationalism, which was one of the extremely/very important values attributed to the American culture in 1999.

BUILDING A CULTURAL (DIPLOMACY) ENVIRONMENT MOVEMENT

In the fall of 1992, I attended a book signing to support my American University professor Hamid Mowlana. He had edited a book, *Triumph of the Image: The Media's War in the Persian Gulf*, with two stellars in the field of critical communications, Herbert Schiller and George Gerbner. This was my first meeting with both, and fortuitously, I remained in touch with Schiller and Gerbner throughout the rest of their lives. George Gerbner influenced my professional development as much as Herb Schiller, always encouraging me to push the envelope of acceptable scholarship in the field of political and international communications. George never talked too much about his background, as most men of his generation did not. There was no need to self-promote. They let their great achievements speak for themselves. He never boasted about all his accomplishments: Dean of the Annenberg School for Communication at the University of Pennsylvania from 1964–1989; a decorated World War II veteran and former officer in the Office of Strategic Services (OSS), the predecessor to the CIA; "best dissertation" award in 1955 for "Toward a General Theory of Communication" from the University of Southern California; Editor, U.S. Information Service in Vienna, Austria, responsible for daily broadcast and print news for all U.S. forces serving in Austria (1946–1947). All of this I learned through our involvement in his last crowning achievement, the Cultural Environment Movement (CEM), often learning about George's history from other admirers. George's legacy after retiring from U-Penn was to take all his academic knowledge and bring it to the people, particularly those serving in the media and information industries—actors, artists, activists, among many other constituencies. He wanted us to understand the "Gerbner" approach to communication. Basically it was that all communication is based in political, social, and cultural action. In other words, it is a learning environment, not an ivory tower model or theory best left to peer-reviewed journals of inquiry. The environment of communication is what everyone is born into and it becomes as integral to our life's direction as parental, religious, or educational teachings and influences.

The rest of my work has built from the influence of those who came before me, persons like Gerbner, who wrote back in 1956 that "The structure of freedom is organized diversity whether it pleases or not."[34] His Cultural Indicators Project, which used empirical data to uncover the lack of diversity in the communications industry, inspired the founding of the Cultural Environment Movement. Both were based in part on how the stories we tell each other about our lives reflect the essence of who we are. Sadly, most of our stories are now commercially produced and propagated through marketing strategies that have more to do with selling than with the telling. The stories we tell are there more to bring eyeballs of consumers to advertisers. Even the so-called public interest in communications is more of a competition among special interests than a reflection of what the people want. What Gerbner called on all who care about communication and media was to liberate ourselves from its marketing imperatives, particularly the stranglehold of tax-deductible advertising expenditures that drive the stories we tell we other. This is taxation without representation so long as the stories told are narrowly defined by what the market will demand. George was able to articulate the problem of our times in a most articulate manner at our founding convention in March 1996:

> Most of what we know, or think we know, we have never personally experienced. We live in a world erected by the stories we hear and see and tell. Unlocking incredible riches through imagery and words, conjuring up the unseen through art, creating towering works of imagination and fact through science, poetry, song, tales, reports and laws—that is the true magic of human life. Through that magic we live in a world much wider than the threats and gratifications of the immediate physical environment, which is the world of other species. Stories socialize us into roles of gender, age, class, vocation and lifestyle, and offer models of conformity or targets for rebellion. They weave the seamless web of the cultural environment that cultivates most of what we think, what we do, and how we conduct our affairs . . . For the first time in human history, children are born into homes where mass-mediated storytellers reach them on the average more than seven hours a day. Most waking hours, and often dreams, are filled with their stories. Giant industries discharge their messages into the mainstream of common consciousness. The historic nexus of church and state is replaced by television and state.[35]

After inspiring us to fight on through the market clutter and noise, George would always caution us to recall the Soviet dissident toast, "And here is to the success of our hopeless endeavor." Coming from a Hungarian-born, anti-fascist who fought for America in World War II, it always got a laugh. But as George once said of his academic and activism work, "If nobody screams, you are not doing anything."

Why I write about George now is that he died Christmas Eve 2005 at his home in Philadelphia, Pennsylvania at the age of 86, and just weeks after his wife of 59 years, Ilona, died. I had last seen George at the International Communication Association annual meeting in May 2004 in New Orleans, Louisiana, where he was being honored for his lifetime work. It was the last time I was in that city before Hurricane Katrina. I said hello to George and Ilona and said, "You are why I flew in from Los Angeles." George and Ilona looked tired, she with Alzheimer's disease of several years, and he with the worried concern of a soul mate. I never saw him leave her side for one minute. He was as devoted a husband as he was devoted to his lifelong achievements. George's CEM did not continue into the 21st century; it suffered, as do many nonprofits, from staff overturns and spotty funding. I'll never forget George's pitch to me to become its new executive director in 2000 as I resisted and sought warmer climes in Southern California. CEM may not have survived, but I know that its visionary leader inspired a multitude of media reform groups including Free Press and the National Conferences on Media Reform organized by CEM "graduates" Robert McChesney and John Nichols. I do hope that these groups will initiate George Gerbner awards in the future that recognize stalwart research and activism on media and culture.

What I take away from my experience with Herbert Schiller and George Gerbner is to keep calling for liberating alternatives to the status quo. In the context of public diplomacy, I believe that we need to promote much more public participation in diplomacy efforts than we do now. We need to equalize these efforts and work outside our traditional hierarchies in government and business, Hollywood, Madison Avenue, and Washington, D.C. We can do that best through cultural diplomacy and educational exchange initiatives. Cultural diplomacy and educational exchange outcomes are very similar to our CEM mission. Cultural diplomacy has been defined as "the exchange of ideas, information, art, and other aspects of culture among nations and their peoples in order to foster mutual understanding."[36] George Washington University scholar Bruce Gregory, director of the Public Diplomacy Institute, refers to cultural diplomacy as a form of discourse communication:

> Discourse communication assumes people can engage in non-manipulative ways that lead to shared understandings and actions compatible with those understandings . . . Discourse theory relates most directly to those elements of public diplomacy that emphasize engagement and the exchange of people and ideas. It is less relevant to elements that emphasize advocacy, persuasion, policies, and strategic communications campaigns narrowly defined.
>
> Cultural diplomats import ideal speech and education norms. In their emphasis on listening and dialogue, they also import methods of hermeneutics. They value learning through questions, reasoned arguments, and orientation toward openness, not seeking to "win" every argument, not talking at cross purposes, considering the opinions of others, shared knowledge and working out common meanings.[37]

The idea of discourse communication in cultural diplomacy in turn supports a cultural mediation orientation in educational exchange, particularly sponsored exchanges like the Fulbright Educational Exchange

Program, International Visitors Leadership Program, and the Edward R. Murrow Journalism Program. These programs are public-private partnerships and include government funding, but not government control. At least this has been my experience as both a Fulbright student, Fulbright program desk officer at USIA, and International Visitors speaker and guest lecturer. The cultural mediation function of such programs is to engage, not dominate, to listen and learn, and to open up one's mind and outlook to another cultural perspective. The cultural mediator seeks to understand first without lecturing, to ask questions in a spirit of intellectual curiosity and not condescension. I wrote about this in the epilogue section of my 1992 doctoral dissertation, *Fulbright Scholars as Cultural Mediators*. At that time, coming at the end of the Cold War, the world was undergoing incredible shifts in democratic participation. The Fulbright program, like other prestigious international exchange programs, offered an opportunity to contribute to the global democracy movements. The United States, more than any other country, had the most to gain from promoting global exchanges at record levels and emphasizing cultural mediation outcomes in the process. Why? Because we were a country that has historically downplayed intercultural factors in communication processes, whether they were our own or others. We have often favored American models that enhanced amplification over active listening, leading to a neglect of the study of interrelationships between culture and communication. What I wrote back in 1992 could just as easily apply today:

> Our own neglect is highly ironic given that the U.S. as a culture is studied worldwide and as a democratic structure has been given much credit for triumphing in the Cold War. Through our example, we have whetted the world's appetite for change and progress. The neglect of our cultural heritage and the cultural heritage of other nations has contributed to some of our most significant foreign policy crises, namely Vietnam, Iran, and most recently, Iraq. Might we have learned more about the changes that were happening which preceded these conflicts had we gotten in touch with expatriates and others outside military circles who were experiencing these cultures firsthand? Did we learn enough from those experiences to better equip ourselves in handling cultural changes in Yugoslavia, the Russian republics, and the fundamentalist Islamic world?[38]

A recent survey of over 1,000 Fulbright alumni concluded overwhelmingly that the program promotes mutual understanding, global leadership, and cultural learning, outcomes that I found in my own survey of several hundred international Fulbright scholars in 1991.[39] The program has an alumni network of 300,000 since 1946, yet few are being asked to contribute to its legacy. The problem may be that our cultural and educational channels are still too bureaucratized, hierarchical, and short-term in their thinking, which leads us to favor crisis communications, mass media broadcasting, and covert propaganda strategies over cultural learning. The 9/11 Commission released its report card of commission recommendations in December 2005, including public diplomacy efforts in scholarship, educational and library programs and it was barely a passing grade: A "D" for increasing our funding overall in educational and cultural exchange, but at the same time closing down more American libraries overseas, and watching numbers decline of young people from the Middle East who are studying in the United States, an obvious fallout from visa and national security restrictions after 9/11.[40] This is not a report card you can bring home to Mom. This follows a September 2005 Congressional Research Service report for Congress that indicated more than half of 29 public diplomacy reports completed between 1999 and 2005 called for an expansion of international exchanges and American libraries overseas, "making it the most common proposal among this group of reports."[41] Ten of the twenty-nine studies called for the White House to take a more involved and coordinated role in public diplomacy promotion, a recommendation with which I strongly disagree. Whether it's a Republican or Democrat in the highest branch of our executive government is not the issue. My worry is that public diplomacy will become too elitist and inaccessible to the public if its activities are monitored too closely by the White House. This is not to say that the White House shouldn't care about public diplomacy—it should, but at an arm's length. Right now public diplomacy is already too closely attached to the war on terrorism as defined by the current leadership in the White House. Washington in general is always focused on short-term policy concerns.

A longer-term solution with less policy focus would be for every member of Congress to have a public diplomacy plan for his/her respective state, including coordinating international exchangees in and out of each state with a public diplomacy plan of action. This would help to improve overall communication between the United States and other countries in the world if we sought to return more public diplomacy function to the state level and at the grassroots. Right now, the global media and global public opinion polls are focused so much on President George W. Bush and his lack of global leadership. A public diplomacy plan that sought to strengthen public diplomacy in the White House would only intensify the anti-American sentiment directed at the American president. Anti-American sentiment is not as often directed at the state level. In fact, when Hurricane Katrina hit the Gulf states of the South, a great deal of international sympathy was extended to its victims, including the hard-hit New Orleans, a much beloved American city to global travelers. The criticism for the hurricane cleanup fell on the president's shoulders once again, including his crony-like supporters like Michael Brown, then head of the Federal Emergency Management Agency (FEMA). It might help diffuse some of the criticism if American citizens took up the cause of public diplomacy for themselves state-to-state and city-to-city. We already do that through international organizations like Sister City International and Rotary Clubs, but we should expand these groups' visibility and membership in our local communities. We should identify all the Fulbright visiting scholars and students at all state universities as well as visiting foreign journalists who are often holed away at our colleges and universities for one or more semesters without much fanfare or awareness on the part of the greater community. Once identified, schools and universities should open their doors at least once a year for a global education day, inviting private citizens, local elementary and high schools, and community leaders to roundtable sessions and lectures on the value of learning about America and the world. This would serve the call for more local engagement, two-way information exchange, and two-way dialogue that so many public diplomacy reports have suggested.

Twenty years ago when I received my Fulbright grant, my hometown newspaper, *The Greenville News*, ran an announcement of the award. Local newspapers love to brag about their home-grown citizens' achievements. As a Fulbright student, I saw my role as part cultural ambassador for the United States, part student ambassador for educational exchange, and part promoter of peace and conflict resolution through exchange. The beauty of the Fulbright program was that when I received the grant, I had no sense that the U.S. government was even involved in the program. My letter of congratulations came from New York's Institute for International Education (IIE) that oversees all U.S. and international student grants through a subcontract with what was then the U.S. Information Agency, which practically no American at the time would have heard of, and now the U.S. State Department's Bureau for Educational and Cultural Affairs. Fulbrighters are given publicly-supported opportunities from home and host governments to pursue graduate-level research. It is this hands off government approach to educational exchange that propelled me toward education in general and international relations study in particular.

Any student who asks me, "What should I do now?" is often met with the quick response, "Leave home." I mean leave your home country and visit the world. If you want to love this country more than you do now, you must leave it to know it better and represent what it really is to the rest of the world. Hollywood, CNN, and even Fox News Channel cannot do that for us. I believed then, as I do now, that culture is the center of our communication process and that cultural exchanges like the Fulbright program expose students from other countries to the great ideas of this country—liberty, economic enterprise, political activism, and advocacy. In turn, American students going abroad have an opportunity to continue to engage in discursive communication with others who may harbor resentment toward Western society, a resentment that we know from research is fueled more by mass mediated messages than personal experience. We have focused this resentment in the Middle East, but that's too narrow a focus. Global opinion tells us that America is losing its leadership acumen in many parts of the world, including Australia, Canada, and parts of Asia and Europe where we were once known as the "good guys" and "liberators" for decades after World War II and the duration of the Cold War.

It is my hope that America will continue to be a leader in international engagement and remain a vital part of global development, humanitarianism, and aid. The world very much needs our know-how, can-do spirit, and our optimism about the future just as we need to learn about the values and perspectives that the world has to offer us. We may not hear it said "We are all Americans" but perhaps we'll be seen again as important and valued members of the global community, as needed and beneficial as any other nation of people with an inspiration and aspiration of diverse and democratic values and voices to share.

NOTES

1. John McDonald, "The Track Not Taken," *Harvard International Review* 22, no. 3, 2000: 68.

2. McDonald, "Track Not Taken."

3. These reports are summarized in a State Department–approved review of 29 articles and studies on public diplomacy, "Public Diplomacy: A Review of Past Recommendations," by Susan B. Epstein and Lisa Mages, Congressional Research Service, September 2, 2005.

4. Al Kamen, "In the Loop: Over Here, An Earful," *Washington Post*, October 7, 2005, A21.

5. www.battelle.org/forecasts/terror.stm

6. Susan B. Glasser, "Annual Terror Report Won't Include Numbers," *Washington Post* April 19, 2005, A17.

7. www.battelle.org/forecasts/terror.stm

8. www.state.gov/r/pa/prs/ps/2006/61268.htm

9. Ting-Toomey and Chung, *Understanding Intercultural Communication*, 9–10.

10. Ting-Toomey and Chung, 13.

11. Barry and Judith Colp Rubin, *Hating America*, ix.

12. Daniel Flynn, *Why the Left Hates America: Exposing the Lies That Have Obscured Our Nation's Greatness*, New York, Three Rivers Press, 2004, 4–5.

13. George Livadas, Review of *Why the Left Hates America: Exposing the Lies That Have Obscured Our Nation's Greatness* by Daniel J. Flynn, Prima Publishing, October 23, 2002, www.academia.org/reviews/why.html.

14. Noam Chomsky, *Hegemony or Survival: America's Quest for Global Dominance*, New York, Metropolitian Books, 2003, 45.

15. Kelly, Final Paper, "Anti-Americanism: Hating America at Home and Abroad," University of Southern California, Annenberg School for Communication, December 8, 2005, 4–5. Students' last names have been dropped to protect their identities.

16. CBC News, "Martin rejects U.S. Ambassador's rebuke," December 13, 2005;   www.cbc.ca/story/canadavotes2006/national/2005/12/13/wilkins-051213.html.

17. Canadian Broadcasting Corporation, "U.S. Ambassador Charms, Irks Local Audience," December 15, 2005.

18. Krystel, Final Paper, "Anti-Americanism: Hating America at Home and Abroad," University of Southern California, Annenberg School for Communication, December 8, 2005, 4.

19. Kristy, Final Paper, "Anti-Americanism: Hating America at Home and Abroad," University of Southern California, Annenberg School for Communication, December 8, 2005.

20. Katherine, Final Paper, "Anti-Americanism: Hating America at Home and Abroad," USC Annenberg School for Communication, December 8, 2005.

21. Adam, Final Paper, USC Annenberg, December 8, 2005.

22. Catherine, Final Paper, USC Annenberg, December 8, 2005, 5.

23. Marissa, Final Paper, USC Annenberg, December 8, 2005.

24. C. Wright Mills, *The Power Elite*, New York, Oxford University Press, 2000, 205–206.

25. C. Wright Mills, Oxford, 303–304.

26. Mills, 304.

27. Report of the Defense Science Board Task Force, "Strategic Communication," Washington, D.C., Department of Defense, September 2004, 12.

28. Media Note, "Suspension of 'Hi' magazine," Office of the Spokesman, U.S. Department of State, December 22, 2005.

29. H.R. 1869, Strategic Communication Act of 2005, Section 2.(c), duties of the Center.

30. Rep. Mac Thornberry, Floor Statement on H.R. 1869, "Strategic Communication Act," April 28, 2005.

31. Anholt, *Brand America*, 48.

32. Mark Leonard, *Public Diplomacy*, London, Foreign Policy Centre, 2002.

33. Charlotte Beers, "U.S. Public Diplomacy in the Arab and Muslim Worlds," Washington, D.C., Washington Institute for Near East Policy, May 7, 2002.

34. *A Different Road Taken: Profiles in Critical Communication*, John A. Lent, ed. (Boulder, CO: Westview Press, 1995), 101.

35. George Gerbner, "Why the Cultural Environment Movement," commposite.uqam.ca/videaz/docs/gegeen.html.

36. As quoted in Bruce Gregory, "Public Diplomacy and Strategic Communication: Cultures, Firewalls, and Imported Norms," American Political Science Association Conference on International Communication and Conflict, George Washington University and Georgetown University, Washington, D.C., August 31, 2005. Available online at cct.georgetown.edu/apsa/gregory.pdf. Original reference in Milton C. Cummings, Jr., Cultural Diplomacy and the United States Government: A Survey, Washington, D.C., Center for Arts and Culture, 2003, 1. Available online at www.culturalpolicy.org/pdf/MCCpaper.pdf.

37. Gregory, "Public Diplomacy and Strategic Communication," August 31, 2005.

38. Nancy Elizabeth Snow, "Fulbright Scholars as Cultural Mediators: An Exploratory Study," American University unpublished doctoral thesis, 1992, 194–197.

39. exchanges.state.gov/education/evaluations/onepagers/UFS.pdf.

40. www.9-11pdp.org.

41. Susan B. Epstein and Lisa Mages, "Public Diplomacy: A Review of Past Recommendations," (Washington, D.C.: Congressional Research Service, 2005), 11.

BIBLIOGRAPHY

SELECT INTERNET SOURCES

Anti-Americanism Pubdip: pubdip-swicki.eurekster.com/anti-americanism/
BBC News: news.bbc.co.uk/
Business for Diplomatic Action: www.businessfordiplomaticaction.org
Common Dreams: www.commondreams.org
Council on Foreign Relations: www.cfr.org
Dr. Nancy Snow's website of American Persuasion, Influence and Propaganda: www.nancysnow.com
Dr. Philip M. Taylor's website of International Communications and Strategic Communications: ics.leeds.ac.uk/papers/index.cfm?outfit=pmt
Eccentric Star: A Public Diplomacy Weblog: eccentricstar.typepad.com/public_diplomacy_weblog_n/
Foreign Policy Centre: fpc.org.uk/topics/public-diplomacy/
Fulbright Association: www.fulbrightalumni.org/olc/pub/FBA/gfn/grants.html
Global Journalist: www.globaljournalist.org
National Council for International Visitors: www.nciv.org
New Perspectives Quarterly: www.digitalnpq.org
Pew Global Attitudes Project: pewglobal.org/
Pew Research Center for People and the Press: people-press.org
Place Branding: www.placebranding.com
Program on International Policy Attitudes (PIPA) World Public Opinion: www.worldpublicopinion.org
The Global Beat: www.bu.edu/globalbeat/
United Nations Educational, Scientific and Cultural Organization: www.unesco.org

USC Center on Public Diplomacy: uscpublicdiplomacy.org
USIA Alumni Association: www.publicdiplomacy.org
U.S. Department of State: www.state.gov
Watching America: www.watchingamerica.org
World Press: www.worldpress.org/bib

BOOKS

Althen, Gary. Ed. *Learning Across Cultures*. Washington, D.C.: NAFSA, Associ-
    ation of International Educators, 1994.
Anholt, Simon, and Jeremy Hildreth. *Brand America: The Mother of All Brands*.
    London: Cyan Books, 2004.
Arndt, Richard T. *The First Resort of Kings: American Public Diplomacy in the
    Twentieth Century*. Dulles, VA: Potomac Books, Inc., 2005.
Barber, Benjamin R. *Jihad vs. McWorld: How Globalism and Tribalism are Re-
    shaping the World*. New York: Ballantine Books, 1995.
Boorstin, Daniel J. *The Image: A Guide to Pseudo-Events in America*. New York:
    Harper & Row, 1964. First published in 1962 by Atheneum Publishers as *The
    Image or What Happened to the American Dream*.
Carlyle, Thomas. *On Heroes: Hero Worship and the Heroic in History*. London:
    H.R. Allenson, 1905.
Chomsky, Noam. *Hegemony or Survival: America's Quest for Global Dominance*.
    New York: Metropolitan Books, 2003.
Creel, George. *How We Advertised America*. New York: Harper & Row, 1920.
De Beer, Arnold S., and John C. Merrill. *Global Journalism*. New York: Pearson,
    2004.
De Tocqueville, Alexis. *Democracy in America*. Volume 1. Contributors: John
    Bigelow, Henry Reeve, translator. New York: D. Appleton and Company, 1899.
———. *Democracy in America*. Volume 2. New York: D. Appleton and Co., 1899.
Ellul, Jacques. *Propaganda*. New York: Vintage Books, 1973.
Fulbright, J. William. *The Price of Empire*. New York: Pantheon, 1989.
———. *The Pentagon Propaganda Machine*. New York: Liveright, 1970.
———. *The Arrogance of Power*. New York: Vintage Books, 1966.
Gass, Robert H., and John S. Seiter. *Persuasion, Social Influence and Compliance
    Gaining*. 2d ed. Boston: Allyn & Bacon, 2003.
Gibson, John. *Hating America: The New World Sport*. New York: Regan Books,
    2005.
Goldberg, Bernard. *Bias: A CBS Insider Exposes How the Media Distort the
    News*. Washington, D.C.: Regnery, 2002.

Habermas, Juergen. *The Structural Transformation of the Public Sphere: An Inquiry into a Category of Bourgeois Society.* Translated by Thomas Burger. London: Polity Press, 1989.

Howe, Stephen. *Empire.* London: Oxford University Press, 2004.

Huxley, Aldous. *Brave New World Revisited.* New York: Perennial Classics, 2000. Originally published in 1958 by Harper & Row publishers.

Kamalipour, Yahya, and Nancy Snow, eds. *War, Media and Propaganda: A Global Perspective.* Eds. Lanham, MD: Rowman & Littlefield, 2004.

Keen, Sam. *Faces of the Enemy.* San Francisco: Harper & Row, 1986.

Kohls, L. Robert. *Survival Kit for Overseas Living.* Yarmouth, ME: Intercultural Press, 2001.

Kurtz, Howard. *Spin Cycle: Inside the Clinton Propaganda Machine.* New York: The Free Press, 1998.

Lederer, William J., and Eugene Burdick. *The Ugly American.* New York: W.W. Norton and Company, 1958.

Lent, John A., ed. *A Different Road Taken: Profiles in Critical Communication.* Boulder, CO: Westview, 1995.

Lippmann, Walter. *Public Opinion.* New York: Free Press, 1997. Originally published in 1922 by Macmillan.

Manning, Martin. *Historical Dictionary of American Propaganda.* Westport, CT: Greenwood Press, 2004.

Maxwell, Richard. *Herbert Schiller.* Lanham, MD: Rowman and Littlefield, 2003.

Maynard, Senko K. *Japanese Communication: Language and Thought in Context.* Honolulu: University of Hawaii Press, 1997.

McIntire, Mike. "New York Wants to Be 2nd Home™ To the World." *New York Times,* February 17, 2005, A25.

Oskamp, Stuart, and P. Wesley Schultz, *Attitudes and Opinions.* Third ed. Mahwah, NJ: Lawrence Erlbaum Associates, 2005.

Pratkanis, Anthony, and Elliot Aronson. *Age of Propaganda.* New York: W.H. Freeman & Company, 2001.

Reeves, Richard. *What the People Know.* Cambridge, MA: Harvard University Press, 1998.

Rubin, Barry, and Judith Colp Rubin. *Hating America: A History.* New York: Oxford University Press, 2004.

Schiller, Herbert I. *Living in the Number One Country.* New York: Seven Stories Press, 2000.

———. *Communication and Cultural Domination.* New York: International Arts and Sciences Press, 1976.

Snow, Nancy. *Information War: American Propaganda, Free Speech, and Opinion Control Since 9/11.* New York: Seven Stories Press, 2004.

————. *Propaganda, Inc.: Selling America's Culture to the World.* 2d ed. New York: Seven Stories Press, 2002.

Ting-Toomey, Stella, and Leeva C. Chung. *Intercultural Communication.* Los Angeles, CA: Roxbury, 2005.

Wolfe, Tom. *I Am Charlotte Simmons.* New York: Simon & Schuster, 2004.

ARTICLES, PAMPHLETS, SPEECHES, AND REPORTS

Abcarian, Robin. " 'War'? Oh, that's over." *Los Angeles Times.* August 1, 2005.

Abdulkareem, Khaled. "U.S. War on Terror—A Middle Eastern Perspective." *Foreign Service Journal.* April 2002.

Aljazeera.com editorial. "Bush issues staunch warning against Iran and Syria," International English Language Edition. February 3, 2005.

Alter, Jonathan. "Truth: The Best Propaganda," *Newsweek*, March 4, 2002.

American Foreign Service Association. *Foreign Service Journal.* Focus on "How is the War Selling?" April 2002. www.afsa.org/fsj/2002.cfm.

Amr, Hady. "The Need to Communicate: How to Improve U.S. Public Diplomacy with the Islamic World." Washington, D.C.: The Brookings Institution, January 2004. www.brookings.edu/fp/saban/analysis/amr20040101.htm.

Banerjee, Bidisha. "GOP Master Plan Revealed." *Slate.* February 23, 2005. slate.msn.com/id/2113945/.

Bush, George W. Press Conference. The White House. January 26, 2005. www.whitehouse.gov/news/releases/2005/01/20050126-3.html.Bush.

————. State of the Union Address, February 2, 2005.

————. State of the Union Address, January 2004.

————. Televised National Press Conference, October 11, 2001.

————. Joint Session to Congress. September 20, 2001.

Campbell, Susan. "Propaganda, Journalism, and Knowing the Difference. *Hartford Courant*, February 2, 2005.

Caro, Mark. "Movie Review: Control Room." *Chicago Tribune*, June 11, 2004.

Center for Public Integrity. "Networks of Influence: The Political Power of the Communications Industry." Washington, D.C. May 2005.

Center for Arms Control and Non-Proliferation. "U.S. Military Spending vs. the World." February 7, 2005. www.armscontrolcenter.org/archives/001221.php (26 Nov. 2005).

Center for Defense Information. "The Billions for 'Defense' Jeopardize Our Safety," Issue 10. March 9, 2000. www.cdi.org.

Colombani, Jean-Marie. "We Are All Americans." *Le Monde*, September 12, 2001.

Cowan, Geoffrey. "Hughes offers steps, not spin." *USA Today*. September 28, 2005.

Culbert, David. "Film (Feature)." Pp. XXX in *Propaganda and Mass Persuasion: A Historical Encyclopedia, 1500 to the Present*, edited by Nicholas J. Cull, David Culbert, and David Welch. Santa Barbara, CA: ABC-CLIO, Inc., 2003.

Dao, James, and Eric Schmitt. "Pentagon Readies Efforts to Sway Sentiment Abroad." *New York Times*, February 19, 2002.

De Grazia, Victoria. "Bush Team Enlists Madison Avenue in War on Terror." *New York Times*, August 26, 2002.

Donsbach, Wolfgang. "Communication and Natural Disasters: What the Tsunami Tells Us." International Communication Association newsletter. Message from the President, 2005. www.icahd.org.

Economist, The. "Anti-Americanism: The View From Abroad." February 19, 2005.

Economist, The. "Selling the Flag." February 26, 2004.

Epstein, Susan B., and Lisa Mages. "Public Diplomacy: A Review of Past Recommendations." Congressional Research Service. September 2, 2005.

Finn, Ed. "Unhip, unhip Al Hurra." *Slate*, February 20, 2004.

Fisher, William. "How Free is the US Press?" *Inter Press Service*, May 6, 2005.

Fitzgerald, Mark. "Freedom House: Press Liberty Declined Worldwide in 2004." *Editor & Publisher*, April 29, 2005.

Freedom House. "Freedom of the Press 2005: A Global Survey of Media Independence." freedomhouse.org/research/pressurvey/pfs2005.pdf.

Friedman, Thomas L. "Read My Ears." *New York Times*, January 27, 2005, A27.

Fuentes, Carlos. "Bush is Giving Latin America the Willies." *Los Angeles Times*, September 26, 2004.

Galupo, Scott. "Positively Clueless." *Washington Times*, March 4, 2005.

Glasser, Susan B. "Annual Terror Report Won't Include Numbers." The *Washington Post*, April 19, 2005, A17.

Gumbell, Andrew. "Bush Turns Us On to Fake Television News." *The Independent*, March 14, 2005.

Hadar, Leon. "Innocent Abroad: Karen Hughes' Mission Impossible." *The American Conservative*. December 19, 2005.

Havrilesky, Heather. "The Selling of 9/11." *Salon*, September 7, 2002.

Hoffman, David. "Beyond Public Diplomacy." *Foreign Affairs*. March/April 2002.

Hyde, Henry. "Speaking to our Silent Allies: The Role of Public Diplomacy in U.S. Foreign Policy." Speech delivered to the Council on Foreign Relations, June 17, 2002.

———. "Public Diplomacy & U.S. Foreign Policy." Text of an address delivered to the Council on Foreign Relations by U.S. Rep. Henry J. Hyde (R- IL), chairman of the House International Relations Committee, June 18, 2002. www.house.gov/hyde/statements2002/diplomacy.htm.

Inglehart, Ronald. "1990 World Values Survey." Ann Arbor, MI: Institute for Social Research, 1990. Question 3 F.

Johnson, Stephen, and Helle Dale. "Reclaiming America's Voice Overseas." Washington, D.C.: The Heritage Foundation. May 14, 2003. www.heritage.org/Research/NationalSecurity/wm273.cfm.

———. "How to Reinvigorate U.S. Public Diplomacy." Washington, D.C.: The Heritage Foundation, April 23, 2003. www.heritage.org/Research/NationalSecurity/bg1645.cfm.

John S. and James L. Knight Foundation. "First Amendment Survey." January 2005. www.firstamendmentfuture.org/main.html.

Kamen, Al. "In the Loop: Over Here, An Earful," *Washington Post*, October 7, 2005, A21.

Kaplan, David E. "Hearts, Minds and Dollars." *U.S. News and World Report*, April 25, 2005. www.usnews.com/usnews/news/articles/050425/25roots.htm.

Karimi, Nasser. "Iran Condemns Bush Speech on Terrorism." Associated Press, February 3, 2005.

Karp, Alexander C., Gary A. Tobin, and Aryeh K. Weinberg. "An Exceptional Nation." *Philanthropy*. November/December 2004.

Kennedy, John F. "American University Commencement Address." June 10, 1963.

Kornblut, Anne E. "Bush Bars Use of Paid Commentators." *New York Times*, January 27, 2005, A18.

Larson, Cedric, and James R. Mock. "The Lost Files of the Creel Committee of 1917–1919," *Public Opinion Quarterly* 3, no. 1 (January 1939).

Luce, Henry. "The American Century," *Life* magazine editorial, February 1941.

McDonald, John. "The Track Not Taken." *Harvard International Review* 22, no. 3, 2000.

Medved, Michael. "That's Entertainment? Hollywood's Contribution to Anti-Americanism Abroad." *The National Interest*, Summer 2002.

Miami Herald staff editorial. "All the Good News that Money Can Buy: Our opinion: Iraq Propaganda Campaign is Counterproductive." December 5, 2005.

Moravcsik, Andrew. "Dream On America." *Newsweek International*, January 31, 2005.

Morgan, David. "U.S. Planning Arab Language TV Broadcasts to Europe." *New York Times*, February 27, 2005.

Morton, Frederic. "From Role Model to International Bully in Three Short Years," *Los Angeles Times*, September 28, 2004.

Moyers, Bill. "Response to CPB's Tomlinson Charges of Liberal Bias: 'We Were Getting it Right, But Not Right Wing.'" National Conference on Media Reform, St. Louis, Missouri, May 15, 2005.

Murphy, Gael. "The Guards Are Sleeping." *AlterNet*, May 2, 2005.

Nader, Ralph. "America's Right to Know War News." *Common Dreams*, May 15, 2005.

Newport, Frank. "Update: Americans and Religion." December 23, 2004. poll.gallup.com/content/default.aspx?ci=14446&pg=1 (15 Dec 2005).

Ostrow, Joanne. "Bush crew feeds 'news,' TV swallows." *Denver Post*, March 18, 2004.

Packer, George. "Name Calling." *The New Yorker*. August 1, 2005. Online version.

Paul, Ron. "Why Do We Fund UNESCO?" Press Release. www.house.gov/paul/tst/tst2005/tst041805.htm.

Pew Global Attitudes Project. "American Character Gets Mixed Reviews: U.S. Image Up Slightly But Still Negative." June 23, 2005. pewglobal.org/reports/pdf/247.pdf.

Pew Research Center for People and the Press. "Trends 2005." January 2005. pewresearch.org/trends/trends2005.pdf.

————. "The Spread of Anti-Americanism" in "Trends 2005." pewresearch.org/trends/trends2005-global.pdf.

Pfanner, Eric. "NGOs gain confidence of public." *International Herald Tribune*. January 24, 2005.

Poniewozik, James. "The Worst TV of 2005." *Time* web exclusive, December 28, 2005.

Powell, Colin Powell. "Testimony Before the House Budget Committee," March 15, 2001.

Pyle, Richard. "From Tonkin Gulf to Persian Gulf: Veteran AP correspondent considers how war reporting has changed." CNN.com. www.cnn.com/SPECIALS/cold.war/episodes/11/then.now/.

Regan, Tom. "Bush Speech Divides Foreign Media." *Christian Science Monitor*, February 3, 2005.

Reinhard, Keith. Testimony Before the House Subcommittee on National Security, Emerging Threats, and International Relations. Hearing on the 9/11 Commission Recommendations on Public Diplomacy: Defending Ideals and Defining the Message. August 23, 2004.

Report of the Defense Science Board Task Force. "Managed Information Dissemination." Office of the Under Secretary of Defense for Acquisition, Technology and Logistics. September 2001. www.acq.osd.mil/dsb/reports/mid.pdf.

Report of an Independent Task Force sponsored by the Council on Foreign Relations. "Finding America's Voice: A Strategy for Reinvigorating U.S. Public Diplomacy," September 2003. www.cfr.org/pdf/public_diplomacy.pdf.

Report of an Independent Task Force sponsored by the Council on Foreign Relations, "Public Diplomacy: A Strategy for Reform." July 2002. www.cfr.org/publication.php?id=4754.xml.

Report of the Advisory Group on Public Diplomacy for the Arab and Muslim World. "Changing Minds, Winning Peace: A New Strategic Direction for U.S. Public Diplomacy in the Arab & Muslim World." Submitted to the Committee on Appropriations, U.S. House of Representatives, October 1, 2003. www.state.gov/documents/organization/24882.pdf.

Report of the Eleventh Annual Aspen Institute Roundtable on Information Technology. "The Rise of Netpolitik: How the Internet is Changing International Politics and Diplomacy." 2003. www.aspeninstitute.org/AspenInstitute/files/CCLIBRARYFILES/FILENAME/0000000077/netpolitik.pdf.

Report of the Center for the Study of the Presidency. "Strengthening U.S.-Muslim Communications, July 2003. www.thepresidency.org/pubs/US-MuslimCommunications.pdf.

Report of the Public Diplomacy Institute and Public Diplomacy Council, George Washington University. "Public Diplomacy for the 21st Century." Submitted by request to the staffs of the Committee on Foreign Relations, U.S. Senate, and Committee on International Relations, U.S. House of Representatives, May 31, 2002. pdi.gwu.edu/.

Report of the U.S. General Accountability Office. "U.S. International Broadcasting: Challenges Facing the Broadcasting Board of Governors." Statement before the Subcommittee on International Operations and Terrorism, Committee on Foreign Relations, U.S. Senate, April 29, 2004. www.gao.gov/new.items/d04627t.pdf.

———. "U.S. Public Diplomacy: State Department and Broadcasting Board of Governors Expand Efforts in the Middle East but Face Significant Challenges." Statement before the Subcommittee on National Security, Emerging Threats, and International Relations, Committee on Government Reform, U.S. House of Representatives, February 10, 2004. www.gao.gov/cgl-bin/getrpt?GAO-04-435T.

———. "U.S. Public Diplomacy: State Department Expands Efforts But Faces Significant Challenges." Statement before the Committee on International Relations, U.S. House of Representatives, September 2003. www.gao.gov/new.items/d03951.pdf.

———. "U.S. International Broadcasting: New Strategic Approach Focuses on Reaching Large Audiences but Lacks Measurable Program Objectives." Statement before the Committee on International Relations, U.S. House of Representatives, July 2003. www.gao.gov/new.items/d03772.pdf.

Rice, Condoleezza. Prepared remarks before the U.S. Congress, Subcommittee on Foreign Operations, House Appropriations Committee. February 16, 2005.

Roberts, Dan, and Alison Maitland. "NGOs Win Greater Trust than Media and Big Business." *Financial Times*. January 24, 2005.

Rugh, William A. Testimony to U.S. Senate Foreign Relations Committee, International Operations Subcommittee, U.S. Congress. April 29, 2004.

Sacci, Kristina. "Brand That I Love." *Fast Company*. November 2004.

Sands, David R. "America Enjoys View from the Top." *Washington Times*. National Weekly Edition. 3–9 January 2005.

Sheridan, Greg. "A Man of His Word Like it or Lump It." *The Australian*, February 3, 2005.

Simon, Roger. "Waging the Spin War." *U.S. News and World Report*, October 22, 2001.

Snow, Nancy. "Media is a Battlefield," *Common Dreams*, May 14, 2005.

———. "The Propaganda Czar From Paris + Texas," *Common Dreams*, March 14, 2005.

———. "The Language Police: Gettin' Jiggy with Frank Luntz." *Common Dreams*, February 26, 2005.

———. "Tall Order, Tough Questions," *Common Dreams*, January 18, 2005.

———. "Marketing America: A Tale of Two Careers." *Asian Times*, June 4, 2004. www.atimes.com/atimes/Front_Page/FF03Aa11.html.

———. "The Real 'Scary Movie' Won't Be on Elm Street this Summer." (Silver City, NM & Washington, DC: Foreign Policy In Focus, May 27, 2004). www.fpif.org/commentary/2004/0405scary.html.

———. "Al Hurra-Al Who? Haven't Heard? We're Free, They're Not!" *O'Dwyer's PR Daily*, March 9, 2004.

———. "Kill Your TV: No Oops, I Really Mean It This Time." *Common Dreams*, January 8, 2004.

———. "When Truth is a Dangerous Thing," *Common Dreams*, May 11, 2003.

———. "While the Propaganda Czar Departs, the Product Pitching Remains," *Common Dreams*, March 4, 2003.

———. "Reweaving Charlotte's Web." *Common Dreams*, December 27, 2002.

———. "What the World Thinks Now." *Common Dreams*, December 6, 2002.

———. "Déjà Vu All Over Again," *Common Dreams*, February 20, 2002.

———. "United States Information Agency." *Foreign Policy in Focus* 2, no. 40, August 1997. www.fpif.org/briefs/vol2/v2n40usia_body.html.

Soriano, Cesar G., and Ann Oldenburg. "With America at War, Hollywood Follows." *USA Today*, February 7, 2005.

Spiers, Ronald. "The Anatomy of Terrorism." *Foreign Service Journal*. September 2004.

Stengel, Richard. "Books: Rival Capitals of Fantasy: The Power and the Glitter by Ronald Brownstein." *Time*, February 4, 1991.

Ungar, Sanford. "Preaching U.S. Supremacy Won't Help Image Abroad." *Baltimore Sun*. October 9, 2005.

United States Advisory Commission on Public Diplomacy. "The New Diplomacy: Utilizing Innovative Communication Concepts that Recognize Resource Constraints." 2003. www.state.gov/r/adcompd/rls/22818.htm.

———. "Building Public Diplomacy Through a Reformed Structure and Additional Resources." 2002. www.state.gov/documents/organization/13622.pdf.

University of Maryland Program on International Policy Attitudes (PIPA). "In 20 of 23 Countries Polled Citizens Want Europe to Be More Influential Than US." April 6, 2005. www.pipa.org/OnlineReports/europe/040605/html/new_4_06_05.html#1.

USA Today editorial. "Sales pitch falls flat." September 28, 2005.

Van Wagtendonk, Reinout. "State of the Union Warning for Syria and Iran." Radio Netherlands, February 3, 2005, www2.rnw.nl/rnw/en/currentaffairs/region/northamerica/usa050203.

Weaver, Gary R. "American Cultural Values." Originally published in *Kokusai Bunka Kenshu (Intercultural Training)* 14 (Winter 1997): 14–20.

Winseman, Albert L. "Who Has Been Born Again?" January 18, 2005. www.gallup.com/poll/content/default.aspx?ci=14632 (15 Dec. 2005).

UNPUBLISHED THESES

Garrett, Amy C. "Marketing America: Public Culture and Public Diplomacy in the Marshall Plan Era, 1947–1954." University of Pennsylvania unpublished doctoral dissertation, 2004.

Snow, Nancy E. "Fulbright Scholars as Cultural Mediators: An Exploratory Study." American University unpublished doctoral dissertation, 1992.

INDEX

ABOUT THE AUTHOR

Nancy Snow is tenured associate professor of communications at California State University, Fullerton and adjunct professor in the Annenberg School for Communication, University of Southern California. A former Fulbright scholar to Germany, Snow served from 1992–1994 as a United States Information Agency (USIA) and U.S. Department of State (DOS) official in public diplomacy and international exchange. She serves as senior fellow in the USC Center on Public Diplomacy where she conducts research and teaches courses on anti-Americanism, American propaganda, press and public diplomacy, and global communications. Dr. Snow is the author of numerous book chapters, articles, and several books, including *Propaganda, Inc.*, *Information War*, and *War, Media and Propaganda: A Global Perspective* (with Yahya Kamalipour). Her writings have been translated into five foreign languages. She was a *magna cum laude* Ph.D. graduate in international relations from American University's School of International Service in Washington, D.C., and a *summa cum laude* political science graduate from Clemson University in South Carolina. Snow is a lifetime member of the Fulbright Association. She edits a website devoted to American persuasion, influence, and propaganda at www.nancysnow.com.